D1061345

WITHDRAWN

REDWOOD
LIBRARY
NEWPORT
R.I.

GOODWOOD'S OAK

The Life and Times of the Third Duke of Richmond, Lennox and Aubigny

The arms of the Dukes of Richmond, Lennox and Aubigny. They show the coat of arms of King Charles II within a border of alternating red and white panels embellished with the Lennox rose. The border indicates illegitimacy, and it distinguishes the Richmond and Lennox arms from those of the King's other natural sons, which bear a baton sinister. The 'escutcheon of pretence' in the centre of the shield is charged with three 'buckles or' for the Dukedom of Aubigny.

GOODWOOD'S OAK

The Life and Times of the Third Duke of Richmond, Lennox and Aubigny

M. M. REESE

Foreword by
His Grace the Ninth Duke
of Richmond, DL

Threshold Books

Edited by Marabel Hadfield

Designed by Tim Higgins

© 1987 M. M. Reese

First published 1987 by Threshold Books Limited
661 Fulham Road, London SW6 5PZ

All rights reserved

Set in Linotron Fournier by
Filmtype Services Limited, Scarborough, Yorkshire
Printed in Great Britain by The Garden City Press Ltd,
Letchworth, Herts

No part of this publication may be reproduced, stored in a retrieval system, or transmitted, in any form or by any means, electronic, mechanical, photocopying, recording, or otherwise, without written permission of the publisher.

British Library Cataloguing in Publication Data
Reese, M. M.
Goodwood's oak: the life and times of the Third Duke
of Richmond, Lennox and Aubigny
1. Richmond, Lennox and Aubigny, Charles Lennox, *Duke of*
2. Statesman – England – Biography
3. Great Britain – Nobility – Biography
I. Title
942.07′3′0924 DA506.R5

ISBN 0 901 366 23 4

DA
506
.R5
R43
1987

138089

Contents

MAR 25 1988

Author's acknowledgements

I wish to record my gratitude and thanks to the Earl of March and Kinrara whose generosity has made this biography possible, and to Barbara Cooper, my publisher, for providing me with the opportunity of writing it.

I would also like to express my special appreciation to David Legg-Willis, House General Manager at Goodwood, for his unfailing efficiency and forebearing, and to his secretary, Valerie Griffiths; to Timothy McCann, Assistant Archivist at the West Sussex Record Office, for his constant help and advice; to Sarah Waters who undertook the picture research and whose editorial suggestions were immensely valuable; to Ben Ramos for his inspired text research, and to my painstaking editor, Marabel Hadfield.

My thanks are also due to Sarah Barter Bailey, Chief Librarian at the Royal Armouries, for her advice on the Ordnance; to De Witt Bailey for his contribution to the text of the chapter on the Ordnance; to John Baynes of the Ordnance Survey for information on early maps; and to David Harding for his advice on arms and regimental history.

All sources are acknowledged in the Notes and Sources, but I am particularly indebted to John Cannon's *Aristocratic Century*, Alison Olson's *The Radical Duke*, and to Mrs Priscilla Napier for references in her manuscript 'My Brother Richmond'.

M. M. Reese

List of illustrations

Colour plates

Monochrome illustrations

List of illustrations

Foreword

by His Grace the Duke of Richmond, DL

AS THE NINTH IN A LINE of which the subject of this book is the third, I congratulate Max Reese on his work. Like my son, I have long wanted to get to know the third Duke better. My father wrote a biography of the second Duke (*A Duke and His Friends*, Hutchinson, 1911), and the detail and delight of that eighteenth-century glimpse is most ably followed by this account of the life of his really remarkable son.

When, in the 1930s, I had to sell much of the family land because of huge Victorian mortgages and two sets of death duties within seven years, it was on the preservation of Goodwood, essentially the creation of the third Duke, that I concentrated. For in spite of the size of Gordon Castle and the Scottish estates, the family has never been in doubt that its home and roots were at Goodwood. For these reasons I am delighted to contribute this Foreword.

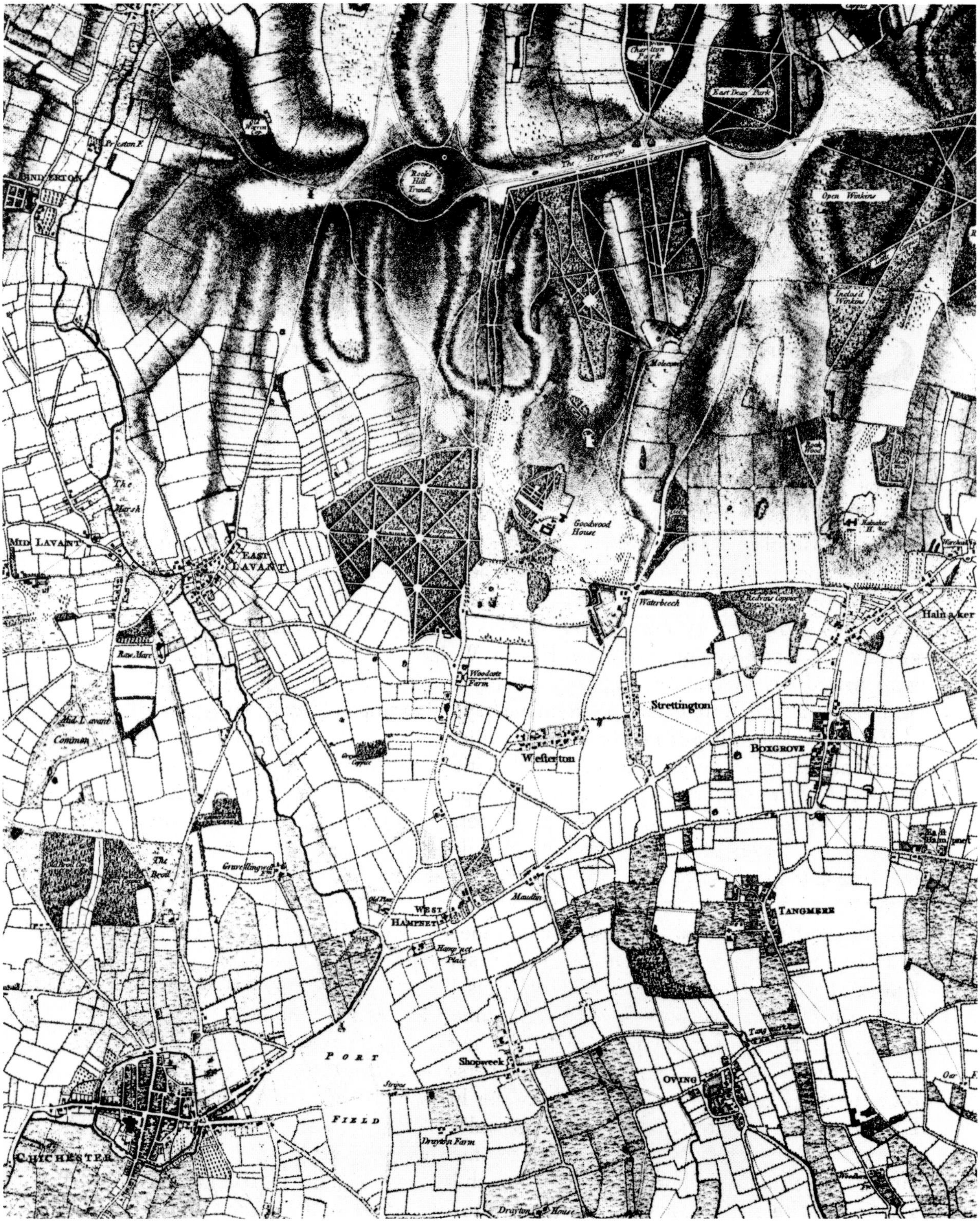

1 Goodwood House and Park as it appeared on the map of Sussex prepared by the surveyors Yeakell and Gardner in 1778.

Introduction

by the Earl of March, FCA, DL

So few personal papers of the third Duke of Richmond, Lennox and Aubigny have survived that the man who laid the foundations of Goodwood as it is now has always been something of an enigma to my family. I have found this very frustrating because I suspect that, in the context of today, I am substantially following in his footsteps.

That is why I am extremely grateful to Max Reese for drawing together so much little-known information about him and discovering within it his fascinating and frustrating character. For the third Duke seems to have been as difficult for his contemporaries to read as he has been for me – until Max took the kaleidoscope and shook it in just the right way. Now, for the first time, we can judge this extraordinary man's achievements so much better against the background of his personality. In a letter, Horace Walpole wrote of the Duke that he worshipped 'his thousand virtues beyond any man's' and then said that he was 'intrepid and tender, inflexible and humane beyond example. (*Letters*, vii, 379).

While we have always realised that the third Duke's accomplishments were great and covered a very wide range of activities, the research for this book has revealed hitherto unknown achievements – particularly those initiatives concerned with his thirteen years as Master-General of the Ordnance. I look at the fine original survey of the Goodwood Estate done by Yeakell and Gardner and realise that the Duke took the same brilliant team to found the Ordnance Survey, which today is world-renowned. I am filled with admiration for this same man who urged the House of Lords to introduce one man–one vote in 1780, some 138 years before it became a reality! Likewise, his spirited championship of peace and independence for the American Colonies has been hitherto largely neglected, though it comes in very useful now with American tourists! Sadly, as yet, no correspondence to or from the Founding Fathers has come to light.

The Grand Tour was not part of my personal upbringing, and it is only recently that I have visited the Duke's former French properties at Aubigny and La Verrerie. It was at the latter I came to realise the significance of the Lennox heritage with which Charles II endowed my family – with genes and titles! The family motto *En La Rose Je Fleurie* meant much less to me until, at La Verrerie, I saw in the cloister a mounted Lennox ancestor in full panoply, bearing on his shield four Lennox roses. That heritage, stretching back before Joan of Arc, was part of the third Duke's very being – and makes much more interesting to me the many French objects and links still remaining at Goodwood, including the French cork oak trees in the park.

Today, Goodwood still boasts 12,000 of the third Duke's 17,000 acres; his Estate is still owned by his family; his House is still lived in by his successors; his House is also still the scene of great events (200 of them in 1987) and of lavish entertainment – from wedding receptions to international conferences; his Park is still used for the activities of horsemanship; his Stables still accommodate horses of all kinds; his Racecourse has become renowned throughout the world as 'Glorious Goodwood'.

I have always regarded the third Duke as a beacon. I want, again, to thank Max Reese for lighting that beacon for me and for others.

March.

The Earl of March, heir of the 9th Duke of Richmond, lives in Goodwood House with his family and is Chairman of the companies which today control the many Goodwood activities.

I

The Planting of the Oaks

Charles Lennox, third Duke of Richmond, was only fifteen when in 1750 he inherited the title. Some twenty years later, Edmund Burke, begging him to give more time to public affairs, reminded him of the responsibilities of his position. 'Persons in your station of life ought to have long views. You people of great families and fortunes are not like such as I am, who whatever we may be by the rapidity of our growth and of the fruit we bear, flatter ourselves that while we creep on the ground we belly into melons that are exquisite for size and flavour, yet still we are but annual plants that perish with our season and leave no sort of traces behind us. You, if you are what you ought to be, are the great oaks that shade a country and perpetuate your benefits from generation to generation. The immediate power of a Duke of Richmond or Marquis of Rockingham is not so much of moment; but if their conduct and example hands down their principles to their successors, then their houses become the public repositories and offices of record for the constitution.'[1]

Although Richmond was intermittently active in politics for forty years, his career has a wider interest than this. It embraces also his unusual and distinguished family and his care and enlargement of the Goodwood Estate which still flourishes in Sussex. For the great aristocratic families of the eighteenth century their participation in central government was only one of their functions, to protect it from royal or populist abuse. They were custodians of social and political order, committed by their vast inheritance to the duty of leading by moral example the communities that depended on them.

On estates running to many thousands of acres these men built their houses with local materials and local labour and enriched them not only with pictures and sculptures acquired on their foreign travels but also with the work of native artists and designers of whom they were patrons. Beyond their parklands and disciplined gardens their ownership of advowsons and manorial rights influenced the appointment and behaviour of parsons and lesser gentry; they controlled the election of parliamentary candidates for county or borough seats;* they mobilised

* Rockingham, for instance, inherited land in Yorkshire, Northamptonshire and Ireland bringing an annual rental of £20,000, nomination to three parliamentary seats, and appointment to twenty-three ecclesiastical livings and five chaplaincies.

and commanded the local militia; their servants and tenantry formed a little community for whose work and welfare they were responsible; they raised cricket teams, they shot and raced and hunted, and those of them who lived round the clock returned from the field for an evening of cards and port. Thus a whole neighbourhood took its character from the personality and interests of the local lord; and in the circumstances it is remarkable that many of these noblemen still found time and energy for public affairs.[2]

It is rash to generalise about a class and a way of life, and the picture has darker aspects. Some aristocrats were merely eccentric, like the fourth Duke of Queensberry who reputedly bathed in milk before it was retailed on the streets, or the sixth Duke of Somerset who carried grandeur to absurdity – he communicated with his servants by hand signals only, his children were not allowed to speak in his presence, roads had to be cleared before he would go out.* Architectural taste sometimes declined from Georgian elegance to the building of 'follies' or the Gothic extravagance of Ashridge and Fonthill. The acquisition of land to enlarge an estate was harmless when, as at Goodwood, it only required the diversion of a highway, but it brought intolerable hardship when it depopulated a whole village. Of the Game Laws that protected the land from poachers the Reverend Sydney Smith wrote: 'There is a sort of horror in thinking of a whole land lurking with engines of death – machinations against human life under every green tree – traps and guns in every dusky dell and bosky bourn – the lords of manors eyeing their peasantry as so many butts and marks, and panting to hear the click of the trap and to see the flash of the gun.'

Although it is said that the first Duke of Newcastle always made careful preparation before attending the Eucharist, to refresh his understanding of what was about to be performed, eighteenth-century noblemen did not seek spiritual elevation. Impatient of revelation or doctrines that pretended to mystical authority, they were as a class content with the unexacting simplicities of Latitudinarianism,** which was unconcerned with dogmatic truth or liturgical precision and equated good churchmanship with a distaste for controversy and acquiescence in the Protestant Hanoverian succession. In their private chapels the nobility observed a formal piety, assured that the parson (in effect an employee) would say nothing politically inconvenient or vulgarised by sectarian 'enthusiasm'. These chapels they maintained in seemly fashion; also their family vaults, as to this favour they all must come.

---

* When Somerset condescended to offer marriage to the widowed Sarah Churchill, he received this classic put-down: 'If I were young and handsome as I was, instead of old and faded as I am, and you could lay the empire of the world at my feet, you should never share the heart and hand that once belonged to John Duke of Marlborough.'

** The Latitudinarians were members of the Church of England who in the seventeenth century took a liberal approach to orthodox doctrines, rejecting the dogma of the High Church and Puritans.

Twenty years of Robert Walpole did not stimulate idealism and, likewise, a pew-oriented piety untouched by living faith produced only a negative morality not strong enough to guard men against the prevailing vices of the age – gambling and drink. At Brooks's and Almack's and other London clubs, or in the assembly-rooms at Bath, younger lords joined their elders in staking thousands of pounds on dice and cards. They bet heavily on horses, too, and on cricket matches and cock fights; although the stakes were lower, the ladies in their salons were just as reckless. 'Society in those days was one vast casino.'[3]

So strong was this addiction that the card-table offered too little excitement and men had to devise preposterous wagers. A bet was regarded as the conclusive way of settling an argument. If 'A' boasted that he could drink more wine in an hour than 'B', the solution was to lay a bet and prove it. But this was too matter-of-fact to satisfy some eager spirits, and they would make wagers on issues not immediately verifiable, such as the sex of the Chevalier d'Eon, who was reticent on the matter,* or the weight of the corpulent and disease-ridden Duke of Cumberland. Men would bet on the life-span of their parents or the sex of the first child to be born to a son who was not yet married. Horace Walpole recorded that his nephew Lord Orford had wagered £500 with the Marquis of Rockingham (who was not a frivolous man) on five turkeys and five geese 'to run from Norwich to London.' The trivial reasons for which men fought duels, where a pretended honour was at stake, sprang from the same gambling compulsion. During the American War of Independence Walpole said that gambling was a vice appropriate to a nation that was losing an empire.

Heavy drinking was in part an accompaniment of the long nights spent at the tables, but it spread wider than that. Gin was the cheap tipple of the mob, who had little else to console them and had to be taxed out of the habit. The nobility drank wine: usually port for the Whigs and, as a contrary gesture, claret for the Tories. Even Dr Johnson, who was not a toper or an aristocrat or a Whig, was known to drink three bottles of port at a sitting. The consequences in disease were appalling. Men wore out their constitutions and were old at fifty, sometimes less, and an agonising attack of gout was welcomed as relief from symptoms yet more painful.

Medicine and hygiene were so primitive that both men and women were unashamedly dirty. Lady Mary Wortley Montagu was sufficiently enlightened to advocate inoculation, but when rebuked for going to the opera with unwashed hands, she only replied, 'You should see my feet.' Executions were spectacles relished by people of all classes, not least by the necrophiliac George Selwyn, who shared the tastes of Louis XV across the Channel. Stern pedagogues ruled the schools with floggings that invigorated the pursuit of a classical education,

* It was settled by a post-mortem when he died in London in 1810. He was a spy who liked to operate in drag.

but the survivors of this regimen could be remarkably credulous. Joanna Southcott, a farmer's daughter from Devon, had society trembling on her promise to deliver a new Messiah; Mary Tofts from Godalming won wide acceptance of her claim to have given birth to fifteen rabbits, she and her litter being drawn by Hogarth; the Duke of York was among the patrons of Elizabeth Parsons, entrepreneur of 'the Cock Lane Ghost'. At a higher intellectual level, Chatterton's 'Thomas Rowley' fabrications had many romantic admirers; 'Ossian' deceived Hume and Adam Smith, not to mention Goethe and Napoleon Bonaparte; the Shakespearean forgeries of William Henry Ireland were popular on the stage until Malone destroyed them. Dr Johnson was not fooled by Ossian, mistrusting anything of Scottish provenance, but even he wrote a preface to William Lauder's book which 'proved' that much of *Paradise Lost* was derived from modern Latin poets.

The frequency of these deceptions in an age that prided itself on submitting all ideas and phenomena to the cool light of reason is puzzling. (It could have strange effects. When the Lisbon earthquake of 1755 destroyed the greater part of the city in fifteen minutes and killed 60,000 people, it was several months before Johnson could bring himself to believe that such an outrage to rational expectation had really happened.) Something was lacking in the critical faculty of the age if to Horace Walpole, one of its keenest and most fastidious minds, Dante meant no more than 'a Methodist parson in Bedlam.'

Every noble household had at its table tutors, parsons and visitors who would, if permitted, bring the conversation to a philosophical plane, but at Goodwood it is likely that discussions, when not of the prospects for hunting and the farm, were of painting, sculpture and building. Here Richmond had taste and knowledge, and he was always eager to learn more. In other respects his pragmatic mind was not given to literary or metaphysical speculation, and probably he was too restless to do much reading outside his official business. Samuel Rogers, prosperous banker, sometime poet and unquenchable gossip, wrote in his *Table Talk* of an occasion when in the company of Charles Fox and Burke the Duke said, '"I prefer reading history to philosophy or poetry, because history is *truth*." Both Fox and Burke disagreed with him: they thought that poetry was *truth*, being a representation of human nature.'

Flawed though it was, and disappointed in its conviction that Man had conquered Nature, English society in the brief Augustan aftermath held a golden prospect for the young Duke of Richmond when he entered it. It was an interlude between the passions and agitations of the seventeenth century and the violence born of industrial poverty and the French Revolution. Landed peers, about 170 of them, presided over a world untroubled by fanaticism, in which they could maintain without challenge their own standards of propriety, culture and social obligation. They were, no doubt, preposterous in some of their behaviour and assumptions, but they were versatile and confident and they had an enviable zest for living.[4]

At the centre of their interests and affections was the family, and it is important to recognise what this meant to a man like Richmond. When he came of age he had two elder sisters married to men of wealth and influence, but as head of the family he was the focus of a close-knit loyalty overriding personal disagreements or conflicting ambitions. In any crisis he was to be consulted and his decisions regarded. The head of the family was *paterfamilias* almost in the old Roman sense, responsible not only for any children of his own but for brothers and sisters, nephews and nieces, all of whom in some degree acknowledged his authority. To Virgil, Aeneas was always *pius.* At any crisis in the family – and there were several – Richmond laid aside other concerns and gave it kindness and understanding. It was to his home and his own people that his thoughts returned at the bitterest moment in his public life when in 1795, he was dismissed from an office that he cherished. He wrote to his Duchess: '*Nous nous consolerons en cultivant notre jardin.*'*

* Probably he had read *Candide* in the contemporary edition of Voltaire's works that is still in the library at Goodwood.

2 Charles I with Queen Henrietta Maria, the future Charles II, and the infant Princess Mary, by Van Dyck. After the King's execution the painting was sold to the Duc d'Orléans, brother of Louis XIV, and when it came up for sale during the French Revolution it was bought by the third Duke of Richmond. In its elaborate French frame surmounted by the emblem of the Sun King, it hangs in the Ballroom at Goodwood.

2

Origins

At Easter 1684 John Evelyn was present to hear the Bishop of Rochester preach before Charles II, and after noting without approval that 'there was perfume burnt before the Office began,' he saw the King accompanied to the altar by three of his natural sons, each born of a different mother: the Dukes of Northumberland, Richmond and St Albans. The younger two were 'very pretty boys', but Evelyn thought that Northumberland showed the greatest promise of manly development.

Richmond's mother was Louise de Kéroualle (1649–1734), known to the English, always impatient of foreign peculiarities in spelling and pronunciation, as Madame Carwell, and hated by them as French and Catholic and a spy. She came to England, a lovely Breton girl of twenty, in the train of Charles's sister Henrietta Duchess of Orleans during the negotiations for the Treaty of Dover (1670). Ousting the mistress in possession, the venomous Lady Castlemaine, and impervious to the sniping cockney impudence of Nell Gwyn, Louise became the best-loved of Charles's mistresses, and the most intelligent. He made her Duchess of Portsmouth, and if it was part of her duties to hold him to the French alliance he was well aware of it and it suited his inclinations anyway.

Charles II created dukedoms for five of his bastard sons,* and a title was found for Louise's infant when Charles Stuart, Duke of Richmond and Lennox and Seigneur of Aubigny, died without issue in 1672.** To give him his full titles, which are still held by his descendants, the young Charles Lennox was created Baron of Settrington, Earl of March, and Duke of Richmond (Yorkshire) in the English peerage and Baron Methuen of Tarbolton, Earl of Darnley and Duke of Lennox in the peerage of Scotland.

The Aubigny title had been granted to Sir John Stuart of Darnley in 1422 for his services as Constable of a Scots army mustered against the English invaders;

---

* The other four were Southampton, Grafton and Northumberland, his sons by Castlemaine; and St Albans, by Nell Gwyn.

** His wife was the beautiful Frances Stuart, commemorated as Britannia on England's copper coinage. As a maid of honour at Court she defended her virtue against prolonged royal siege before suddenly eloping with Richmond. Furious, Charles banished them to a Danish embassy and hurried Clarendon to his fall for having allegedly engineered the elopement.

3 (ABOVE) Louise de Kéroualle, by Lely (detail). She came to England at the age of twenty as maid of honour to Henriette d'Orléans, and was to be the best loved of Charles II's mistresses.

4 (RIGHT) Charles II, by Lely (detail). The King granted the title of first Duke of Richmond and Lennox to his natural son by Louise de Kéroualle, one of thirteen acknowledged illegitimate children.

and although the line of descent was immensely complicated, his heirs were related to the Stuarts of Lennox and Darnley and, through Henry Darnley's marriage to Mary Queen of Scots, to the Stuart Royal House.[1]

On the death of Charles Stuart in 1672, claim to the seigneury of Aubigny had passed to Charles II. After negotiation with Louis XIV it was agreed that the estate and the title Duchesse d'Aubigny should be held by Louise de Kéroualle during her lifetime on condition that the seigneury passed to her son by Charles II.

The first Duke of Richmond in the new creation (1672–1723) was not a satisfactory person, though in Kneller's portrait he was handsome enough; 'good-looking but good for nothing' was a later Duke's candid assessment. His mother took him to France and brought him up as a Catholic. After serving in the French army against the English in Flanders, he returned to England in 1692, changed his religion and his allegiance and looked for wealth and honours as his reward. Being still suspected of Jacobite sympathies, he received only a few military and political appointments too modest to interrupt a career of debauchery and debt. He was, however, interested in freemasonry, becoming Grand Master of England, and with the Chichester Lodge he attended their annual assembly on St Roche's Hill, later known as Rook's Hill, and now as The Trundle.[2]

Having frequently visited the celebrated hunts in Charlton Forest, Richmond bought for £4100 a Jacobean hunting-lodge at nearby Goodwood, and it became his favourite country resort. It was there that he died. He was buried, unfittingly, in Westminster Abbey, but his remains were later removed to the family mausoleum which his son constructed under Chichester Cathedral. He left a son who succeeded to the dukedom, and two daughters: Louise, married to the third Earl of Berkeley, and Anne, who married William Keppel, second Earl of Albemarle, and had fifteen children. In old age 'Aunt Albemarle' settled near Goodwood and was much loved by all the Lennox family.

The marriage of the first Duke's son, the Earl of March* in 1719 to Lady Sarah Cadogan is said to have been arranged by the respective fathers in settlement of a gambling debt. It took place at The Hague and the bridegroom, unenthusiastic about the frumpish little girl of thirteen who was suffering from a cold, set off at once on the Grand Tour. Returning three years later, he was at the theatre when he asked of a friend who the young woman attracting the attention of everyone in the house was. That, came the reply, is the toast of the town, the beautiful Lady March.

This marriage so unpromisingly begun, brought lifelong happiness to them

* The title, together with the forename Charles, always borne by the eldest son of the Duke.

both. They had twelve children and the Duchess survived her husband by only a few months.

The career of the second Duke (1694–1750) reflects the characteristic versatility of the eighteenth-century aristocrat. In the service of the Crown he was Lord High Constable at the coronation of George II in 1727 and a Lord of the Bedchamber; Master of the Horse from 1735 until his death; Privy Councillor, Knight of the Bath and Knight of the Garter; and on four occasions one of the Lords Justices appointed to govern the realm during the King's absences in Hanover. As a soldier he became Colonel of the Royal Horse Guards; he accompanied George II in the European campaign of 1743 and fought at Dettingen; and during the Jacobite rebellion in 1745 he was made a full General with responsibility for the defence of London. When the Scots turned back after reaching Derby, he chased them north and assisted in the recovery of Carlisle.

Other distinctions conferred upon him reveal the extraordinary breadth of his interests. Cambridge made him Doctor of Law and Doctor of Medicine; he was Grand Master of Freemasons in England; Fellow of the Royal Society; Fellow of the Royal College of Physicians; Fellow, later President, of both the Royal Society of Antiquaries and the Society of Arts; an Elder Brother, later Master, of Trinity House; Lord Lieutenant of Sussex and High Steward of Chichester. No doubt some of these offices were due to his rank, simply because he was a duke; on the other hand they were not just empty titles bestowed honorifically on a non-participant in the work of the institutions that elected him.

Locally Richmond was active against the smugglers, violent men who were a menace in the area. They would ride unmolested over Goodwood Park, and the plot that brought some of them to the gallows was hatched in their lair in Charlton Forest. This was to break into the customs house at Poole and seize a quantity of tea and spirits. Two murders were committed during the enterprise, and the judges were received at Goodwood before opening the assizes at which the smugglers were convicted.[3]

In national politics the second Duke was relatively inactive. Unlike his son, he was not a man much dedicated to high causes. An unquestioning adherent of the Hanoverian dynasty, he supported those Whig ministers – Robert Walpole, Carteret, the Pelhams – who shared this loyalty, and he did not involve himself in factions or intrigues or the pursuit of office. This was due in part to lack of personal inclination but more particularly to his position as Master of the Horse, which he held for longer than any man in the eighteenth century. This was a Royal Household appointment requiring attendance on the monarch on ceremonial occasions and a certain harmony of interest and outlook. No statesman, however powerful, held this office in his gift, and the Master has nearly always been a crossbencher, detached from the political struggle. In wartime the duties were not just ceremonial. When George II went personally to war, the last English monarch so to do, the Master organised a baggage-train of 662 horses with a due complement of carriages, wagons and fodder.

Richmond was content to accept the Duke of Newcastle,* his Sussex neighbour, as his political mentor. Newcastle was the supreme 'jobber' of the age. He had direct control of fifteen parliamentary seats, seven of them in Sussex, and by distributing offices, pensions and emoluments he always had a body of dependants in the Commons. He lacked the brains and steadiness of purpose to develop consistent policies, and contemporaries used him unkindly. Horace Walpole has a cruel account of his performance at George II's funeral, 'spying with one hand and mopping his eyes with the other,' and treading on Cumberland's train 'to avoid the chill of the marble'. In another gleeful anecdote Walpole tells how at the coronation of George III a special retiring-chamber was provided for the Queen, and when she sought to make use of it, it was only to find Newcastle in session. Smollett in *Humphry Clinker* has him rushing to tell the King of his discovery, when in charge of the country's foreign affairs, that 'Cape Breton is an island;' and Chesterfield concluded that he was 'as jealous of power as an impotent lover of his mistress.'

In Newcastle's copious exchange of letters with Richmond, despite the fussiness and obsessive concern for pettifogging detail, a warmer and more attractive character emerges. That Richmond will influence West Sussex in the Whig interest is mutually assumed, and this undress correspondence shows both men at their best. They discuss neighbours and families and life's *minutiae* as well as more solemn affairs. Although Newcastle himself was childless, he enquires after Richmond's Duchess, whom he affectionately calls his 'Sussex Queen', and the well-being of his children. Richmond in turn hopes Newcastle will share his satisfaction in the capture of the Sussex smugglers, or begs him to take care of the Duchess, 'the person in the whole world you know I love the best,' when in her anxiety for his safety during the 'Forty-five she tried to follow him to Lichfield: 'I acknowledge women are often figgitingly troublesome.' During the Dettingen campaign he regrets that George II prefers to wear the yellow sash instead of the red of the Order of the Bath, and he lets off steam about 'Monsieur Freechappel', a Hanoverian stableman who tried to usurp his authority as Master of the Horse. These letters explain Walpole's comment that Richmond was the only man who managed to love the Duke of Newcastle.

Richmond was a liberal patron of painting, architecture and sport, enthusiasms

---

*Thomas Pelham-Holles (1693–1768) was Secretary of State 1724–54 and First Lord of the Treasury 1754–6 and 1757–62. His Sussex seat was at Halland but he was more often at Claremont at Esher, which was closer to London. He was created Duke of Newcastle in 1715. His brother Henry Pelham (1695–1754) was First Lord from 1743 until his death.

5 (LEFT) The second Duke of Richmond, wearing the ribbon of the Order of the Garter. Attributed to Zoffany, this painting is the only known view of the interior of Richmond House. The document on the table refers to the Duke as Master of the Horse to King George II.

6 (BELOW) Carné's Seat, the Palladian-style garden temple designed by Roger Morris in 1743 for the second Duke and built by him for his Duchess. From the windows of the first-floor banqueting room the Duke and his guests could enjoy a magnificent panorama across the Chichester plain to the Cathedral and the Isle of Wight.

7 AND 8 (ABOVE AND OPPOSITE) The second Duke commissioned these two views of London by Canaletto in 1746. Both were painted from the windows of Richmond House (ABOVE) from the Drawing Room: the Holbein Gate of Whitehall Palace, and the Privy Garden. (ABOVE RIGHT) from the Drawing Room: the Thames with St Paul's Cathedral in the background. The gentleman being ushered towards the house by a footman (detail, LEFT) is the second Duke. The small boy in the family group on the terrace (detail, BELOW RIGHT) is probably the third Duke when still Earl of March.

9 (BELOW) Detail from a painting by Wootton showing the South Front of Goodwood House as it was in the 1740s. The groom holding the chestnut hunter Sheldon is wearing the blue and gold livery of the Charlton Hunt.

10 The third Duke by Batoni. Painted in Rome in 1755, it shows Richmond at the age of twenty. It was the custom among the English nobility to have their portraits painted while in Italy on the Grand Tour. Batoni and the German painter Mengs (whose portrait of the third Duke is also at Goodwood) were two of the most fashionable artists in this field at the time.

11 (LEFT) This painting of *A Young Artist*, attributed to John Hamilton Mortimer (1741–79), is dated 1761 when Mortimer would have been about twenty. He is known to have attended the Duke's academy, and it is likely that the picture was painted while he was a pupil there.

which he communicated to his son. From his father he inherited a house in Whitehall which, typically, was falling down, 'from top to bottom full of brick mortar dust', and he had Lord Burlington draw up plans for a new building. He rented other houses in London while the work was going on, and although it is not certain that Burlington's design was used, the new Richmond House in Privy Gardens is commemorated in Canaletto's paintings of the Thames and Whitehall as seen from its windows.

For Goodwood the second Duke had ambitious schemes which foundered through lack of money. An equestrian portrait painted by John Wootton in the 1740s has in the background a solid but smallish house which externally cannot have changed very much since the ninth Earl of Northumberland built it in the reign of James I. Alessandro Galieli, Colen Campbell and Matthew Brettingham were all invited to prepare schemes for its enlargement, but probably only minor alterations were made in the Duke's lifetime. He could afford no more, being, as he told Henry Pelham when an embassage to Paris was proposed in 1748, one who 'never saved a penny in my life, but on the contrary was always in debt.'[4]

Much of this indebtedness must have been due to his expenditure on the interior of the house and on the estate. He bought or commissioned paintings, either on his own travels or through agents working for him abroad. In 1734 the Duchess of Portsmouth died, and in the following year Richmond and his wife did homage to the French Crown for the possession of Aubigny, as had all its owners since the braw Scots Constable received the property from the Dauphin in 1422. There the Duke found china and furniture and works of art, much of which he transported to England. Unfortunately, administration of Aubigny through factors and stewards came to be a liability rather than a hoped-for source of profit.

The original Goodwood estate was small, consisting only of the immediate park and farms in Boxgrove and Westhampnett. The residue of the marriage settlement made by Lord Cadogan enabled Richmond to buy Charlton and Singleton, and with other purchases he extended the estate to 1100 acres, of which two hundred were parkland. On top of a hill with a magnificent view of the sea and some forty miles of coast he built 'Carné's Seat', an elegant stone lodge in Palladian style on the site of a wooden cottage formerly occupied by Philippe de Carné, a retainer of Louise de Kéroualle who stayed in England. (From this eminence the third Duke sent signals to Itchenor to have his ship ready for launching.) The charming Shell House near by, a grotto lined with multi-coloured shells from the West Indies, was created by the Duchess and her daughters. Another unusual adornment of the park was the Temple of Neptune and Minerva, enclosing a fragment discovered during excavations for the building of a council chamber in Chichester. It was a slab of stone, about six feet long, of grey Sussex marble, and when it was presented to the Duke, he erected a pedimented temple in the High Wood to preserve it. The inscription attributes it

13 (ABOVE) The second Duke (1694–1750) while still Earl of March by Dahl.
14 (ABOVE RIGHT) Sarah, his Duchess, by Jervas (detail). The marriage, said to have been arranged in settlement of a gambling debt, brought them lifelong happiness.

12 (LEFT) Charles Lennox, first Duke of Richmond (1672–1723). The painting by William Wissing shows the ten-year-old Duke in his Garter robes.

to King Cogidubnus, who ruled under the authority of the Emperor Tiberius. Cogidubnus, whose palace was at Fishbourne, was chieftain of the Atrebates, who were re-named the Regnenses for their loyalty to the Roman occupation.

In the park Richmond introduced exotic animals and exotic trees. In a decorated subterranean den he kept a menagerie including wolves, tigers, a lion, two 'lepers', a 'Jack all', vultures, eagles, bears, a monkey, Greenland dogs, an armadillo, '1 peccavere and 7 caseawarris': an attraction that, according to his steward, drew from among the visitors some 'rude company. Sunday last we had 4 and 5 hundred good and bad.'[5] With the help of Peter Collinson, an American merchant who became a distinguished naturalist, he planted some remarkable trees, notably some Lebanon cedars on the downs behind the house. However, the cedars did not survive in the chalky soil, and it was not until the third Duke planted more seedlings in the fertile soil of the park that the famous Goodwood cedars flourished. The park had also thirty varieties of oaks and four hundred different American trees and shrubs.

Richmond's young daughter Sarah, peering through rainswept windows as the hunt set out, asked, 'Does Papa *like* hunting, or does he have to?'[6] In a sense he had to, because hunting was an obligation of his class, but he liked it.[7] Charlton, which is in the manor of Singleton in the lee of Goodwood hill, had long been famous for its hunting. The Duke of Monmouth, a regular patron, declared that when he was king, he would come and keep his court at Charlton. The hunt became the property of the third Duke of Bolton until his recreational interests were diverted when Lavinia Fenton, the original Polly Peachum in *The Beggar's Opera*, became his mistress (and later his second wife). He gave his hounds to Richmond, who in 1731 became sole proprietor of the hunt until it was formed into a society. The hunt, with the grooms in their blue liveries with gold trimmings, was one of the most important sporting and social events in the country, seventeen peers and their retainers with 143 horses being quartered in the village for a meet(ing) in 1743. Richmond had his own hunting-lodge in Charlton, known as Foxhall, part of which – the Duke's personal quarters – has lately been restored. The banqueting hall has completely disappeared.

In 1738 occurred a celebrated chase in which a bitch fox was found in East Dean wood before eight o'clock in the morning and eluded its pursuers until nearly six in the evening when in the January darkness 'the glorious twenty-three hounds put an end to the campaign.' The only riders in at the death were Richmond, Billy Ives (pricker-in) and General Hawley, 'to the immortal honour of seventeen stone, and at least as many campaigns.' It is of interest that a chase of ten hours' duration would not have happened in the third Duke's day because he always desired to give fair play to a fox that had given good sport. He would not allow any assistance to be given to the hounds by a 'view holloa'. The cry of the hounds and the sound of the horn was all the notice to be given when a fox broke cover; and when a fox was run to earth, or sought refuge out of reach of the pack, the huntsman was ordered to whip them off, 'or I must send for a candle and lantern for you.'[8]

Sussex was the cradle of cricket and several noble households had their own teams: Richmond's outstanding players were Thomas Waymark, a groom, and Stephen Dingate, a Surrey professional whom he employed as a barber. In 1725 he challenged Sir William Gage's team at Lewes and two years later, at Peper Harow near Godalming, he played a match in which the laws of the game were formulated for the first time. The opponents were led by Alan Brodrick, Viscount Midleton, an Irish jurist, and since heavy wagers were always a feature of such contests, the two captains drew up rules to avoid disputes. Provision was made for lengthy intervals for refreshment, and it was stipulated that 'gamesters' (players) who should 'speak or give their opinion' were to be 'turned out and voided in the match': the captains being expressly exempted from this clause.[9] In 1977 the two hundred-and-fiftieth anniversary of this match was celebrated in a meeting of the village teams of Goodwood and Peper Harow. The match was played in contemporary costume and according to the original rules, with only two stumps.

Richmond also sponsored and sometimes led the famous team at the little Sussex village of Slindon, where the manor house had once been the summer palace of the Archbishops of Canterbury. The team was built round Richard Newland, a Chichester surgeon, and his two brothers, and the 'England' team which played Kent in 1744; the earliest match recorded in *Scores and Biographies*, was virtually the Slindon side. Slindon might have been more famous in cricket history even than Hambledon if Richard Nyren, Newland's nephew, had not crossed the border to keep 'The Bat and Ball' on Broad-Halfpenny Down and if his son John had not been the first great writer on the game.*

The second Duke died in 1750 at the house in Godalming where he used to break his journeys between Sussex and London. His mother thought him 'extremely rattle-headed', but mothers say these things. Harder to understand is the verdict of George II's Queen Caroline, a clear-sighted lady who smiled at the tantrums of her peppery little husband, talked bawdy with Robert Walpole and held erudite conversations with Lord Hervey. She described Richmond as 'so half-witted, so bizarre, and so grand-seigneur, and so mulish, that he is as troublesome from meaning well and comprehending so ill, as if he meant as ill as

* Cricket continued to be a favourite pastime with the family. In 1768 the third Duke led a Sussex team against Hambledon and won 1000 guineas. The fourth Duke, an all-round athlete, was an early patron of Lord's and the MCC. At a military posting in Edinburgh he had his men playing with the uncomprehending Scots; at Brussels in 1815 he organised matches for the Brigade of Guards; and when he was Governor-General of Canada, cricket was played on the Heights of Abraham. See E. V. Lucas, *The Hambledon Men*, 1907, and H. S. Altham, *The History of Cricket*, 1926.

he comprehends.' Probably these unkind words were an exasperated response to Richmond's well-intended efforts to soften the quarrel between Caroline and Frederick Prince of Wales, the son whom she detested beyond all reason. After her death in 1737 he worked with occasional success to reconcile Frederick with the King.

George certainly valued his disinterested service. 'I couldn't have lost anybody more affectionate, and a more sincere friend,' and he did not expect to find a Master of the Horse worthy to replace 'the poor man that is gone.' Abraham Trembley, the Genevan scholar whom he appointed to tutor his sons, described him as 'a man even more remarkable for the manner in which he lived in the distinguished rank he held in his country, than for the rank itself.[10]

His career has been outlined here because it pointed the way for the inexperienced boy who succeeded him. The Goodwood dukes were newcomers compared not only with their Scottish forebears in the mediaeval mists, but with long-established families at places such as Arundel, Penshurst, Knole, Chatsworth and Woburn. The Pelhams dominated East Sussex, and even in West Sussex Richmond was able to nominate only one of the two members for Chichester,* and his efforts to promote candidates at New Shoreham and Arundel were unsuccessful.[11] But the family's local influence was becoming stronger as the 'proud' Duke of Somerset at Petworth grew older, testier and less active (he died in 1748), and meanwhile Richmond had a useful base in London where his re-edified house in Whitehall was close to the centres of power. At Goodwood he had extended and transformed the estate, and invitations to ride with the Charlton Hunt conferred social as well as sporting distinction. That he was a Duke of royal descent gave an edge to his aspirations, as also to his eligibility among his fellow-grandees. His awareness that Goodwood House itself was not yet a worthy 'ducal seat' is evident in the frequent preparation of schemes that a man 'who never saved a penny in my life' unfortunately could not afford.

For his heir the foundations were firm and the direction clear: he must cherish the family's prestige and influence and build on the improvements that had been made even if he too could not always afford it. Financial prudence not being part of the legacy, all this was honourably and willingly undertaken. But the third Duke had also a strong political drive and ambition that sought a responsible place in government; and sooner than most men of his kind he had a sense of impending change and of the reforms that would be necessary if families such as his were to retain their privileged position in society.

---

* Newcastle even held the nomination to the Chichester bishopric.

3

The Family

OF THE SECOND DUKE'S TWELVE CHILDREN only seven outgrew their nursery years. The third Duke, born in 1735, was seventh in the sequence, two earlier brothers having died in infancy; and another boy, George, was born in 1737. The surviving daughters were Caroline (1723), Emily (1731), Louisa (1742), Sarah (1744) and Cecilia (1750), a shadowy figure who died at the age of nineteen.

Lord George was a soldier, becoming a general in 1793 after an honourable career which began with service in Europe throughout the Seven Years War. He was member of Parliament for Chichester 1761–7 and for Sussex from 1767–90, when his son succeeded him in what was virtually a family seat. He was also a Privy Councillor, and his last appointment was as Governor of Plymouth, where he died in 1805.

His relations with Richmond were conventionally fraternal, with reconciliation soon following periods of misunderstanding and disagreement. The disagreements – so at any rate the sisters felt – were usually promoted by his wife, Lady Louisa Kerr, whom he married in 1758 against the wishes of her father, the fourth Marquis of Lothian. Lady George may not have been a very attractive person but her character was blackened by the Lennox ladies, who regarded her as a sharp-tongued intriguer always stirring up trouble from her home at West Stoke, only a few miles from Goodwood.

The Lennox ladies were formidable, and between them they caused more family complications than any mischief contrived by Lady George.[1] In 1744 Lady Caroline, the eldest, scandalised fashionable London by eloping with Henry Fox. The second Duke and his wife, who had refused their permission, would not speak to them for four years, and the friend who had lent his house for the ceremony faced social ostracism.

The bride's sister Emily thought Fox 'an ambitious, vain toad,' and his rapacity and cynical self-interest were startling even by contemporary standards. His father, Sir Stephen Fox (1627–1716), having lost all the sons of his first marriage, and being still, at the age of seventy-seven, 'of a vegete and hale constitution,' married the daughter of a Lincolnshire parson and sired four more children: Lord Ilchester, the first, and then Henry, paired with a twin sister Christian, and Charlotte, the youngest.

Service under Henry Pelham as Secretary at War provided Henry Fox with a few lucrative pickings, a foretaste of what was to come. He made his vast immoral fortune during eight years, 1757–65, as Paymaster of the Forces. All the funds to pay, equip and supply the Army came into his department; and having taken the commission demanded of the contractors and their bankers, he made a further profit by investing this public money during the considerable period between his receiving and disbursing it.*

Having enriched himself by war, Fox was equally willing to sell his services in the cause of peace, this time for the promise of a title. The young George III and his chief minister, the Earl of Bute, were determined to end the war now that the French were defeated, and they saw this also as a means of purging the administration of the corrupting influence of the Walpole and Pelham régimes.** The agreements that ended the Seven Years War were attacked as a betrayal of Britain's allies (as if it were possible to 'betray' Frederick of Prussia) and the sacrifice of national advantage. It is true that some territorial gains and trading possibilities were handed back to the enemy, but there were good hard-headed reasons why peace should be made. Pitt, superb organiser of victory by his leadership and strategy, had become overbearing, an unslaked carnivore seeking further prey. The Duke of Bedford – the Russells have seldom been 'king's men' – argued the unwisdom of campaigning for more territories and commercial surrenders that would be costly and difficult to defend, and would provoke other nations to envy and retaliation.

So in the autumn of 1762 it fell to Henry Fox to persuade the Commons to accept the peace preliminaries agreed at Fontainebleau earlier in the year. For this purpose the King was willing to postpone the promised purification of the system: 'We must call in bad men to govern bad men.' With the Crown's patronage at his back, Fox's adroit mixture of bribes, promises and intimidation broke even the Duke of Newcastle's political machine and the peace proposals were carried by 319 votes to 65. Fox then fell upon the errant 65 who had resisted the Royal will. 'Fox's Martyrs', harassed and deprived for a hostile parliamentary vote, sealed his disgrace. His work done, he was abandoned by the King, whose sensibilities were now offended by 'the scene of corruption' he had helped to create. (Thus early in his reign George had discovered that the cleansing of Augean stables is not necessarily good for the horses.) In 1763 Fox received the

* In a will made before he took the Pay Office, Fox left his wife £1100 a year and securities of £8000. At his death he left her £2000 a year, Holland House, and securities of £120,000; and to his three sons estates and annual incomes, plus some £50,000 in cash to be shared between them. He had earlier spent thousands on settling their gambling debts, Charles losing £140,000 in three years. Auditors' attempts to separate Fox's private wealth from money properly belonging to the public domain continued for eight years after his death. See Trevelyan, pp.24–5, 268–71.

** For George III's constitutional policies, see Chapter 8.

15 (RIGHT) The third Duke of Richmond (1735–1806), when Earl of March, aged five.

16 (BELOW) Lady Caroline Lennox, aged ten, with her pony and a groom, by Wootton. In a letter dated August 1733 the artist advised her father, the second Duke, to remove any dust from the painting by using 'a clean Spunge and water,' and he hoped that 'my lady Dutches recd no great harm from . . . the highwayman that rob'd her Grace and company on Rook's Hill.'

17 (LEFT) Henry Fox, Lord Holland. Lady Caroline Lennox married him against the wishes of her parents, the second Duke and Duchess.

18 (BELOW) Holland House, Kensington, from an engraving by P. Foudrinier, 1751. Henry Fox took the title of his barony from this Jacobean mansion, which he bought when he was Paymaster of the Forces.

19 Meissen snuffbox with a portrait of Caroline Holland on the inside of the lid. Caroline eloped with Henry Fox in 1744, and the snuffbox was a reconciliation present from Fox to the second Duchess.

barony of Holland, named from the house in West London that he had bought with the plunder of the Pay Office, where he was allowed to remain for another couple of years, but his public career was over. He consoled himself at 'Tully's Formian villa,' an architectural absurdity with imitation castles, abbeys and ruins that he had built at Kingsgate, in Kent, on the North Foreland.

In Fox's own view he had done the State some service and he never could understand his unpopularity and political isolation. He spent his last years brazenly soliciting an earldom which he never received. He had debased politics in an age when most men had their price, and probably this influenced his talented son Charles. When Charles lost heavily at the tables, payment of his gambling debts was a point of honour. He saw less reason to behave honourably in politics.

Yet in his marriage Henry Fox was as happy as anyone in England. For thirty years he had Lady Caroline's unwavering love and confidence, and if he did not always have her understanding also, this was because she did not care about politics and refused to discuss them. She preferred books and gardening and the amateur theatricals which brought her friends to Holland House. She enjoyed her responsibility for her younger sisters and shared the joys and troubles of her own three sons. Henry, the second, had died in infancy, and the survivors were Stephen, dull, deaf and overweight; Charles, heir to his father's deviousness but not his financial acumen; and Henry Edward, who became a successful soldier and diplomat. Their parents loved them deeply and spoiled them outrageously. Caroline's dutifulness to her husband as *paterfamilias* was shown when in 1768 he ordered her to cease her correspondence with her sister Emily in Ireland on account of a political disagreement with Emily's husband, the Duke of Leinster. She kept her promise for four years, resuming her letters only when she learned that Leinster was dying.

Henry Fox died in 1774, followed by Caroline three weeks later and Stephen by the end of the year – but not before Stephen's wife had borne him a son whose belated arrival prevented Charles from inheriting the Holland title. Although Caroline had lived down the shame of her elopement, her marriage to Fox was politically unfortunate for Richmond because, however unfairly, Fox's unpopularity rubbed off on to him. Even after an open rupture in 1768, when Fox supported government policy over the Middlesex election, Richmond could not escape the suspicion that he and his brother-in-law were natural allies. With young Charles soon displaying his wayward political ambitions, the suspicion lingered. Although by the 1780s they were on opposite sides about almost everything, in earlier days their attitudes and interests sometimes coincided. Richmond's connection with the Fox family was one of the reasons why he had a reputation for unreliability.

Caroline was the most worldly of the Lennox sisters, forthright and often censorious in her opinions, with a touch of steel that the others lacked. She could be critical of the frailties of her sex, wondering whether beauty was always an advantage: 'I seriously think people are so often disagreeable with it. Good sense and a pleasing manner is so infinitely preferable.' Men's vanity fed women's illusions: men 'fancy they are so mighty necessary to a woman's health and happiness; it's abominably indelicate and I don't believe a word of it. I'm sure one sees many an old virgin mighty well and mighty comfortable'.

Contemporary portraits suggest that Lady Emily was the most beautiful of the Lennox sisters. She was only fifteen when in 1747 she married James Fitzgerald, twentieth Earl of Kildare, who subsequently became Viscount Leinster in the English peerage and, in Ireland, Duke of Leinster, Ireland's only duke and premier peer. Polyphiloprogenitive even beyond the habits of her adopted country, Emily bore him nineteen children in twenty-six fecund years, not counting a miscarriage here and there. In her great house at Carton in County Kildare there was endless gaiety of balls and parties, and when her husband built Leinster House in Dublin, the revels continued there. It did not seem that Emily's opulent and contented way of life could ever embarrass her brother living on a more modest scale in distant Sussex.

James Leinster was a serious-minded man, an enlightened landlord and wealthy enough to offer to equip a regiment from his own pocket when the Jacobites invaded England in 1745. Although loyal to the Crown, he was sensitive to Irish grievances and resentful of the intolerant Protestant ascendancy maintained by Archbishop Stone at Dublin Castle. He wished the Parliament in London to grant to the Irish the liberties already enjoyed by their own people and to repeal the embargoes that crippled Irish trade: the policy of a liberal and civilised man, not of a perfervid nationalist. In 1753 he went in person to London to petition George II on behalf of a people oppressed by a corrupt and factious government. 'Lord Kildare has deceived himself or been deceived egregiously,' was Henry Fox's reflection on this.

A particularly harsh Lord Lieutenant, the first Duke of Dorset, was recalled, but not until Henry Grattan's time was there any substantial improvement of the system. Complaining about 'the Castle' was knocking one's head against a wall, and although he did not change his views, Leinster had to be content with improving the condition of his tenants and people within his immediate care. In 1762 he was in London again to try to persuade the government to prepare against a possible Franco-Spanish invasion through a virtually undefended Ireland. News that in his absence Emily had given a ball at Carton produced a tender admonition on wise behaviour in a crisis: 'I think you were quite right in drinking near a pint before your ball, but should have advised madeira rather than hock, lest the effect might have occasioned your going forth oftener than you would have chosen upon such a day.'

The second Duke had wished that, until they came of age or married, his younger daughters should be in the care of their two elder sisters. With the estate to look after, and his public business and presumably children of his own, the heir would not welcome energetic young ladies overrunning the house. For a period, therefore, Emily had the care of Louisa and Sarah as well as of her own family. Now and then she and some of her children travelled to England to stay with Caroline in London or with the Richmonds at Goodwood, and in the meantime Caroline's frequent letters, until Fox forbade them, kept her informed of family affairs. 'I hope to see a great deal of my dear brother Richmond,' Emily wrote on the eve of one of her visits, 'for I do love him monstrously and he is so good to me.'

Her brother's heartfelt goodness brought her such consolation as was possible on the death in 1765 of her first-born child and heir, George, Lord Offaly. Aged nineteen, he had just been commissioned in a cavalry regiment when he died at Richmond House in London, stricken by a sudden fever. After providing every medical care in an effort to save his life, Richmond was 'forced to take upon me that miserable task of acquainting his father with it.' He arranged for the boy to be buried at St Martin's Church but he feared to think how Emily would take the news. 'Whichever way she hears it I dread the consequences,' he wrote to Henry Fox.[2] 'You know how much she had placed her affections upon him . . . and surely with the greatest reason for I never saw such sweetness of temper, sense and everything that was amiable in any person stronger than in this poor boy.' The letter ends: 'Adieu, my dear Lord. My best love to my sister. You are happy indeed to have such children and to preserve them! Next to you I am happy in having none, for surely it must be infinite misery to lose them.' In Offaly, perhaps, he saw the son that he would never have. The Duke's concern for all members of his family remained constant throughout his life. In 1780 he wrote to Lord St Vincent from Ranmer Camp near Dorking, thanking the admiral for his kindness to Emily's son Gerald:

> As it is by no means a matter of indifference to me whether my nephew receives the best education possible at sea, or the common one which is very bad, I must rejoice at his being with you, where he will be made both a Seaman and a Gentleman. Good sense in education is rarely met with; an unreasonable severity or total neglect are the extremes which are much oftener fallen into, than that just medium absence on board the *Foudroyant*.

RICHMOND'S FAVOURITE among the sisters is said to have been Louisa, and she was loved by all. Without being unworldly she was one of those rare women who found natural happiness in bringing love and strength and comfort wherever they were needed. 'That self-same unalterable, dearest of sisters, who is ever and

22 (RIGHT) Lady Louisa Conolly with her hunter and her dog Hibou, by Robert Healy, 1768. Said to be Richmond's favourite among the sisters, she married Thomas Conolly of Castletown, County Kildare, in 1758.

20 James Fitzgerald, Duke of Leinster, by Allan Ramsay. Fitzgerald married the fifteen-year-old Emily Lennox in 1747.

21 Emily Leinster, by Francis Cotes. She was reputedly the most beautiful of the Lennox sisters.

for ever the same in affection and tenderness,' Sarah described her. In a life not free from trouble she would never 'let anybody see that she was suffering, lest they should be sorry too.'

Her own greatest sorrow was that after an early miscarriage she was told that she would never have children. In 1758 she had left Emily's care at Carton to marry Thomas Conolly of Castletown in County Kildare,* a commoner with a large estate and £27,000 a year with which to maintain it. Conolly was indolent and hypochondriac – not an inspiring man – and although he represented Londonderry in the Irish Commons for forty years and occupied a few minor offices, he lacked the Fitzgeralds' energy and sense of responsibility. He also appeared in the English Parliament. In 1759 Fox procured him a seat at Malmesbury, and from 1768 to 1780 he was a member for Chichester, but as he seldom spent more than a couple of months a year in England, his contribution was modest.

Soon after their marriage the Conollys were in London and Caroline told Emily of the impression they had made on her. Louisa was 'a sweet pretty-behaved girl, indeed people don't reckon her very handsome, I find, but everybody likes her . . . in short, a mighty amiable girl, and of a most pleasing disposition.' With Conolly it was another matter. 'You must indeed be partial not to think him immensely silly, dear sis; sure he is a tiresome boy, and one feels sorry he is so, he seems so exceeding good-natured. I can but think how miserable I should have been at Louisa's age to have had such a husband. I hope and believe she won't find it out ever.'

She never did find it out although distressed by his attachment to a neighbouring Irish widow. With her serene gift of seeing good in everyone, she nursed him through all his manifestations of ill-health, and cherished him until he died. Besides, he had several sisters, so that as well as an overspill of Emily's children Castletown was always full of nephews and nieces to receive her love. (One of Conolly's sisters was married to General Howe, whose involvement in the American campaign caused needless anxieties for his safety – he did not take risks; another to 'the Fighting Fitzgerald' of County Mayo, a privileged bandit who led a private force of armed thugs and eventually was hanged for murder.) Social life at Castletown lacked the sparkling gaiety that Emily brought to Carton, but Louisa managed her household with unobtrusive efficiency, and visitors were always the better for being there. Her impact on her brother Richmond's career was unimportant in so far as she never brought him social or political embarrassment. In a wider sense it was considerable because she was a life-enhancing influence on all who knew her.

The fourth sister, Sarah, has a larger part in the story.

---

* The house, built in the 1720s to designs by Galieli, is now the headquarters of the Irish Georgian Society.

4

Westminster School and the Grand Tour

THE YOUNG EARL OF MARCH entered Westminster School* in about 1745 and his brother George soon afterwards. Pupils more or less contemporary with them included Rockingham (then Viscount Higham), Cowper, Gibbon, Warren Hastings and the satirist Charles Churchill. Cowper later recorded that it was March who 'set fire to Vinny Bourne's greasy locks and box'd his ears to put it out,' but this has been attributed to other scholars, Higham included, and Vincent Bourne being an eminent Latinist but a mild man, it may have happened more than once. That March was early adept in schoolboy ingenuity is evident in his excuse for not writing regular letters home. Lord John Sackville reported that 'he desir'd me if I saw the Duchess of Richmond to beg she would excuse his writing to her every week, and that his Master was of opinion it took up too much of his Lordship's time, and thought that once a fortnight was sufficient; Ld George too desir'd me to tell her Grace that if she would write to him he knew somebody would write to her in return.'[1]

The difficulty in finding time to write was mentioned again in March's letter to the Duchess a year later.

I received your letter, and would have wrote to you on Thursday as you desired, but what with busines and masters I could nott; Saturday and Sunday it was the same: to day I have found one hour leager [?leisure] to write to my dear Mama. I saw Papa who was so good as to beg us a play. I hope he and you are both well. Pray tell my Sister that I received her letter and would have answered it if I had had Time. Doctor Johnson is with us about the Rules of Verses which is faging work. I have heard some time ago that Jamaica was taken by the French, but it is no more talk'd of.

It will be remembered that the second Duke managed to talk himself out of an official embassy to Paris, arguing that he could not afford to maintain an

---

* The eighteenth century saw a marked shift from private education by tutors towards the public schools, notably Eton, Westminster, Winchester (despite a taint of Jacobitism) and Harrow. Westminster, especially, was known as a nursery for statesmen, including Carteret, Pulteney, Chesterfield, Newcastle, Henry Pelham, Mansfield, Bedford, Grafton and Portland. Attending the same school created an identity of outlook. Newcastle, who never neglected his opportunities, was always careful to surround himself with Westminster men on whose support he was confident he could rely. See John Cannon, *Aristocratic Century*, 1984, pp.42–4.

establishment fitting the dignity of the King's representative. Later in 1749, however, he made one of his regular visits to Paris and Aubigny, leaving his two sons in England in the care of a tutor, Thomas Gibberd. During the summer holiday they stayed with the Cadogans at Caversham and also visited Oxford, where, according to Gibberd, 'one of the present Proctors was extremely pleased with Lord March's curiosity and attention to everything that was shown him.' Clearly not everything was as agreeable as this, because March's own letters have a slightly apologetic or defensive tone as though in reply to some parental reproof. Thus in August he writes: 'I am very much obliged to you for your kind letter which I hope will have a proper effect upon me. By this time I hope your passage has been as favourable to France as it was to Holland . . . Goodwood, *considering your absence from it*, has been tolerably pleasant. I hope that you are very happy abroad and that at your return home you will find everything to make you happy here, as your kind indulgences have always made your most dutiful and obedent son.' Writing a few weeks later he says: 'At my return from Oxford, I received your letter and was very sorry I gave occasion to you to caution me about my writing well, which was in some measure owing to my not having good pens, but chiefly to my own negligence, concerning which I shall take greater care for the future.'

This letter goes on to describe 'an accident from a large dog who flew at my face after I had been giving him some meat, and pinched it, but did not fetch

blood. It has pretty much swelled but it is quite gone down again and remains now only a little black.' The same post carried Gibberd's version of the accident, which arose from March's 'teasing, or playing too roughly with him, tho' frequently cautioned against it.' The victim had been in more discomfort than he had admitted, but the swelling had been reduced by 'an ointment I brought with me from London, for fear of an accident.' Doctors had been consulted and there was no cause for anxiety.

An undated letter at this time shows March's salutary respect for his father's displeasure and hope in his mother's willingness to shield him from it. He tells her that:

> . . . I have reflected with great concern upon the uneasiness I gave you at dinner by a behaviour which I am extremely ashamed of, and sorry for. I scarce know with what face to ask your pardon, after having had occasion to desire it so often, but shall esteem it as a particular favour if you would so far oblige me as not to mention my ill behaviour to Papa, but forgive your most penitent, dutiful and obedient son.

The Duke was home at Goodwood for what was to be the last Christmas he would spend there, and in the final weeks of his life he was much concerned by hints which Henry Fox had passed about March's behaviour. As he was able to live at Richmond House, March did not board at Westminster and had freedom to spend weekends and evenings as he pleased. In a long, boastful and exuberant letter to Henry Fox he had set out his philosophy for dealing with the female sex; and Fox had said only enough to make the parents anxious.

Richmond thought that Fox 'must have some strong and recent reasons for saying you dread his staying another year at school . . . We therefore beg you would explain what you mean by it; are you apprehensive of drunkenness, or what is worst of all, marriage? . . . If there is risk of what I have mentioned, the only step to take would be sending him abroad.'

March's offence was neither drunkenness nor an intention to be married, but even a man as case-hardened as Fox felt that if March already had so much of his royal great-grandfather in him, it would be prudent to remove him from the temptations of Vauxhall Gardens and Ranelagh; and kinder for the ladies.

March's letter[2] opens saucily enough by reminding Fox that as he is 'Secretary at War and consequently know all the business of the state, and how to keep it secret, I shall beg you never to mention anything of this to anybody; at least not to anyone but those you are sure will never speak of it again.' Much is said about a Miss Townsend, who 'is a great coquette' but is March's 'angel' and he wrote a semi-blasphemous poem to be placed in her prayer-book:

> *'Tis Love, the noblest passion of the mind*
> *The gospel bids, love bold and unconfin'd . . .*

23 (LEFT) Watercolour based on eighteenth-century etchings of Richmond House in London, by the ninth Duke. The house can be seen between the towers of Westminster Abbey and the small skiff in midstream.

A VIEW *of the* FIRE-WORKES *and* ILLVMINATIONS, *at his* GRACE *the Duke of* RICHMOND'S
Perform'd by the direction of Charles Frederick Esq.

N°. 1 Pavillon beautifully illuminated.
2. The Duke of Richmond's House.
3. The Boats and Barges for the Aquatic Fire-works.
4. His Majesty's Barge.

Vue des FEUX *d'*ARTIFICE *et des* ILLUMINATIONS *donnés par Monseig*
sur la TAMISE *et vis a vis de son Hotel, Lundi le* 1

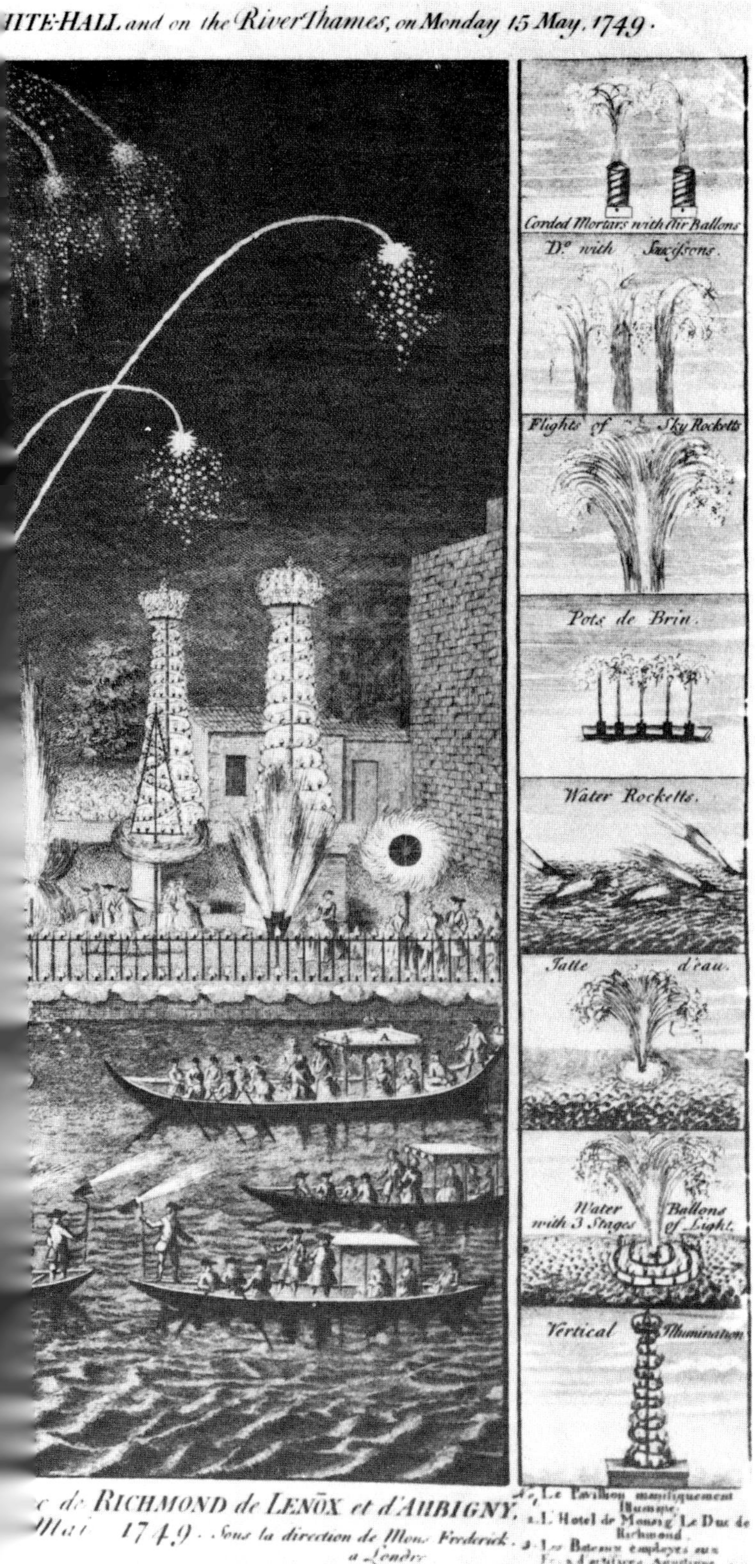

24 The grand illuminations of Monday 15 May 1749, when the second Duke of Richmond entertained the Duke of Modena at Richmond House. A contemporary account in *The Gentleman's Magazine* describes how 'four hundred persons of distinction were present and a magnificent display of fireworks contained in the Privy Garden and on the Thames.' The fireworks included 200 water mines, 200 air balloons, 200 fire flies, 5000 water rockets, 5000 sky rockets, 100 fire showers, 20 suns, 100 stars. Richmond House is on the left of the picture, and the Royal Barge carrying King George II and Queen Caroline, is on the right.

Then there is a Miss Rigby who mistook brother George for a boy she had kissed the night before but offered to redeem her mistake by a similar token. George ran away 'and said he left me his proxy, which office I acquitted very tolerably with half a dozen more of my own . . . , for I was soon acquainted . . . For God's sake never mention Miss Rigby's name to any one mortal, not even to Lord Kildare. For one should never kiss and tell.' Then '. . . in the midst of my jollity I was packt to Hampton Court for a week, but I diverted myself as well as I could in so mussy a place, especially one day in the maze with a very pretty girl.'

This is the young philanderer's philosophy:

> I have learnt from the little experience I have, not to care a farthing for one woman more than another, so as not to make myself uneasy about her or anyone else. I say everything that is fine, squeeze their hands, tell them they are angels, &c., never meaning a word I say, and not caring for them when they are out of my sight. I have sometimes err'd from this rule, but upon the whole am not captivated by one woman. I always make myself, wherever I am, as easy as possible.

'Love them and leave them' is not altogether reprehensible in a boy of fifteen, and no doubt March tailored his account to appeal to Fox's salty character. In this brother-in-law thirty years his senior he probably found a confidant to whom he could say things – not necessarily things that were wholly truthful – that he could not say to a rather stern father. But Fox was sufficiently uneasy to hint to the parents that all was not well. The outcome is not known, because a few weeks later both parents were dead.

It would be five years before the new Duke of Richmond came of age, and five guardians were appointed to administer his estate: two uncles, the Earls of Albemarle and Cadogan; two brothers-in-law, Henry Fox (Lord Holland) and Emily's husband James Kildare (Duke of Leinster); and as a sort of political godfather, the Duke of Newcastle. Debts of £17,000 owing on the estate were in due course settled, and Richmond was sent to Geneva in the care of Abraham Trembley.

Trembley had made a European reputation by his researches on coelenterates, and his observations on polyps collected by him at Bognor, were first published in 1742. He had lived for some years as tutor, secretary and valued friend in the household of Count Bentinck at The Hague. Bentinck's wife was Lady Margaret Cadogan, Duchess Sarah's younger sister, and as the families were closely linked the second Duke chanced to have witnessed some of Trembley's experiments, confirming them in a letter to the Royal Society in 1743.[3] The Duke had such a high regard for Trembley's wide-ranging abilities that he secured him a diplomatic appointment at the congress at Aix which ended the European war in

1748, and his services there earned him a pension of £300 from the British government. He was then invited to Goodwood, where he studied fresh-water organisms on the Sussex coast and demonstrated that the marine polyp was not, as had been thought, a plant but an animal.[4]

Having left the Bentinck household, Trembley had no settled purpose when the second Duke was taken ill 'and expressed in the last moments of his life his hope that I would be attached to the person of a son whom he was leaving at the age when a father is always necessary . . . I seized the opportunity with eagerness and gratitude. I followed it with delight; and my happiness increased when I found myself attached to both the sons of the illustrious father for whom I grieved.' For five and a half years the young Richmond was in Trembley's full charge.

At Geneva he was instructed by Trembley's own former tutors, and Trembley was well pleased with his development: adding, 'He loves dogs prodigiously. He loves also the human race and the *feminine* race.' In September 1752 they set out on the Grand Tour, and apart from a stay in England the following year and a few months at Leyden University, they were steadily on the move until January 1756. The Tour was a perambulation obligatory for young men of wealth and position. From it they would acquire a sense of the unity of civilisation, of a cultural heritage older than any national strivings. French and English families did not cease their civilised association just because their countries happened to be at war.

For many young men the Tour meant a succession of balls, amours and parties interrupted by sometimes perfunctory inspection of statues and ancient buildings, but Trembley's intellectual interests and his fame as a scientist ensured a more rigorous application to duty. Their travels[5] started in the South of France, where the great Montesquieu discussed viniculture as well as laws and constitutions, and continued by way of Paris (visiting La Condamine, explorer of the Amazon, and Fontenelle, still needle-sharp at 95); Leyden, where Lord George joined them for scientific studies under Jean Allamand, Brussels, Brunswick, Berlin (an interview with Frederick the Great), Bohemia, Vienna (some fifty mornings spent at the new museum constructed by Emperor Frances I), Venice, Rome, Naples (Vesuvius obligingly erupted), Florence, Pisa, Turin (for discussions with the great geologist Donati), Berne and home through the Rhineland cities to join the Bentincks at The Hague.

Two portraits at Goodwood show Richmond as he was at this time. They were painted, rapidly and to order, by Batoni and Mengs, craftsmen who made a profitable business of catching noblemen on the Grand Tour as a photographer would today, and indeed the two portraits are photographic in style. They show a handsome, reflective young man who may have been somewhat overwhelmed by the richness of his experiences. He had quick perceptions and high artistic taste, but he was not an intellectual. In scholarly erudition he fell some way behind many of the English politicians he would meet in later years.

What was his response to all those European polymaths with whom Trembley discoursed so learnedly? What did he make – assuming he had to attend them – of all those mornings in the museum at Vienna, with the Emperor himself sometimes a student at Trembley's feet? To artistic achievement of any kind his response would be genuine and immediate, and the experience stayed with him, but at times he must have been overstretched.

We do have occasional glimpses of him. An English visitor who met the tourists in Hanover reported to Fox that 'he has not lost one bit of his amorous disposition, I assure you.' More seriously, he was deeply impressed at Berne by Albrecht von Haller, a multi-faceted man who was botanist, anatomist, physiologist and a poet with a lyrical response to the splendours of Alpine scenery. Near Strasbourg they found armies on manoeuvre, and Richmond insisted on pitching his tent near the centre of the action and studying the operations: to the inconvenience of Trembley, who was appalled by the noise. At Herculaneum he surveyed the ruins with books by Latin authors in his hand to test the accuracy of their descriptions: he was always one to check his sources.

These are only fragments, but in Italy we hear his own voice in some letters to Fox which have been preserved.[6] War is said to be imminent and he is determined to be part of it, even if it means going to sea. From Rome in March 1755 he hopes the French will realise we are in earnest, but he would rather the war came soon 'while we have the superiority at sea and that we may destroy their navy and trade now that we can.'

'If there is a war, remember me,' he writes, assured that Fox will exert his ministerial weight in the making of appointments. 'Remember I shall be immensely happy to serve anywhere, and if it is a sea war and we poor soldiers are useless,* I should even like to go board a fleet out of curiosity if there is any likelihood of their meeting with the French.' A few weeks later he apologises for troubling Fox again, 'but the excessive desire I have to see some service, and the fear I have of being absent when there is anything going on in the defence of my country, makes it impossible for me to let one post go by without desiring you not to forget me.'

In May, now at Florence, he has been told of the official view that although naval fighting might be imminent, a land war was not expected that summer. He 'should vastly like to see a naval fight, which tho' it seems at first to have no connection with the business by land, yet I am persuaded may give one some ideas. At least I should see fire, which the sooner one is broke to, the better.'

* Richmond had been given the rank of captain in the 20th Regiment of Foot in June 1753, four months before graduating at Leyden.

English admirals might not have welcomed ducal bystanders in the heat of battle, and of course Richmond's view of himself as a committed soldier had as yet very little foundation, but it would be improper to question or disparage the sincerity of his declarations. An active young man was eager to flesh his sword in defence of his country, and if called upon, he would drop all other plans and come home.

Meanwhile, as the land forces would not be immediately engaged, Richmond thought of attending the military academy at Turin, which perhaps set itself out as a tourist attraction rather than a serious training-school. 'I should not think of staying there longer than three weeks unless I find anything there worth learning.'

His concerns in Florence were not exclusively military. A mischievous postscript to a letter of 3 May tells Fox: 'I am in love with the Venus and take great pleasure to stroke her bum and thighs.' (Emma Hamilton's first attraction for her archaeologist husband was that she reminded him of certain Etruscan vases.)

Fox suggested that Richmond and Lord George come home in the autumn by way of Vienna and Hanover, where they might observe the military reviews, but Richmond replied that more yet was to be learned in Italy 'where every inch of ground is famous for some military action, and where I am sure we may learn a great deal of the many wars that have been in these countries.' After inspecting Piedmont, Lombardy and Genoa, he intended to return to England for the winter 'if the appearance of war increases.' Otherwise he would go back to Vienna, 'where the way of living and the people please me vastly' (Lord George preferred the French) and there would be opportunity to visit training-camps. Here he would like to be accompanied by a Captain Carleton rather than Trembley, and he asks Fox to communicate this as he does not wish Trembley to be offended. 'I think that to live together I should prefer Mr Trembley, but for the short time I should spend at Vienna and in the environs I should like Mr Carleton as I could learn more of him as a soldier and he is in that way more active. In short they are both excellent in their different ways and I love and esteem them both exceedingly.'

The choice did not arise, as Carleton was given a staff appointment with the Duke of Cumberland, and so 'I will jog on with Mr Trembley for I know it would hurt him not to return to England with me ... He is really the best and most honest man alive and has an infinite deal of learning and good sense.' Richmond's regard for his tutor was sincere and lasting. They became regular correspondents, Trembley was secured against financial need, and Richmond became godfather to his daughter. Their apparently unruffled companionship during five long years is a tribute to the qualities of them both, and no one could have discharged a responsibility more honourably than this good and amiable man.

25 (RIGHT) *View of Geneva*, by R. Gardelle. The young Duke of Richmond spent two years of his Grand Tour here, under the supervision of his tutor Abraham Trembley.

26 (BELOW LEFT) Portrait of Abraham Trembley, aged sixty-two, taken from the frontispiece of his book, *Instructions d'un Père à ses Enfants sur la Religion*.

27 (BELOW RIGHT) A page from Trembley's work on polyps. Some of the experiments leading to his discovery that the marine polyp is an animal and not a plant were conducted at Goodwood, using polyps collected at Bognor.

28 (OPPOSITE, BELOW) The Forum, painted by Van Lindt at about the time that Richmond visited Rome on the Grand Tour.

MÉMOIRES
POUR L'HISTOIRE DES POLYPES.

PREMIER MÉMOIRE.

Où l'on décrit les Polypes, leur Forme, leurs Mouvemens, & une partie de ce qu'on a pu découvrir sur leur Structure.

DES Faits auſſi ſinguliers, auſſi contraires aux idées généralement reçues ſur la nature des Animaux, que le ſont ceux que m'a fait voir l'Inſecte dont je vais donner l'Hiſtoire, demandent, pour être admis, les preuves les plus évidentes. Il eſt arrivé plus d'une fois, que la précipitation, & l'amour

A du

29 (LEFT) The *Apollo Belvedere*, commissioned by the third Duke from Joseph Wilton. This was one of a number of statues and busts acquired for the Duke's academy at Richmond House. Now at Goodwood, the *Apollo* was damaged during demonstrations by students deprived of their gratuities while the Duke was abroad on military service.

30 (BELOW) *A Dance in Raiatea*, by Giovanni Cipriani. The painting was probably commissioned by the third Duke when the artist was director of painting studies at the Richmond House academy. It is based on a drawing by Sydney Parkinson who sailed with Captain Cook on his voyage in the *Endeavour*.

31 *The Artist, Joseph Wilton RA, and a Student*, attributed to John Hamilton Mortimer, who at one time was a pupil at the Duke's academy when Wilton was its director. The picture must have been painted shortly before his death in 1779.

During his travels the Duke acquired some treasures for Goodwood, and a painting of Venus came, too, for purposes educative rather than erotic. In Rome in 1755 he had met three young artists, William Chambers, Joseph Wilton and Giovanni Cipriani, all of whom came soon afterwards to London and helped him to set up a small academy at his London house.* Opened in 1758, it welcomed 'any painter, carver, sculptor or other artist and youth over twelve years of age, to whom the study of statuary might be useful.' Chambers constructed a new gateway at Richmond House and also the gallery where the pupils, who included the young Romney, worked on plaster casts of Italian statuary. These casts provided a base for engravings, models, decorative sculpture, and even paintings, in the neo-classical style. Wilton, an English sculptor who created the monument of Wolfe in Westminster Abbey, was the academy's first director and he chose further casts to supplement those which the Duke had brought home from Italy. The Florentine Cipriani taught the pupils whose primary interest was in painting and decoration.

In February 1758 Walpole told Sir Horace Mann[7] 'that he had been pleased with a very grand seigneurial design of the Duke of Richmond,' who had assembled fine antique casts, had placed them 'in a large room in his garden, and designs to throw it open to encourage drawing. I have offered him to let my eagle be cast.' *The Daily Advertiser* noted at the same time that 'on Saturdays Messrs Wilton and Cipriani are to attend to see what progress each [student] has made' and to select the best models and drawings for annual prizes.

Many great collections of antiques were put together during the eighteenth century, but these were not accessible to the public, and artists who could not afford to travel had no opportunity to study the originals at first hand. Richmond's gallery helped to overcome both these difficulties, and the private drawing-masters of the period such as William Shipley and the brothers Henry and William Pars sent their pupils to make copies of great masterpieces. Richmond bought more casts from Wilton and the younger Matthew Brettingham, and the remarkably varied 'stock' included the *Apollo Belvedere* and the *Medici Faun* (both sculpted in marble by Wilton), Michelangelo's *Bacchus* and the feet of his *David* and also work by Duquesnoy, Bernini, Giovanni Bologna and Sansovino.[8]

Unhappily the offer of premiums, or prizes, led to difficulties when the Duke was called to his regiment and was unable to award them. According to the antiquary John Thomas Smith,[9] on his return he found a notice posted by the students:

---

* All three were engaged in the construction of the Gold State Coach, still used at Coronations: Chambers to design it, Wilton to carve the panels and Cipriani to paint them. This monstrous wagon cost £7661, weighed four tons and required eight stallions to pull it.

... apologizing for his poverty and expressing his sorrow for having promised premiums. For this most malicious conduct of the students concerned, his Grace, for a time, shut up the gallery, and some of the casts became the property of the Royal Academy, upon its establishment. The above account I received from my father, who was one of the many other students who suffered by the misconduct of his disorderly companions. The Duke's liberality was extolled by Hayley in his epistle to his friend Romney, who was one of the most constant and well-behaved students in his Grace's gallery.

The Duke relented, as he often did after impulsive gestures, and in 1764 the Society of Arts awarded its first prize of 20 guineas to Lewis Pingo* 'for the best engraving, on cornelian, of a Venus from one of the statues in the Duke of Richmond's Gallery.' But the students were still dissatisfied and in another demonstration 'some young men among them mutilated many of the statues by wantonly breaking off fingers, thumbs or toes; this naturally produced an exclusion of the innocent with the guilty.'** Perhaps the exclusion was permanent as far as the Duke was concerned for, with other things on his mind, he had a way of losing interest in ideas and enterprises he had initiated and he could be easily discouraged. But the gallery continued to function despite the foundation of the Royal Academy in 1768, and two years later it was taken over by the Incorporated Society of Artists, the Duke receiving a warm letter of thanks from the well-known engraver William Woollett. When Richmond House burned down in 1791 the newspapers recorded that its 'unrivalled collection' of artistic objects had been saved, and it is unlikely that in the intervening years the collection had only been gathering dust.

In his posthumous *Anecdotes of Painting* (1808) Edward Edwards regretted that the gallery had not received the recognition that it deserved. 'It was in this school that young men acquired a purer taste in the knowledge of human form than had before been cultivated by the artists in England.' If he had never done anything else, Richmond would deserve to be remembered for an imaginative and disinterested attempt to make available the work of foreign artists and craftsmen in an age when travel was restricted to the wealthy and the treasures of country houses were not open to the public. Walpole was right to call it 'a very grand seigneurial design.' This kind of enlightened patronage fostered a climate in which beauty could spread and flourish.

---

*Pingo, a medallist, later succeeded his father as engraver at the Royal Mint.

** The *Apollo Belvedere* can be seen in the colonnade at Goodwood today.

5

Marriage and the Military

GENERAL HENRY SEYMOUR CONWAY (1710–95) both as soldier and statesman was a victim of his own scruples and hesitations: as Edmund Burke aptly said of him, he was 'a Little Red Riding-Hood who could not tell a wolf from his grandmother.' A nephew of Robert Walpole, he was in the Commons for more than forty years for a succession of pocket boroughs. As a soldier he fought at Dettingen, Fontenoy and Culloden, but his failure in an expedition against Rochfort in 1757, due to his congenital hesitations, led to a series of pamphlets in which his bravery and judgment were alternately defended and impugned.

Absolved of the graver charges, he served under Prince Ferdinand of Brunswick, but when he began to take a serious part in politics he continued to be a prey to conflicting principles and indecision. Subsequently he was for more than twenty years Governor of Jersey, where he was only occasionally resident, and the island offered little resistance when the French twice raided it during the American war. Yet he was always in some degree respected for his inconvenient honesty, and his cousin Horace Walpole on two occasions offered him half his fortune. Conway retired from politics in 1784 because he could not accommodate himself to the younger Pitt. His home was at Park Place at Henley-on-Thames, where he built the bridge across the river, for which his daughter Anne Damer sculpted some of the heads. In old age he wrote a drama, *False Appearances*, in which Elizabeth Farren appeared at Drury Lane.

This was the man who became Richmond's stepfather-in-law. Conway was married to Lady Caroline Campbell, third wife of the late Earl of Ailesbury, whose only child was Lady Mary Bruce. 'Every time I see her I like her better and find in her everything I could wish,' Richmond wrote to Conway during 1756.[1] He was eager to know if there were any obstacles to the realisation of his happiness, and if there were not, he would like to 'accelerate it as much as possible.' He would be grateful if Conway and Lady Ailesbury would acquaint Lady Mary with his feelings, so that she should not be surprised or embarrassed when he addressed her.

They were married on 1 April 1757, when Richmond was twenty-two and his bride seventeen. Horace Walpole was ecstatic about 'the perfectest match in the

32 The third Duchess of Richmond, by Angelica Kauffmann. The Duchess is wearing a Turkish costume of gold-embroidered white silk with a purple, ermine-trimmed cape. This may be *A Lady in Turkish Dress*, exhibited by the artist at the Royal Academy in 1775.

33 Detail from a hunting scene by George Stubbs, showing the third Duke and Lord George Lennox out with the Charlton Hunt on the Sussex downs. Richmond was the first patron of Stubbs, who painted several outstanding pictures when he stayed at Goodwood in the early 1760s.

34 (RIGHT) Duchess Mary with, on her right, Richard Buckner, the bailiff, and Lady Louisa Conolly. (Detail from Stubbs' *A Study of Horses Exercising*, c. 1761.)

35 (BELOW) Foxhall, in the village of Charlton, was the hunting lodge where the Duke entertained his guests. A weather vane above the chimney stack activated a dial over the fireplace in the Duke's quarters so that His Grace could observe the direction of the wind while lying in bed.

world; youth, beauty, riches, alliances, and all the blood of all the kings from Robert Bruce to Charles II. They are the prettiest couple in England.'

An early Reynolds portrait shows Mary severely dressed, with braided hair, intent upon her sewing: the image of placid domesticity. That was not exactly the impression of the Duchess which Caroline conveyed to the other Lennox sisters. She was disturbingly 'giddy', or flirtatious, and apart from her good humour, 'she don't improve in the least,' proving that a pretty face is nothing 'without other *agréments*.' She was 'always routing about with men,' and when Richmond was absent at the wars, Caroline told Emily of an indiscretion reported by Lord George. At the play Mary stayed behind to watch the farce (a comic postlude) 'after the other ladies had left, with a Mr Medows and some other gentlemen . . . She means no harm, she says, and there is no persuading her a young woman's character may be vastly hurt without her meaning the least harm . . . George thinks too, and I agree with him, that racketing about the way she does, my poor dear brother abroad, is not quite decent. We don't mean she should shut herself up, but it's too much. She is beautiful this year, more admired by the men than anybody, which she likes.'

The Duchess accepted rebuke 'with infinite good humour,': not the response to which Caroline in her role of universal governess, was accustomed. She would not have the Duchess criticised by Lady George, whose observations on the matter were 'very impertinent', but she was baffled by a character who was new in her experience. 'She is an odd composition. George says she has good sense, which I doubt; that she has good humour, no envy in her temper, is certain; and yet she has one quality that makes a sort of contradiction to the rest, a vast deal of pride. Feelings, what you and I mean by them, to be sure she has none.' It is the difference between sense and sensibility: the Lennox sisters were apt to wear their hearts on their sleeves. The Duchess's 'pride' was in refusing to be bullied by Caroline or to take her seriously.

On Richmond's return, however, Caroline was able to give Emily a more consoling report. 'You can't imagine how much the Duchess improves. She seems to have discarded all her lovers. If my brother stay always at home for these next two or three years at least, she will do vastly well. She has the most perfect confidence in him, tells him everything in the world, the least trifling event, loves him as well as she can love anything.'

Possibly Caroline dare not to be too critical, with the husband around, but even this diluted praise lacks real warmth. Always there is the unspoken criticism – and it does indicate an honest anxiety – that instead of 'racketing about' in London, the Duchess should have been performing her first duty, which was to stay at home and have children. This she could not do. The marriage was childless, but even the *Dictionary of National Biography*, never enthusiastic in making such admissions, allows that Richmond had four illegitimate daughters.

36 (LEFT) Charles James Fox, aged thirteen, walking in the garden of Holland House with his cousin Lady Susan Fox Strangways. Leaning out of the window is Lady Sarah Lennox, who was to marry Charles Bunbury before Sir Joshua Reynolds completed the painting.

37 (LEFT) Portrait miniature of Mary, third Duchess of Richmond, probably painted shortly after her marriage in 1757.

38 (RIGHT) The third Duke of Richmond, by Sir Joshua Reynolds. A receipt from Reynolds himself, dated 1759, records payment of thirty guineas for the portrait and 'six guineas for a Miniature copy.'

Although neither partner was 'faithful' to the marriage in the common meaning of the word, it lasted for forty years with every appearance of total harmony. The only surviving pages of correspondence in the last years of the Duchess's life suggest a compatibility of interest and understanding founded on deep affection. The Duke loved children, but except in the few heartbroken words to Fox when young Offaly, his nephew, died, he is not known ever to have revealed in word or action how deeply it grieved him that in marriage he would have none of his own. To use a facile *cliché* and say that he and Duchess Mary 'came to terms with their situation' would be inadequate because they seem to have done more than that. Instead of driving them apart, misfortune strengthened the bond between them and made it a true 'union of hearts.'

ON THE GRAND TOUR Richmond had shown his enthusiasm for military affairs and his eagerness to take the first opportunity of testing himself in action. In 1756 he was made lieutenant-colonel in the 33rd Foot* and in the spring and summer he was with his troops in Holland and Germany. Here he kept very detailed accounts of expenditure on coaches and postilions, servants and board wages,

---

* Now the Duke of Wellington's Regiment.

103

even his disbursements for paper and pens (amounting at The Hague to four ducats). Officers won or lost quite heavily on gaming, and Richmond kept a careful record of his ventures 'at play'. There was a debit of 800 ducats to Colonel Beckwith, but during a week in April he won 190 ducats against reverses of only 19. This winning streak did not continue, because in the first half of June he lost 675 ducats against successes of only 403. When this fragmentary account closes he is recording a deficit of 458 ducats on 7 July.[2]

His mind was kept on more serious business by an interesting correspondence with Colonel James Wolfe, who appears to have found in him an officer capable of rescuing the country from disaster. 'I have fix'd upon you as the man by whose knowledge and example a solid and substantial degree of discipline will be introduced into the British Infantry,' he wrote in June 1756. The correspondence[3] began at the end of 1755 and ended in the summer of 1758 when Wolfe was in Canada and hoping that, if he should find good fur, he might present a muff to the Duchess, 'notwithstanding her manifest contempt for the *Militaire*.'

The two men had met in Paris in 1752 when Wolfe was on leave and they had discussed the organisation and 'discipline', in its original meaning of training, of Continental armies. Richmond's letters to Wolfe have not survived but he appears to have been equally despondent about Britain's prospects, and Wolfe endorses his complaint that youthful talent is not recognised: it is 'a foible of the time ... to exclude sound sense from all heads but grey.' It is fortunate that Richmond is in the Lords to warn Britain of its peril, or 'the affairs of this country will every day decline.'

During manoeuvres on Salisbury Plain Wolfe is pleased that Richmond has found time to write to 'a country acquaintance', as he calls himself, but he is still pessimistic. 'We decline visibly, our captains are almost all invalids and our subalterns have but a small portion of knowledge, spirit and authority.' He commends Richmond's own resolution under the restraints imposed by obstinacy and ignorance, but at the same time he is pleased that the young man should have taken some leave in order to hunt. Such 'country diversions' build up health and strength and are 'becoming recreations for a soldier.'

Early in 1757 Richmond must have offered a shrewd, and also prophetic, military analysis, because Wolfe is agreeing with him that 'the reduction of Quebec is the only effective blow that we can strike' in North America. It would give us 'the advantage of the war', and he is amazed that so far it has not been projected. A few months later, when the war was still going badly, he stated the essentials of total victory. 'Every honest man in the kingdom should take arms, dismiss his superfluous servants and equipages; keep his family in the country and give one half of his estate into the Exchequer. We must do this or submit – only denial and sacrifice will preserve our blessings to posterity.' This was astonishing language considering that 700 years had passed since a foreign

* the words are missing –
But since ignoble age* must come.
Disease & Death's inexorable Doom,
That life which others pay let us bestow
And give to Fame what we to Nature owe:
Brave let us fall, or honor'd if we live,
Or let us glory gain, or glory give –
Such, men shall own deserve a Sovereign State
Envied by those who dare not imitate.

39 General Wolfe, by Elizabeth, Duchess of Devonshire. This portrait in pencil and watercolour is based on a drawing by Sir Hervey Smyth thought to have been made on the Heights of Abraham in 1758. The verses below were found in the pocket of Wolfe's uniform after his death in the battle.

invader caused serious disturbance on English soil and that traditional warfare involved only a small part of the nation's manpower and resources. It is little wonder that senior commanders always thought that Wolfe was slightly crazed – though the King did wish that something of his madness might infect his fellow-officers.

Wolfe was sure that Richmond would do his duty and 'lend your money freely to support the constitution; but the bulk of our nobility are riding at horse races or shooting grouse when all the rest of the world are in arms.' Writing from the Isle of Wight six weeks later, Wolfe regarded a French invasion as inevitable, and laid down principles of defence that Richmond would ponder in later years. The enemy must be stopped at Canterbury because the Medway towns were too near London to make a safe defensive position. With 'a hidden thunder ready to break in upon this mass of ignorance,' Richmond should 'urge the ministers to put our docks into a better state of defence; fortify them so that the enemy must necessarily open trenches before them; and keep strong garrisons in Portsmouth and Plymouth, and a corps in Kent.'

The mutual attraction of these two young men is easy to explain. They had strong ideas and forceful natures and they could be sure of themselves to the point of obsession. Wolfe fulfilled his destiny at Quebec, seeming to leave Richmond to inherit his struggle against the torpor and ignorance of the military mind. Meanwhile a tiny incident[4] in September 1758 suggests that Richmond had already acquired some reputation as a pundit on matters of defence.

John Smith, a native of Hull now in Amsterdam, wrote to inform the Hull postmaster, John Wray, of a pending Dutch attack on the city. It was inspired by the French and its intention was to set fire to the port, the shipping and the magazines, to seize a vessel as a prize and to spare no man, woman or child. Wray was sufficiently alarmed to bring the letter to official notice, adding his own opinion that in Hull's present state of defencelessness a single 30-gun ship and 400 men might easily carry out these threats.

Wray's letter proceeded through the official channels until it reached Pitt himself; and Pitt, busy directing wars in Europe, North America and Asia instructed Richmond* to take whatever action should be necessary. His letter of 23 September said that although the threatened raid seemed unlikely, it would be improper to neglect the possibility. The condition of Hull required immediate attention, and 'I recommend to your Lordship to make instant provision for the defence of the place.' Perhaps it would be possible to spare some men from Newcastle or Berwick, or to make use of two troops of Light Horse that were on their way from Scotland. Richmond must decide what was best to be done but it was made clear to him that he must do something. The document ends at that

---

* He had been made a colonel in the 72nd Regiment of Foot in May 1758.

point, but no doubt Richmond responded energetically and, on paper at least, Hull was in a very short time rendered virtually impregnable.

Richmond had been fretting for months because his regiment had not been posted back to Europe, and he threatened to go to London to browbeat ministers or even the King himself. Orders were changed without this impulsive intervention, and in August he had taken part in a raid on Cherbourg. Pitt had a policy – described by a critic as 'breaking windows with guineas' – of launching commando raids on the French coast to compel the enemy to keep troops in the area who might otherwise have been sent to the main battle zone in Germany. The Cherbourg expedition was led by General Thomas Bligh, born in 1685 and still a year off retirement, an embodiment of the principle that military virtue resided only in greybeards. The town was occupied and much damage was done, but there were not the resources to hold it permanently and it had to be abandoned.

1759, the *annus mirabilis*, was a happier time for Richmond. His brother Lord George with him, he was in the British contingent supporting Prince Ferdinand of Brunswick in the great victory at Minden which was a turning-point in the Continental war. It liberated Hanover (which for George II was the primary, if not the only, object of the war) and relieved the pressure on Britain's ally Frederick of Prussia. The French escaped total rout only because Lord George Sackville failed to send his cavalry in pursuit. For this he was court-martialled and declared unfit to serve again in any military capacity: a verdict to be read to every British regiment to show that a title was no protection against charges of incompetence or irresolution. It did not, however, preclude Sackville, now calling himself Lord George Germain, from being given military direction of the war in America nearly twenty years later and being savagely criticised by Richmond.

At Minden Richmond distinguished himself. Prince Ferdinand thanked the whole army for the bravery they had shown and in conclusion commanded that 'it may be known to those who were immediately in touch with him whose behaviour he especially admired, namely the Duke of Richmond [and a few other officers], that he has great reason for satisfaction with their bearing.'

Actively this was the end of Richmond's short military career, and perhaps he chose the wrong course. With his expert interest in strategy, training and fortifications, he might have become a distinguished soldier duke. But the pull of Goodwood and the Lennox interest was too strong, and he also felt that his duty lay in political service. More immediately, however, he had to face the prospect of becoming brother-in-law to King George III.

6

Sister Sarah

In November 1759 Lady Sarah Lennox, rising fifteen, departed from Emily at Carton for the more sophisticated social life of Holland House. She was presented at Court, where the rancid old King wanted to cuddle her and the future George III fell in love with her.

George was only twelve when his father, Frederick Prince of Wales, died in 1751, and the dominating influence in his life soon became his tutor and mentor the Earl of Bute.* Bute was a family man with a Scotsman's respect for learning but he was politically inexperienced and had neither aptitude nor inclination for the uneasy eminence that he would presently reach. He taught his pupil history, set and corrected his exercises, and acquired an extraordinary authority over that slow-developing mind.

George's letter on the embarrassing topic of sex was written in general terms.[1]

> I mean to lay my whole breast naked before you and therefore shall in the course of this epistle touch on a spring that prudence bids me be silent on . . . You have often accused me of growing grave and thoughtful, it is entirely owing to a daily increasing admiration of the fair sex, which I am attempting with all the philosophy and resolution I am capable of to keep under . . . You will plainly feel how strong a struggle there is between the boiling youth of 21 years and prudence. The last, I hope, will ever keep the upper hand, indeed if I can but weather it but a few years, marriage will put a stop to this combat in my breast.**

A few weeks later he was more specific: Sarah had arrived. 'I was struck with her first appearance at St James's, my passion has been increased every time I have since beheld her; her voice is sweet, she seems sensible . . . in short she is everything I can form to myself lovely.' This was not just a royal flirtation or a would-be seduction as intended by George's brother Edward of York, who hoped that Sarah would be inclinable to his pawing attentions. Marriage was the object. 'I protest before God I never have had any improper thought with regard

* Sir John Stuart, third Earl (1713–92); Secretary of State 1761, First Lord of the Treasury 1762–3; widely unpopular and retired into private life after 1766 despite George's protestations.

** Not everyone believed in George's professions of continent virtue. Pamphlets accused him of having married Hannah Lightfoot, a Quakeress from Wapping, and of having had a child by her. Years later, in the ravages of his illness, he uttered strange intimacies about the Countess of Pembroke in the belief that he was married to her.

to her; I don't deny having often flattered myself with hopes that one day or other you would consent to my raising her to a Throne.' But he assured Bute that if this consent were withheld he would 'grieve in silence . . . for if I must either lose my friend or my love, I will give up the latter, for I esteem your friendship above every earthly joy.'

Bute had no intention of allowing the Prince to marry a relative of Henry Fox, a member of the war ministry of which he disapproved; their later association in engineering the peace was not yet anticipated by either of them. The Dowager Princess of Wales, Augusta of Saxe-Gotha, was equally determined that her son should not marry any English girl. George meekly trod the line. His 'dearest friend' had 'thoroughly convinced me of the impropriety of marrying a country woman; the interest of my country ever shall be my first care, my own inclinations shall ever submit to it; I am born for the happiness or misery of a great nation, and consequently must often act contrary to my passions.'

It was not to be as easy as that. Lady George Lennox entered the competition by producing her brother Lord Newbattle as Sarah's suitor, a brash youth who was heir to the Lothian titles. But Henry Fox did not give up hope and was still assiduous as a marriage broker. George came to the throne in October 1760 and the agents who scoured the German courts for suitable princesses produced Charlotte of Mecklenburg-Strelitz for the approval of Princess Augusta. Sarah was sent to the country estate of her uncle Lord Ilchester, where she broke a leg: occasioning from Lord Newbattle the comment that she was ugly enough already and now she would be worse. But Fox lost no opportunity of assuring the King of her courage, cheerfulness and expectation of an early recovery. When she returned to London, he instructed her in appropriate responses and expressions if the King should address her, and in the hope of a royal visit he bade her linger in the gardens at Holland House 'dressed in a fancied habit making hay.' Only a few days before his engagement was announced the king approached Sarah at Court, and it was remarked that he spoke warmly and intimately, 'had eyes but for her and hardly talked to anyone else.'

George III and his plain little German princess were to have fifteen children, and their loyalty to one another was unique among England's Hanoverian monarchs. With its draughts, its plain food, homely pleasures and unyielding etiquette their court was uncomfortable and dull, but it was decent: a fact of some importance when profligate thrones were toppling all over Europe. Sarah bore her disappointment if such it was with a dignity and good sense that was most creditable to a girl of her age. 'I can't go jigitting for ever.'*

* The King's repudiation of Sarah had a sequel in the Royal Marriage Act (1772). Two of his brothers, Cumberland and Gloucester, had secretly married commoners without his approval, and certain rather impracticable conditions were now laid upon members of the Royal Family in their choice of a mate. Among the opponents of this measure was Charles James Fox, an unexpected champion of the pieties of the domestic hearth.

40 (ABOVE)
King George III
at the age of about
twenty-two. (Studio of
Allan Ramsay). The
painting, which is at
Goodwood, is a version
of the portrait in
the Royal Collection.

41 (RIGHT) *Lady Sarah Bunbury sacrificing to the Graces*, (1765) by Sir Joshua Reynolds. The seated figure is Lady Susan Fox Strangways. Around the pedestal are garlands of roses, a device frequently used in paintings of the period to symbolise friendship. The picture was exhibited at the Society of Artists in 1765. (Oil on canvas 242 cm × 151.5 cm. Mr and Mrs W. W. Kimball Collection, 1922–4468. © 1987 Art Institute of Chicago. All Rights Reserved.)

She showed something of her feelings to her cousin Lady Susan Fox-Strangways, Ilchester's daughter, her confidante for many years.

Does not your choler rise at this? You think I dare say, that I have been doing some terrible thing to deserve it, but I assure you I have not . . . He always took pains to show me some preference by talking twice, and mighty kind speeches and looks; even last Thursday, the day after the orders were come out [about the official engagement] he had the face to come up and speak to me with all the good humour in the world . . . I shall take good care to show I am not mortified to anybody, but if it is true that one can vex anybody with a reserved, cold manner, he shall have that, I promise him.

Now as to what I think about myself, excepting this little revenge I have almost forgiven him; luckily for me I did not love him, nor did the title weigh anything with me, so little at least that my disappointment did not affect my spirits above one hour or two. I did not cry, I assure you, which I believe you will as I know you were more set upon it than I was. The thing I am most angry at is looking so like a fool.

If Sarah was not mortified, Henry Fox was. He blamed Lady George for intruding Lord Newbattle, a 'vain insignificant puppy,' but most he blamed Bute: 'Every man has at some time or other found a Scotchman in his way.' Although some advised against it, he insisted that Sarah be a bridesmaid at the royal wedding. 'You are the first virgin in England and you shall take your place in spite of them all, and the King shall behold your pretty face and repent.'

Richmond had none of this vehemence and he appears to have kept his own counsel throughout the whole embarrassing episode. If Sarah had married the King, his own future must have been different. On many subjects he could not have shared George's opinions, and yet it would have been improper for him to have gone, as it were, into public opposition. He would have been obliged to accept honorific posts – perhaps Master of the Horse like his father – which would have curbed his freedom. There was an ardency in him, a need to be up and doing, that would have been stifled in a mere appendage of the Court; and all the good and valiant things he attempted would never have happened.

Her elders meanwhile were sure that something must be done about Sarah, and quickly. Her portraits suggest that she was no great beauty. She seems to have had small eyes, a large nose and a rather doughy countenance. Yet Walpole observed that, 'with neither features nor air' she outshone all the other bridesmaids at the wedding, and Fox made a shrewd comment of a similar kind. To record her features 'is not describing her, for her great beauty was a peculiarity of countenance that made her at the same time different from and prettier than any other girl I ever saw.'

Reynold's stylised painting of her 'Sacrificing to the Graces' (1765) has none of this magnetism. As Mrs Thrale robustly remarked, sacrificing to the Graces was not her style: 'Her face was gloriously handsome, but she used to play cricket, and eat beefsteaks on the Steyne at Brighton.' But to certain susceptible men she was as terrible as an army with banners. Lord Errol, as mighty in his person as in the Scottish acres he commanded, was on his knees for an hour beseeching her to marry him. Horace Walpole thought that at the wedding 'dressed in tissue, he looked like one of the Giants in Guildhall, new gilt,' and it was not easy for a young girl to turn down a prodigy such as this, with his money and his influence. The sooner she was married, the better, before any more noble hearts were broken or knees worn out in fruitless solicitation, but no one would have expected her to marry Charles Bunbury.

Heir of a well-endowed Suffolk baronet, Bunbury was among the aspiring young men who frequented Holland House, ostensibly to discuss politics with Fox. He would be a member of the House of Commons, where Walpole referred to him as 'a chicken orator', and also of Dr Johnson's Literary Club, a distinction that argues some intellectual suppleness. He gambled in the London clubs and was seen on the social round, but he was always eager to get back to his dogs and his horses and his country pursuits. In the racing world he is still well esteemed. He was an active member of the Jockey Club, established in the 1750s to regulate the sport and keep out unscrupulous intruders; and although he always raced to win, he was known for the humanity that ordered his riders to use the spur seldom and the whip not at all. In 1780 his Diomede would win the first Derby.*

To Sarah he was politely attentive, which distinguished him from the suitors who had been hotly insistent, and she seems to have drifted into marriage rather than making a conscious choice. Louisa from Ireland, whom nothing could disenchant, said how lucky she was to 'meet with one who has such a universal good character,' but those nearer to events saw the auspices differently. Richmond thought Bunbury a coxcomb and said in a letter to Fox[2] 'how very bad a match this is! And 'tis the greater pity as I think one may say from past observation that Sarah's temper is not so unalterable but she might have done without him . . . But it is in my opinion necessary for her to marry him for her own reputation. How difficult it is to persuade one's friends to do what is for their own happiness! Well, my two thousand pounds is ready for the day of marriage.'

Even this promise may not have been fulfilled because Richmond complained that the French war would prevent his bringing in funds from Aubigny. He even became reluctant to contribute towards Sarah's trousseau. 'He has no great opinion of his pretty sister's attachments,' Caroline told Emily; and Lord Cadogan, Sarah's uncle, agreed that 'this is a very poor match, but the young lady is so apt to be in love it's better to secure this than venture her making a worse.' Caroline was reassured by Bunbury's placid good nature, but 'he is not

* The name of Bunbury has since been immortalised by Oscar Wilde, but it might have been remembered for something else. It has been said that when this great race was run for the first time Bunbury and Lord Derby, the promoters, tossed a coin to decide after which of them it should be named. What is in a name? Would the race have become world-famous if it had been called the Bunbury instead of the Derby?

lively . . . one of those people one can't find fault with and yet don't grow more pleasing on acquaintance.' She complained of a 'cold insipidity that disturbs me. His passions are not very strong.'

Bunbury was not the marrying sort, but married they were, in June 1762, in the private chapel at Holland House, Bunbury twenty-two, Sarah seventeen and now to be known to Emily's younger children as 'Aunt Bum'. Before long her unlucky habit of arousing the wrong sort of publicity fed the gossips once again when in 1764 her cousin Lady Susan eloped with an Irish actor, William O'Brien. The circumstances were furtive and, according to Walpole, Sarah had been an unwitting party to them. Lord Ilchester had forbidden the lovers to correspond, but 'the swain had learned to counterfeit Lady Sarah Bunbury's hand so well that Lord Ilchester himself had delivered several of O'Brien's letters to Lady Susan.' O'Brien's claim to kinship with the Clare viscounts was blarney, but he was not the opportunist down-at-heel mummer that has been suggested. No less a judge than Garrick brought him from Dublin to Drury Lane, where he played leading roles in plays of the period and such Shakespearean parts as Mercutio, Lucio and Prince Hal. The theatregoing public were sorry to lose him. But for a wealthy heiress like Susan, marriage with an actor was a dreadful thing and the couple had to disappear. Fox generously settled £400 a year on them and found O'Brien a job in North America. Lady Ilchester paid the bridegroom's debts of £2000 and Fox also settled the bill for a portrait which he had commissioned but omitted to pay for.

The departure of her closest friend – now to be 3000 miles away – was a blow to Sarah because inevitably their correspondence became slower and less frequent. At Barton, in slow-paced Suffolk, she missed the children and the gaiety of Carton and the sophisticated company of Holland House. Although Bunbury was always kind and considerate, she was fearful of 'tagging after him' as he pursued his masculine activities in the card-room and the field. Her house and gardens were lovely but she had no children to occupy her and, try as she might, her letters to her sisters, full of trivialities, could not hide her boredom.

7

Cultivating the Garden

GEORGE III HAD BEEN ON THE THRONE only a few weeks when a foolish incident soured the high promise of Richmond's career. In the new reign he had been appointed a Lord of the Bedchamber, a Household office of some importance to those who held it – about a dozen of them – because their personal attendance on the Sovereign brought them inside knowledge and they were watched as barometers of royal opinion. But Richmond was angry because Lord Fitzmaurice had been preferred to Lord George and to Charles Fitzroy, a kinsman of the Duke of Grafton, as Aide-de-Camp to the King.

As Fox tells the story,[1] 'he declares publicly he will resign and make his brother resign if it is so, and what not! Lady George Lennox, whose love of mischief and want of judgment will I fear appear in more instances, flies to Goodwood and away comes the Duke . . .'

Richmond paused to try to enlist Bute's help in the matter but the reply was discouraging.[2] Bute would do all in his power 'to assist your wishes concerning your brother. At the same time I must not conceal from your Grace that I think it a very difficult point to carry.'

In Fox's account, 'the Duke of Grafton has an audience, asks for Fitzroy with good breeding, is refused and comes out in 3 minutes. The Duke of Richmond stays 20 minutes, makes the King exceedingly angry, and comes out in a passion' and announces that he has resigned the Bedchamber, although not his regimental command:

> It was hard to guess exactly what passed. The King says he will never repeat it, it is too bad to be repeated. I find by the Duke of Richmond the King behaved with firmness and with dignity, tho' very angry . . . The Duke was much dejected and is gone to Goodwood, Dec 10th, sorry as we all are for him to have quarrelled so unreasonably and unprovoked with a young King capable of great resentment where his dignity is trenched upon. The Duke's not resigning his Regiment is much wondered at and makes everybody see that he must know himself in the wrong . . . He has not been at Goodwood a week before he writes to Lord Bute to complain that the King has not spoke to him. He has been to Court since, and spoken to, and upon that foot of civility will remain, as I fear the too justly conceived ill opinion of him will too.

42 Aerial photograph of Goodwood from the south-west taken in 1934. The wing behind the house and slightly to the right of the portico was demolished in 1969. The stables are to the left, and behind them is the old 'gothic' laundry, which has been converted into a canteen for visiting stable-hands. In the distance are the former kennels, now the headquarters of a local golf club.

Walpole had a similar view from the Earl of Hertford, who 'cannot be very sorry for the Duke of Richmond; I have no opinion of his Grace's judgment, and his temper will bear humbling.' Caroline had no doubt that it was the importunity of Lady George that caused this indiscretion and the King was right 'not to be bullied by silly boys who go over people's heads.' Richmond 'had indeed made a fine *tripotage* altogether . . . I am very sorry, for it's a thousand pities with so many good and pleasing qualities as he has, to give himself such a *travers dans le monde* and throw away the prospect (at least of a most agreeable situation in life) before him.'

George was self-willed and obstinate and he could be rancorous. Some contemporaries believed that he never forgave Richmond for conduct which constitutionally was outrageous; and possibly, with Sarah in the minds of both men, things were said at that meeting that could never be forgotten or forgiven. It would not be the last time that Richmond would regret the hasty anger and impetuosity that turned his wounded victims into enemies.

The Rockingham group to whom he attached himself politically could never come to terms with Bute, nor with the Grenville ministry that followed, so that it was nearly five years before he had any prospect of office. He became so impatient that in 1762 he sought a military staff appointment in Portugal. He failed because he made his application too late, and afterwards, so Caroline informed Emily, he and the Duchess were in London and behaving irresponsibly. With their cronies 'they play and sit up at one of their houses every night till four or five in the morning; then instead of their own equipages they come home, six or seven together, in hackney coaches . . . They are, as you may suppose, finely abused.' It was no way to embark upon a serious career.

London Society was undisturbed by behaviour much more culpable than this, and the years until 1765 were sufficiently rewarding because Richmond was continuing with the improvements he had earlier begun at Goodwood. 'I have come here to sweeten myself for a few days,' he wrote to Rockingham in 1775 after a wearisome session in London. Goodwood had this effect on him, and he was always working, at enormous cost in money, time and energy, to enrich and beautify it. During his lifetime he expanded the estate from 1100 to 17,000 acres, with a mainly enclosed park at the centre. Altogether his land purchases cost about £120,000, and at his death the estate employed 1200 workers and cost £4000 a year to maintain.

His first action was to divert the main Chichester–Petworth road, which ran close to the eastern side of the house. Some of the original milestones, although overgrown by trees and bushes, can still be seen. By 1765 he had acquired the manors of Halnaker and Westhampnett and land at West Lavant, Stoke, Tangmere, Singleton and East Dean, the very considerable funds being available as a result of the careful stewardship of his guardians during his minority.

In about 1757 Richmond brought William Chambers to Goodwood to build stables for his hunters. Chambers was the son of a Scottish merchant trading in Sweden, and he was brought up for the same line of business until his travels gave him a taste for architecture. His most famous building was to be Somerset House (1775). It was purpose-built because of the expansion of the government's administrative work and is certainly the most spectacular accommodation ever designed for the use of Civil Servants. The same might almost be said of the stables at Goodwood, designed for the accommodation of horses. Still used for the equestrian competitions held in the park, it is a huge quadrangular building with stalls for fifty-four horses and quarters for the grooms, built of local knapped flint with stone dressings to the arches and a Tuscan portal. The diapered red brick of the inner walls is an attractive feature of a building whose size and splendour dwarfed the main house which it adjoined and suggested that the Duke's horses were more spaciously boarded than he was himself.

Chambers did some work on the house itself, designing the entrance hall from the garden which is now the large library in the middle of the South Front.[3] The villa design that he seems to have intended was superseded later by the more ambitious schemes undertaken by James Wyatt, possibly under the direction of the Duke himself. Chambers's accounts include a bill for five guineas for 'attendance on his Grace to teach him architecture.' Chambers also designed a gateway, and decorations for the ceiling of the gallery at Richmond House in London, and following his work at Goodwood he received commissions from three of the Duke's sisters, Emily at Leinster House in Dublin, Louisa at Castletown and Sarah at Barton.

To adorn the interior of the house, Richmond was not content with the paintings, sculptures and tapestries which he brought home from his visits to France. He was always anxious to patronise native artists such as George Smith, son of a Chichester tradesman, whose work he encouraged and recommended to his friends. Some of Smith's delicate landscapes may be seen at Goodwood today.

Then in about 1761, George Stubbs was invited to Goodwood and stayed for nine months. One of the pictures he painted there, *A Study of Horses Exercising*, has been sensitively examined in an article by David Piper:[4] 'This is a picture of horses and horsemen set in a green saucer high on the Sussex downs. In the centre of the painting are a man and a woman, husband and wife, in deep blue touched with gold, on grey horses so dark that they are almost blacks. These two, with a third figure, a woman also in the same blue and on a chestnut horse just to the right of them, are the deepest tone in the picture, and the dominant one; they are the proprietors, in charge of the picture still, as they were of the grooms and the jockeys and the horses when it was all painted just over 200 years ago. To left and to right of them their servants, humans and horses, are busy.' On the right, grooms are rubbing down a horse, and on the left, following the line of the

43 AND 44 (OPPOSITE) The stables at Goodwood, designed by Sir William Chambers, have changed very little since they were built for the third Duke in the late 1750s. During race meetings the first-floor dormitories still provide sleeping quarters for the stable-lads. (ABOVE) The main entrance showing the Tuscan arch. (BELOW) A view from the garden. Covering the wall to the left of the archway is a descendant of Peter Collinson's *Magnolia Grandiflora*.

45 (RIGHT) Sir William Chambers, by Reynolds.

central figure's extended whip, are 'three horses, a grey, a chestnut and a bay, nose to tail and each at full stretch, at full rock it almost seems, up the slope, diminuendo in perspective, and all clad, horses and riders alike, in the clear yellow of the Richmond livery, touched with scarlet.' The spire of Chichester Cathedral, with white sailing-ships on the Channel beyond, gives a hazy background. The three central figures are now thought to be Richard Buckner (a bailiff), the Duchess Mary, and Lady Louisa Conolly, all wearing the dark blue of the Charlton Hunt. His stay at Goodwood came at a crucial stage in Stubbs's career; the works he did there under the Duke's patronage were the first paintings of his maturity, before his classic *The Anatomy of the Horse* (1766) made his reputation and enabled him to obtain higher prices than Reynolds from the same buyers.*

The Duke inherited his father's enthusiasm for 'plantations' and in 1764 he bought from Peter Collinson about one thousand four-year-old cedars which he planted in the park. In the same letter in March 1762 in which he gave his opinion

* Stubbs later painted horses for the Marquis of Rockingham. The most celebrated was the stallion Whistle-jacket, the pride of the Wentworth stables, whom Stubbs was required to paint life-size and doing what he did best, standing on his hind-legs preparing to mount. The painting was so large that a special room was built to house it.

of Sarah's marriage to Bunbury, Richmond asked Fox, when next he wrote to Lord Ilchester, 'to desire him to procure for me if possible the cones of the Great Cedar of Lebanon that is somewhere near Farley. I would willingly hire the tree by the year to have all the cones it produces saved for me.'

Three cork trees grew in front of the house, a species rare in England, and a magnolia planted in 1759 had grown during Kent's early days with the family to a height of twenty-two feet and a girth of eighteen inches. There were also 'splendid specimens of the Pillirea, a kind of evergreen oak, the growth of which has been extraordinary. They even overtop huge timber trees, to the astonishment of those who have in other districts seen them only as shrubs.'

From old servants who spent their lives on the estate Kent gathered several stories about the Duke's dealings with his employees.[5] A military touch was evident here, with the Duke as commanding officer intent on personal supervision. His workers were disconcerted by his habit of early rising, notably those who once lingered overlong at a festivity in Chichester and walked home in the early hours to find their master awaiting them and ironically commending their diligence in reporting for work so promptly.

The day's work began at 7 o'clock and the foremen would be expected to meet the Duke before that hour to take the day's instructions. Charles Tapner, in charge of the Pheasantry, had to be on duty at 4 a.m. because the birds needed to be fed early, and the Duke would sometimes be present to ensure that this was done. When flints and stones were being gathered for the building of the stables, the Duke constructed a mill in which the mortar was pulverised. Thinking that some of the men were not doing the work properly, he attached a bell to the mill which rang after a prescribed number of revolutions. It was suspected, too, that he deliberately advanced his own timepiece a few minutes ahead of the estate clock, to give workers an uncomfortable feeling of being late on parade.

Kent had no doubt that the servants loved and respected their rather eccentric master, and these do not have to be regarded as the proceedings of a petty martinet. Richmond would not demand of his people anything that he would not perform himself, and he expected their devotion to the estate to be equal to his own. He would always, according to Kent, hunt early in the morning, especially in the cubbing season, and one day Tom Grant, the huntsman, went to the house before daybreak to get his instructions. To his surprise he met the Duke crossing the park with a load on his shoulders. 'This is too fine a morning, Grant, to go out hunting while there is corn to harvest. We had better get that field of corn in; so I have brought some rakes and forks for the men to work with.'

He forbade his servants to accept gratuities from visitors. The evidence for this is not in Kent's reminiscences but in the steward's account-book for the Michaelmas quarter in 1764.[6] 'At midsummer 1764 the Duke of Richmond positively forbade any money to be left in the house for the use of servants as he had long before that [words missing here but the sense is clear] of taking tips; in consideration whereof he made augmentations in the wages of several and ordered sums to each in lieu of tips [to provide] shoes, white stockings, powder, etc.'

In 1763 the King appointed Richmond to be Lord Lieutenant and Custos Rotulorum for Sussex, offices under the Great Seal that he was to hold for the rest of his life. As the sovereign's personal representative in a county, the Lord Lieutenant had wide powers, and the position was much sought after. He summoned the militia and, when necessary, directed its service outside the county. From his original duty to supervise the work of local magistrates he had by the eighteenth century virtually acquired the right to nominate them. He was in effect responsible for law and order and the execution of justice, including the collection of local taxes, within his area, and he had the right to call in troops to enforce his will.

With this extensive authority, the Lord Lieutenant was in a position to influence local elections, and Richmond decided to exploit this. Whereas his father had reconciled himself to nominating only one of the two members for Chichester, he wanted both, and after a heated conflict he succeeded.[7] Chichester being a port, the votes of customs officers were significant in an electorate of about 500 and they tended to support the government that appointed them. In view of the complaints he was to make in future years about ministerial corruption and the malign influence of placemen, it is interesting to find the youthful Richmond seeking Treasury help to secure the Custom House vote. In 1754, even before he came of age, he told the Duke of Newcastle that 'it is absolutely necessary for my interest that I should have the sole nomination to the places depending on the Custom House and Treasury at Chichester.' This he did obtain if he was speaking the truth when he informed George Grenville ten years later that 'since my father's death . . . every Lord of the Treasury has given me the disposition of these employments.'

The crucial engagement was fought over the election of 1761. The sitting members were Augustus Keppel, the future admiral, who was Richmond's cousin, and John Page, who had been Member of Parliament for Chichester since 1741 and for Grimsby before that. Keppel was now being nominated for Windsor and Lord George Lennox would take his place. Page was an independent and wanted to retire, but not if this meant delivering both the borough seats to Richmond. He found Richmond overbearing and warned him not to push his claims too far. Thomas Miller of Lavant, whose father, an enthusiastic horticulturalist and planter, had been a close friend of the second Duke, refused to commit himself to either side, and so Newcastle was appealed to as mediator. Inevitably he further vexed the troubled waters on which he tried to pour oil, but his negotiations gave the essential victory to Richmond. Page would keep his

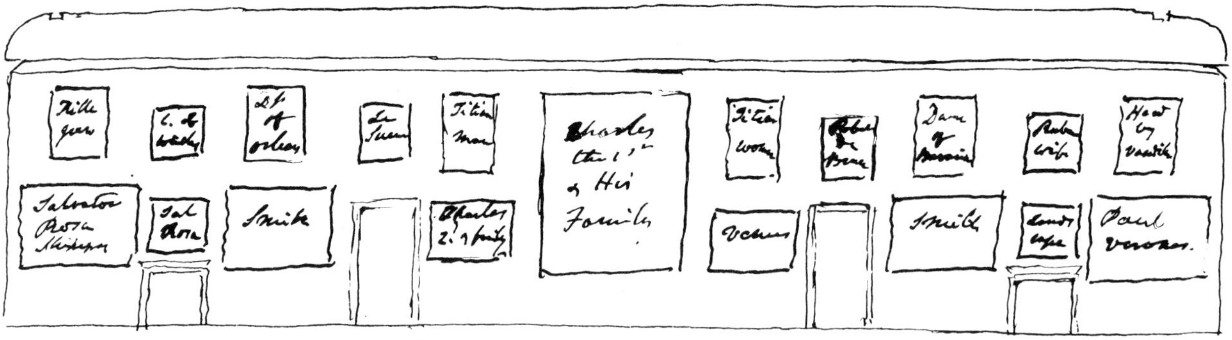

46 AND 47 (ABOVE) A rough sketch by Richmond showing how his pictures were to be hung in the Ballroom at Goodwood. (BELOW) Photograph taken in 1987 of the same wall of the Ballroom shown in the sketch above. The Van Dyck of King Charles I and his family occupies the position proposed by the Duke.

seat for a further term but Richmond was to have the recommendation to all Custom House vacancies.

In 1768, and again in 1774, another Keppel kinsman and Thomas Conolly from Castletown were returned unopposed, as in 1780 were Keppel and Thomas Steele, a Chichester lawyer. But the Chichester voters were getting restive. There had not been a contested election in the borough for many years and the old feeling persisted that Goodwood House should not monopolise both the seats. In 1784 a Richmond nominee, the treasurer of the Ordnance, was heavily defeated by an independent.

Richmond was not politically very active during these years when he was busy on his estate or manipulating the local elections. In 1762 the King feared that what he called 'a league of dukes' (Newcastle, Cumberland, Devonshire and Richmond), along with Rockingham and a few other peers, were intriguing against Bute, but he was jumping at shadows. When Richmond and the Duchess were in London, it was usually to distress Caroline by enjoying themselves. Walpole describes a masquerade which they gave for some six hundred guests in the summer of 1763.[8]

> Last night we had a magnificent entertainment at Richmond House, a masquerade and fireworks ... The Duchesses of Richmond and Grafton, the first as a Persian sultana, the latter as Cleopatra (and what a Cleopatra!), were glorious figures, in very different styles ... The whole garden was illuminated, and the apartments. An encampment of barges decked with streamers in the middle of the Thames kept the people from danger and formed a stage for the fireworks. The ground rooms lighted, with suppers spread, the houses covered and filled with people, the bridge, the garden full of masks, Whitehall crowded with spectators to see the dresses pass, and the multitude of heads on the river, who came to light by the splendour of the fire-wheels, composed the gayest and richest scene imaginable, not to mention the diamonds and the sumptuousness of the habits.

The *Daily Advertiser* reported that 'at least 10,000 spectators' gathered to enjoy the glories of an evening that played havoc with Walpole's prose.

In sympathising with Henry Fox on his dismissal from the Pay Office Richmond wrote: 'I cannot but admire your tranquillity and ease, but I own I could not put up with ill-usage tho' I did not not care a darn for the place, and I do hope you will show some resentment.' This was in June 1765, when Rockingham was about to form a ministry and Richmond would find himself with responsibilities in a political atmosphere unpropitious for a man of his restless idealism. For him there would be little 'tranquillity and ease'; instead a frequent sense of ill-usage, and too much resentment.

8

Burke and the Proper Ends of Government

THE CONSTITUTIONAL DEBATE in the second half of the eighteenth century[1] arose from shared delusions: King George III had been taught that since 1714 unscrupulous Whig grandees had been usurping the Crown's authority, and the Whigs believed that after George's accession the constitutional balance established by the Revolution of 1688, traditionally Glorious, was threatened by the calculated misuse of royal influence. This is to oversimplify an issue that has agitated historians for a very long time; but although no one any longer thinks that the King intended to subvert the constitution, Edmund Burke persuaded the Duke of Richmond and his party that he did so intend.

George was educated by Bute in a proper regard for the English constitution,[2] but there were influences in his youth to make him suppose that the constitution was being perverted by factious conceptions of party. Hanoverian heirs disliked their fathers, and their household accordingly became centres of the so-called 'reversionary interest', with statesmen out of office urging them to overthrow the existing ministry and its policies. Sir Robert Walpole's long tenure of power between 1721 and 1742 produced a considerable number of men, some of them very able, who objected to the methods by which they had been excluded from office. George II's first act on coming to the throne in 1727 was to replace Walpole by Spencer Compton. This was a short-lived disaster and Walpole was soon back in the saddle, but after Walpole's retirement disaffected politicians gathered at Leicester House to assure Prince Frederick that Henry Pelham and his brother the Duke of Newcastle were persisting in the same evil ways.

The young George may not have read Bolingbroke's* *Idea of a Patriot King* (1738), which pretended to be a work of political philosophy but was only the standard complaint of those who had not personally benefited from Walpole's ascendancy. It appealed to 'A PATRIOTIC KING' who 'instead of putting himself at the head of *one party* in order to govern *his people*, he will put himself at the head of *his people* in order to govern, or more properly to subdue, *all parties*.' Frederick died (1751) before having an opportunity to observe these nebulous precepts, but

* Henry St John, Viscount Bolingbroke.

his son received much similar advice. For example, John Douglas, a polemical Scot who later became Bishop of Salisbury, warned him that 'the scheme of putting the sovereign into the leading-strings of party' must be abandoned and a determined sovereign must 'shew his resolution to break all factious *connections* and *confederacies*.' It has then to be remembered that Douglas had for years been a client of William Pulteney, rejected by Walpole and an irreconcilable opponent. Too much of George's early tuition came indirectly from critics of the regime that had governed England peacefully and efficiently since 1714.[3]

So he came to the throne 'in the midst of a bloody and expensive war,' convinced of his duty to end it, and with it the domination of men motivated by 'ingratitude, avarice and ambition.' He was resolved 'never upon any account to suffer those ministers of the late reign who have attempted to fetter and enslave him ever to come into his service while he lives to hold the sceptre.' An ill-expressed note to Bute soon after his accession reveals a frightened young man in the toils, to Pitt especially: 'I plainly see, if every ill humour of a certain man is to be soothed, that in less than a couple of months I shall be irretrievably in his fetters, a state of bondage that an old man of 70-odd [i.e. George II] groaned, and that 22 ought to risk everything rather than submit.'

With Henry Fox as his instrument he made Parliament agree the terms of peace, but the consequent execration appalled him. Bute, 'the Boot', was an easy target because he was a favourite and a Scot and he spoke a braw heathen tongue; so was Princess Augusta, reviled for her petticoat influence. The satirists were not obliged to content themselves with innuendo. Lampoons, ribald verses and caricatures (many of them drawn or inspired by George Townshend, whom the unsuspecting Bute brought into the Privy Council) left nothing to the imagination in announcing an adulterous relationship between 'Sawney the Scot' and the Princess. When insults to his mother and his 'dearest friend' were followed by the *North Briton's* assault on his ministers and his prerogative, George had reason to suspect a conspiracy against his Royal Office.

His vanquished opponents also had cause to fear that the system which had governed England for the past two generations was breaking down. Pitt and Newcastle were gone, the peace had been carried by bribery and intimidation, and those who opposed it had been vindictively punished. The King seemed to be bending Parliament to his will by taking into his own hands the patronage that formerly had been shared with the ruling classes, and he was creating a race of lickspittles known as 'the King's Friends'.

The reality was less dramatic. At worst there had been only a temporary disruption of the essential partnership between the Crown and the governing caste. Divinity still hedged a king, in both his person and his office, and his legitimate powers were still enormous. He had the final decision in the making of war and peace; he could appoint or dismiss ministers, who were responsible to him rather than to Parliament; he could bestow peerages, pensions, sinecures, Household offices, bishoprics and other clerical preferments; as head of the armed forces he could influence army and navy promotions; and although the normal expenses of government were in theory covered by the Civil List voted by Parliament, he was not accountable for expenditure from the Privy Purse or the 'secret service' money. The most effective limitation on his powers was that he could not for long sustain a government or an individual minister who had lost parliamentary support.

Traditional respect for the sovereign meant also that before introducing a measure, a ministry would often consult him beforehand to find whether it had his approval, and members of the Commons would try to discover his opinion before deciding on their vote. The Whig Rockingham did this when in 1766 he wanted to repeal the Stamp Act, the measure that started the quarrel with America; and when George stated that he would not oppose repeal, Rockingham allowed this to be made public. It was not far removed from the 'rumours and messages' about the royal wishes to which Peter Wentworth had objected in the days of Queen Elizabeth, and it significantly illustrates the Crown's continuing influence on legislation. It has been argued[4] that, although he might seem to have been straining his rights, George was not acting unconstitutionally when in 1783 he let it be known that any member of the Lords who supported Charles Fox's India Bill would incur his personal disfavour.

Historians who took the old-fashioned view of George III's policies wrongly supposed that party government in the modern sense already existed in the eighteenth century and that the King was obliged to accept the decisions of elected parliamentary majorities. (In practice no ministry supported by the Crown ever lost an eighteenth-century election.) Party rivalry under William III and Anne was contested on clear-cut distinctions. To quote Bolingbroke's ironical description of this, a Tory in general, 'is a Jacobite or a Papist; a friend to arbitrary government, and against the liberties of the people, both in Church and State.' In the Tory view a Whig is 'a man of republican principles; a Presbyterian; and a sworn enemy to the Church of England and the royal prerogative.' Shorn of rhetorical exaggeration, the Tories supported the Church and the Crown, and those of them who were 'non-jurors' refused the oath of allegiance to William and Mary or, later, to the Hanoverians; and they disliked wars that raised taxes to the apparent advantage of financiers and merchants. Whigs wished to impose restraints on the royal prerogative, sought allies among Dissenters by tolerating their practices, and in an embryonic way were moving towards a credit economy.

How long these distinctions lasted into the eighteenth century is still debated. In 1714 the country had a scare when Bolingbroke came close to achieving a Stuart restoration: according to him, Queen Anne died just a week too soon for the fulfilment of his plans. If the 1715 rising had been even adequately led and organised, King George I might have withdrawn at once from a country where he was so little welcome. Immediate measures were taken for the preservation of public order: the Riot Act (1715); the Septennial Act (1716), since elections could be an excuse for conspiracy and disturbance; the suppression of Convocation (1717) to prevent meetings of angry parsons; the proscription of Bolingbroke; the imprisonment of Bishop Atterbury for Jacobite intrigues. It should be evident, incidentally, that this would have been no time for weakening the monarchy, as the Whigs are alleged to have done. A show of unity and strength was essential, and the powers of George I remained intact. He chose all his first ministers during his reign, he was allowed to consult his German advisers and he guided English foreign policy in the interests of Hanover.

Such Tories as were elected to the Commons were implacable backbenchers, hopeless of promotion or reward because they were branded as Jacobites,

48 'The Loaded Boot', a satirical drawing of the Earl of Bute and Augusta, Princess of Wales. The huge jack-boot – the 'Scotch state Machine' – is drawn by a white horse and a zebra ('the Queen's Ass'), which represent George III and Queen Charlotte. The driver, wearing a plaid waistcoat, is thought to be the Duke of Bedford, who negotiated the peace with France 1762–3.

crypto-Papists and potential rebels. An effective blow was the sermon 'My Kingdom is not of this World' preached in 1717 by Benjamin Hoadly, Bishop of Bangor, the first Englishman appointed to the see since John Bird in 1539. In this he adroitly defused High Anglican passions by denying the visible authority of the Church and so removing it from the political arena.* The Bishop of London, Edmund Gibson, was a learned theologian but he co-operated with Walpole in the appointment of Latitudinarians to significant ecclesiastical positions, and this gradually took the fierceness out of religious controversy. (It was already quite a while since Addison's Foxhunter realised that 'there is scarce a Presbyterian in the whole county, except the bishop.') The new Regius Professorships at the universities guided young minds towards support of the dynasty, and it was hoped that the old Tory doctrine of 'non-resistance' to the Crown would change into positive acceptance. 'Non-juring' is not an attitude that is easily heritable, and the next generation of Tories were willing to accommodate themselves to the world as they found it. Walpole reduced the land tax which the squires had always resented and he kept out of the wars demanded by the merchant interest. The whole country could enjoy the prosperity that his pragmatic policies engendered. Besides, although they were annually suspended, the Test and Corporation Acts, treasured survivals of the Clarendon Code, were kept on the statute-book as a sop to Anglican prejudice.

The assimilation of the Tories into the rest of English society is denied by historians who have insisted that traditional Toryism continued to be an active force until late in the century. In that event it is necessary to explain why the 'Forty-five rebellion had little or no support in England, where it merely seemed that a glamorous but unreliable young man was to be borne to the throne by Highland savages on a programme of restoring Popery and reneging on the National Debt. The Tory squires, and indeed the Tory parsons, who appear in Fielding's novels nowhere give the impression of constituting a political movement hostile to their surroundings. Romantic Toryism no doubt lingered in toasts to 'the King over the water' and in some treasonous words as the port went round, but the 'parties' and 'factions' rather than being between Tory and Whig were between the various Whig groups that occupied themselves in wheeling and dealing for office. Even if the old Toryism was not virtually dead by 1750, the policies of George III cannot be interpreted as a Tory revival aimed at restoring the Stuart prerogative.

A successful ministry of the period had to work in harmony with the Crown, with the independent country gentlemen and with the 'placemen' (those whose votes could be won by titles, offices and pecuniary rewards) in Parliament. Of these three the Crown was much the most important, and George III was wrong

---

* Hoadly's rewards were terrestrial: from Bangor to Hereford, to Salisbury, and finally to Winchester.

to believe that his predecessors had surrendered their rights. Their concern for Hanover, the 'beggarly Electorate' which most Englishmen would cheerfully have abandoned to any fate that German politics arranged for it, ensured their personal attention to foreign policy, and the Secretaries of State had to carry out their orders. George II had not fought personally in the Austrian Succession war in order to lose the peace, and at its close he insisted that Hanover's interests be safeguarded. His concern for Hanover was in no small way responsible for the 'Diplomatic Revolution' of 1756. The Austrians having failed to protect it in the 1740s, it was necessary to look for an ally who would.

Although Whig ministries were able to make use of royal patronage to get their measures through Parliament, George kept control of major appointments, and when conflict arose, the ministers usually gave way. A complete breakdown in co-operation was rare, but in 1744 the Pelhams forced George to dismiss Carteret, whose aims in foreign policy were not acceptable to Parliament. Two years later they confronted him with a mass resignation to compel him to give office to Pitt. More serious instability followed the death of Henry Pelham in 1754. This was a difficult and anxious period. George was ageing and increasingly irritable; although not officially at war, the British and French were fighting each other in India and North America; Austria's inevitable attempt to recover Silesia would renew the continental war and Britain – and Hanover – had no certain ally. In 1757 a succession of military and naval disasters obliged George to turn again to Pitt (the elder) only a few weeks after dismissing him.

The King had been cornered by events, and the impact of this royal failure was felt at Leicester House, where Bute may have had some hand in it.[5] It perhaps explains George III's almost hysterical determination to overturn the ministry as soon as he came to the throne, and in particular his fear and hatred of Pitt. It was an exaggerated demonstration of his authority and it was not typical. Horace Walpole might detect 'a change in the language of the court' and 'the prevalence of prerogative prejudices', but historians now are mostly agreed that constitutional conventions did not change. Certainly in one respect George III was less intrusive than his grandfather. As he told his first Parliament, he gloried in the name of Britain (although he never travelled farther north than Cheltenham) and he was not hog-tied to Hanoverian interests. He respected the rights of Parliament and when he had appointed a ministry, he expected it to govern. He was available for advice and support but he did not force his own opinions or try to direct their policies. This was particularly true of the American conflict, although it has been described as 'King George's war'.

His style of government was described by Lord Hillsborough, who was Colonial Secretary from 1768 to 1772: 'The King will always leave his own sentiments and conform to his Ministers', though he will argue with them, and very sensibly; but if they adhere to their own opinion, he will say, "Well, do you choose it should be so? Then let it be." And sometime he would add, "You must take the blame upon yourself."'[6] In his early days George III could be coltish and unwise, but he matured with experience and mostly he acted with scrupulous propriety. During the uncertainties over the repeal of the Stamp Act, the Duke of Bedford offered, through an intermediary, to take office and put things right. George refused to see him or to consider the offer: 'I cannot take notice of it as I do not think it constitutional for the Crown personally to interfere in measures which it has thought proper to refer to the advice of Parliament.' He would not betray his ministers, at that time the Rockinghams – against whom, in Whig mythology, he was constantly intriguing.

On the surface his conduct over the Royal Marriage Act (1772) looks to be aggressive and unconstitutional. On grounds of public policy there were good reasons for opposing this ill-thought measure,* but George declared that he had 'a right to expect a hearty support from everyone in my service, and shall remember defaulters.' He expected that 'every engine' would be employed to pass the measure smoothly, and after the division he asked to be told of 'abstainers and deserters.' The distinction here is that George, although perhaps mistakenly, saw this as a private issue concerning himself and his family that was outside the domain of public policy: 'it is not a question that immediately relates to Administration but personally to myself.' Therefore he applied pressure on men in his personal service that he would not have applied in matters of wider importance. His conduct was attacked at the time by the Whig opposition and it has often been offered as evidence of his arbitrary inclinations, but in fact it proves the opposite.

Support from the independent country gentlemen was necessary to any administration. The ambitions of these men were local rather than national, and they favoured the interests of their religion, their class and their territory. Their instinct was to mistrust central authority and to represent 'the Country against the Court' or, more simply, the 'Us against Them' that traditionally characterises the Englishman's attitude to his rulers. A speaker in the Lords in 1781 rather splendidly described them as 'men neither to be frowned into servility nor huzzaed into faction.'[7] Eccentrics among them could raise difficulties about almost anything, and it was imprudent to arouse their concerted opposition because then they could be formidable. Neither Whig nor Tory, they preferred order to incompetence and confusion and they would support any administration

* It forbade members of the Royal Family to marry without the King's permission before they reached the age of twenty-five (or twenty-six with permission from Council and Parliament). In consequence only four of George III's fifteen children had legitimate offspring, and his six daughters had only one child between them, that still-born. The death of Princess Charlotte in 1817 left the throne without an heir in her generation; with the result that three middle-aged dukes (a fourth, Sussex, refused) had to lay aside their existing arrangements and marry German princesses for the purpose of begetting a lawful heir.

that avoided chicanery, worked for the general good and did not flout their particular interests.

It was the placemen, or the 'King's Friends' as they now came to be known, who disturbed the constitutional purists. By 1760 between a fifth and a quarter of the Commons* held offices of profit in the gift of the sovereign, either in the Royal Household or distributed through the Treasury. Several Place Acts had been passed with the object of reducing their number, but the frequency of these measures showed that they were ineffectual because governments could not carry on without the placemen's support. As the scope of public administration widened, so did the powers of patronage and the possibility that an unscrupulous king or minister would use it to debauch the members and extinguish the freedom of Parliament.**

There was never the money nor the number of offices available to make this possible, and the placemen themselves would not have consented to it. Macaulay, writing of the reign of George III, described the King's Friends as 'a reptile species of politicians never before and never since known in our country:' which is incorrect in all three of its particulars. There have been King's Friends ever since government began. They existed when the monkish chronicler known as Ordericus Vitalis wrote of the men whom King Henry I 'raised from the dust to do his service': dedicated men whom every monarch needed, lawyers, clerks, accountants and sometimes close personal advisers. Readers of Shakespeare's *Richard II* will remember Bushy, Bagot and Green, marginal figures whom Shakespeare took from Holinshed without developing their character or function. They appear just as followers of the King swept aside by the usurper Bolingbroke. Bushy was Speaker of the Commons, then a royal appointment, and he and Green were 'knights charged to attend the King's council at his pleasure' at a salary of £100 a year, more than was paid to a judge. Whether we call them King's Friends or favourites, minions, 'evil counsellors' or 'caterpillars of the commonwealth,' such men existed in every reign to perform the King's business. Some fell with their master, some grew corrupt or rose above their station and had to be knocked down, some were charged by their enemies with embezzlement, witchcraft, unnatural practices, giving the King diseases, seducing his Queen, or any extravagance that animosity could devise. These were the handful who found their way into the history books, which do not record the hundreds of unnamed men whose quiet service enabled the administration to work.

---

* In the House of Lords also about half the peers had offices or pensions (see Cannon, *Aristocratic Century*, pp. 96–8). The bishops, too, were loyal to the patrons who had assisted their promotion, sometimes with financial help – mitres did not come cheap.

** Some of the money went to such harmless purposes as providing pensions for Dr Johnson and Abraham Trembley.

The eighteenth-century House of Commons contained time-serving sinecurists who would vote for the government on any issue, but it is now acknowledged that the King's Friends were the genesis of the Civil Service, although this term was not used until the following century. Whether members of Parliament or not, these men earned some reward for the time and talent which under their ornamental titles they gave to public business, and even the lesser gifts of ecclesiastical or military appointments made provision for dependants who might otherwise have been a financial burden. It was not an ideal system and it could be abused; but government could not survive without it and it would continue until, in the patient English way, a method was evolved for rewarding professional servants without requiring also their political affiliation. Because these men were professionals their interest was in administrative discipline and continuity. Thus they withheld support from unstable ministries like the Pitt-Devonshire combination in 1756–7 or Rockingham's in 1765–6, knowing that Crown and Commons lacked confidence in them and they would not survive. They had an eye for political realities and – like the King – were always seeking a working partnership with viable administrations. Wise statesmen, therefore, looked for the respect and co-operation of such 'King's Friends' and did not waste breath complaining of their supposed pliancy and corruption.

To summarise a system that was fluid and informal, the Crown and the aristocratic caste were mutually dependent and had to work together, not in opposition, at a time when administrative tasks were expanding and the powers of government had therefore to increase rather than to diminish. The eighteenth-century constitution developed from the experience of the previous century and was not trying to equip itself for the problems of the next; and it evolved not from the dreams of sectaries and levellers but from the common-sense of men of affairs like Clarendon, Halifax and in the new generation Robert Walpole. Nor must we forget the personal equation: the simple fact, overriding constitutional niceties, that some kings and ministers get on well together and others do not. Walpole understood this perfectly, as in his advice to Henry Pelham on handling King George II: 'The more you can make any thing appear to be his own, and agreeable to his declarations and orders, . . . the better you will be heard.' If George III had better understood the arts of man management, he would have had a happier reign.

This appraisal of eighteenth-century government, although summary and superficial,[8] is important for an understanding of Richmond's public career. His own liberal inclinations and his friendship with General Conway, the Duchess's stepfather, led him to 'the Pelhamite succession,' the group attached to the Duke of Newcastle and the Marquis of Rockingham. By age and experience Newcastle was its leader, but its patron – and by his influence at Court its most significant member – was the King's uncle, the Duke of Cumberland, commander of the

English force at Culloden. The younger members included the fourth Duke of Devonshire, until his early death; the third Duke of Portland,* a Bentinck who married into the Chatsworth stable; Lord John Cavendish, his brother-in-law; Sir George Savile, a baronet with large estates in Yorkshire who took the liberal side on every issue of the day without regard for personal or political advantage; and William Dowdeswell, by upbringing a Tory from the apple counties but a shrewd parliamentarian and financier.

Charles Watson-Wentworth, second Marquis of Rockingham (1730–82), was Richmond's friend and ally for many years. A descendant of Thomas Wentworth, Earl of Strafford, he succeeded to the Rockingham title by one of those accidents not uncommon in an age of youthful mortality: he was the fifth but only surviving son. His great wealth and influence in Yorkshire caused him to be wooed by the Pelhams and in 1751 he was made a Lord of the Bedchamber and Lord Lieutenant of the North and West Ridings. His uncle William Murray,** then Solicitor General, planned a political career for him, instructing him to study Demosthenes for oratory, and in general to model himself on Sir Walter Raleigh. No statesman less like Raleigh could be imagined, and Rockingham refused to undertake the recommended studies. For ten years his concerns were provincial. He rebuilt Wentworth Park, where his famous ancestor had lived in a wooden house; bred horses; opened a coal mine and devised agricultural instruments to improve the yield of his estates. During the Seven Years War he raised three militia regiments to defend the Ridings in the event of invasion. Although he used his ample patronage to protect Whig interests in the county – in 1758 spending £12,000 of his own money to defeat a Tory candidate in a by-election at York – he did not involve himself in national politics until George III and Bute began to undermine his territorial influence. In 1762 he resigned from the Bedchamber in sympathy with colleagues who were being removed from office and he was deprived of his lieutenancies a month later. His path was now clear to him and for the rest of his life he would be opposed to the policies of the Court.[9]

He and Richmond had surprisingly much in common. Both were at Westminster School and both had childless marriages, but Rockingham too had four sisters, with all the responsibilities they might create; both loved sport and horses, Richmond for hunting, Rockingham for racing; both found in their domestic life refreshment from political strains at Westminster and were apt to find excuses for

---

* William Henry Cavendish Bentinck (1738–1809), First Lord of the Treasury 1783 and 1807–09; led 'the Old Whigs' to the side of the younger Pitt during the French Revolution; Home Secretary 1794–1801; supported union with Ireland.

** William Murray, first Earl of Mansfield (1705–93), Lord Chief Justice 1756–88; an outstanding lawyer but unpopular for the supposed severity of his judgments, especially in libel cases, and for his coercive policy towards America.

49 (LEFT) William Augustus, Duke of Cumberland, *c.* 1758–60 (studio of Reynolds).

50 (RIGHT) The second Marquis of Rockingham, by Reynolds.

prolonging their absences in the country; and both made rather a profession of their ill-health. Rockingham claimed a chronic disorder with chest pains and was always doctoring this 'old complaint'. As early as 1761 Savile told him that no habit, 'not even the confirmed avarice of old age, is more incorrigible than this game of quacking.' Richmond, too, was inclined to 'quack', and to impatient observers ill-health and a commanding passion for horses must have appeared to be characteristic ducal infirmities. Yet Richmond would accuse Rockingham of malingering. 'You are so often ill without being dangerously so,' he wrote in 1772, 'and are so often doctoring yourself that when I first heard you were not

well I concluded it was only a surfeit of Physic, and I am told that it might possibly be owing to your not letting yourself alone when you have been ill.'

Their affection for their own firesides, at the expense of the calls of public duty, was a lasting bond. On holiday in 1767 Rockingham wrote to Lord Dartmouth, a member of his recent ministry: 'Since I came here I found so much real private business & so much amusement in riding about inspecting farming & other occupations, that I own I took up such an indolence of mind that I dreaded the idea of setting down to write on political matters.' He had company in the house for the past ten days, and he is about to attend York races.[10] In 1769, when

London was in a furore about Wilkes and the Middlesex election, he said in a letter to Richmond:

> I most perfectly agree with your Grace that the pleasures one enjoys at one's own place in the country very far exceed the scenes which we have been used to in public life . . . I feel here as your Grace does at Goodwood: I think I have everything wherewithal to gratify my wishes within the bounds of reason and moderation . . . I often think that I could set down here, attend & watch on the wants & necessities of those who are near to me, be of use and assistance to many & finally secure to myself the comfort of thinking that I have done some good.[11]

Horace Walpole thought Rockingham 'a poor creature', but poor creatures do not write and feel in this way. Neither Rockingham nor Richmond was continuously successful in politics, but success – and happiness – in life depend upon a man's relative values; and the judgment of historians likewise will depend upon their own yardstick. The patrician families who ruled in Georgian England were a different species from the modern politician because in sport and the arts and the pleasure of watching things grow they found a way of life that mattered as much to them as 'the endless adventure of governing men.'

The degree of political commitment varied, nonetheless, and temperamental differences showed more strongly when, after Newcastle's death in 1768, Rockingham became the accepted leader of their group. One of the Marquis of Halifax's aphorisms might have been written with Rockingham in mind: 'State business is a cruel trade; good nature is a bungler in it.' Rockingham was dilatory, procrastinating, and such a poor speaker that he seldom asserted any authority in the Lords. When in 1769 he demanded to see the Civil List accounts before voting to pay the outstanding debts, he was speaking for the first time in three years, and he confessed that 'I was from beginning to end in a violent agitation . . . I got a good draught of madeira before I went to the House.' Richmond, himself a ready speaker, had no sympathy with such hesitancy. 'Indeed, my dear Lord, you owe it to yourself, to your friends and to the cause which you stand at the head of, to deliver those sentiments in public which have made you so many private friends.' His value as a leader was in his ability to hold men together when more forceful methods might have divided them, and the impetuous Richmond discovered this when for a period in 1771 he was temporary leader while Rockingham was nursing a sick wife in Bath. 'The want of you to keep people together, particularly the H of C gentlemen, is too apparent. There are many of them who will upon most occasions vote with us, but want to be spoke to . . . The thing that influences them is the personal regard they have for you which will make them do for your speaking what they will not do for another man's.'[12] For Richmond, who did not lack self-confidence, this was a considerable admission. In the long run Rockingham's flexibility and quiet conciliatory tactics probably did more for the cause than Richmond would have achieved by more dynamic leadership, even if a man so easily discouraged had been able to sustain this. Rockingham's patent honesty removed all suspicion of self-seeking, and he did not have Richmond's unhappy knack of making enemies.

It was as Rockingham's secretary that Edmund Burke first made his mark in British politics as the guru of the Whigs. Burke had that eloquent command of the English language with which certain fortunate Irishmen have been endowed, and he was not sparing in the use of it. He spoke nobly on conciliation with America,* and in his *Reflections on the French Revolution* (1790) he early foresaw the tyranny that would follow when the levellers had done their work. He warned that Charles Fox and his raffish little friends would be among the first *à la lànterne* if, as they professed to hope, revolutionary principles were brought into England. 'A state without some means of change is without the means of its conservation,' but he knew that the bonds of society were still religious and semi-mystical and he condemned the secular liberalism that would question law and tradition and pull up society by its roots. There is a perennial attractiveness in his appeal to prescriptive rights and what Clarendon called the 'wisdom that is learned by tract of time.'

Burke's disservice to the Whigs was an idealism that misread the signs. He dismissed as 'cant' the prevailing system of 'men, not measures': the choice of ministers of loyalty and competence more concerned with efficient government than the promotion of personal or sectional policies. This was the political dogma of the age. Pitt and Newcastle and the majority of parliamentarians were as anxious as George III himself to destroy 'those unhappy distinctions of party called Whigs and Tories.' The concept of 'party', of a body of men with a legislative programme they would carry out as soon as they had the chance, was as yet unconstitutional and 'factious'. To 'storm the Closet,' to confront the sovereign with a list of demands as a condition of ministerial co-operation, was a gross breach of propriety.

For Burke, however, membership of a party was almost a sacred trust, consonant with his belief that 'the principles of true politics are those of morality enlarged.' Party meant 'a body of men united, for promoting by their joint endeavours, the national interest upon some particular interest in which they are all agreed.' A speculative philosopher will 'mark the proper ends of government,' and it is the business of the politician, 'who is the philosopher in action, to find out proper means towards those ends . . . and carry their common plans into execution with all the power and authority of the state.' Halifax, a wiser man than Burke, had observed during the heated conflicts of the previous century that 'the

* Speech on Conciliation, 22 March 1775.

best party is but a kind of conspiracy against the rest of the nation.'* With their shifting combinations and opportunist alliances eighteenth-century politicians simply did not operate at Burke's high-minded level. His notion of party was an invasion of the King's right to choose his servants for their usefulness rather than their principles.

Thus the constitutional innovators in this period were not George III and the King's Friends but the Rockinghams, with premature conceptions of party government. In their short ministry in 1782 they faithfully carried out the programme they had promised, but the final establishment of their principles had to await an overhaul of the electoral system, the social and economic changes consequent upon the spread of industrialism, improved communications, the enlarged responsibilities of empire, and the growth and re-distribution of population, ominously concentrated in northern factory towns. With the French example introducing a sort of radicalism unknown to the eighteenth century, these changes brought in a different world. 'Party' in the modern sense may have originated in the movement leading to the 1832 Reform Act, but parliamentary reform in various guises had long roots. Arguably the first real manifestation was the Anti-Corn Law League. Its motives were questionable and had little to do with Burke's enlargement of morality, but its class, regional and occupational context is not unfamiliar today.

Meanwhile Burke's ideas had an emotional appeal for the rich and influential men who looked to Rockingham for guidance. Portland declared that 'for the young men of property, and independent people in both Houses, it is holding out a banner for them to come to, where interest cannot be said to point out the way, and where nothing but public good is to be sought for, on the plainest, honestest and most disinterested terms.'[13] Unfortunately Burke thought that the great obstacle to his schemes was the corrupt influence of the Treasury and the Crown. He did more than anyone to consecrate, if not to invent, the myth of a young King led into unconstitutional actions by his 'Friends', men who exploited his patronage to undermine Parliament's will. Chief of these was Bute, whose pernicious intents long outlasted his retirement; and even the Dowager Princess Augusta (a lady narrow in her horizons but much maligned – liberal in her charities and founder of the Royal Botanical Gardens at Kew) was riding her broomstick until her death. To explain why men opposed to these methods had become '*les enfants perdus* of politics', Burke published in 1770 his *Thoughts on the Cause of the Present Discontents*.

Ten years later Burke claimed that Richmond had been responsible for this

---

* Halifax said this also: 'I cannot forbear to put in a *caveat* against men tied to a party. Such a man can hardly be called a free agent, and for that reason is very unfit to be trusted with the people's liberty when he hath given up his own.'

51 Edmund Burke, by Reynolds.

pamphlet, which was 'written at your Grace's very particular and pressing desire, printed by your command, and sanctified with your public approbation in the House of Lords, where you said that it contained your Creed.'[14] Burke's main contention was that 'the power of the Crown, almost dead and rotten as Prerogative, has grown up anew, with much more strength, and far less odium, under the name of Influence.' He was equating Stuart prerogative, with agencies like Star Chamber to enforce it, with George III's use of his supposedly corrupt 'influence' to ensure ministerial stability. (The historian and philosopher David Hume drew attention to the 'paradox' of influence. 'We may give to this influence what name we please, we may call it by the insidious appellations of *corruption* and *dependence*; but some degree and some kind of it are inseparable from the very nature of the constitution, and necessary to the preservation of our mixed government.')[15] The opposition's remedy was 'economical reform': close accounting of the Civil List, fewer placemen, and reduction of the money available for corruption. All through the 1770s the Whigs complained of the government's methods, and tried to win support for a cause that would do little to assist them if they ever came to office. They had their small triumph when, in 1780, Dunning's resolution that 'the influence of the Crown has increased, is increasing, and ought to be diminished' was carried by 233 votes to 215. In a speech on reform Burke showed that in ten years he had learnt nothing. He complained of 'corrupt influence, which is itself the perennial spring of all prodigality and all disorder; which loads us more than millions of debt; which takes away vigour from our arms, wisdom from our councils and every shadow of authority and credit from the most venerable parts of our constitution.'

Thus in the long years of opposition between 1766 and 1782 the Rockingham party were victims of a 'conspiracy theory'. This is an enervating condition to be in, because it puts a gloss on one's own failure by blaming it on the wickedness of other men. They were able to persuade themselves that they were excluded from office by an administration under Lord North which was sustained by misuse of the Crown's authority; and this restricted their efforts to concert a united opposition with other disaffected groups who nevertheless had a more sober perception of political realities.

The Duke of Richmond was then in the prime of his argumentative powers, as he showed in his consistent mastery of issues that affected him. His party meanwhile, whenever they were halted, could only echo Burke's plangent futilities; and Richmond, too easily thrown off course when things did not go his way, never lacked excuses for threatening to withdraw from the struggle.

9

Embassy and Office

In 1763 Bute resigned, having had his fill of public contempt and execration – and also perhaps of royal prompting behind the scenes – and the King turned without enthusiasm to George Grenville, a precise and sombre man whom he described as having 'the mind of a clerk in a counting-house.' Grenville was Pitt's brother-in-law and had influential friends, but any ministry at this time was precarious unless Pitt was a member of it, and the King had to accommodate himself to the idea that he and Pitt, in their dislike of party combinations and party programmes, had similar aims.

Grenville was unfortunate in his policies. As a conscientious economist burdened with heavy debt from the recent war he decided to enforce the regulations against smuggling between the New England colonies and the West Indies, and in order to make the Americans contribute to their own defence he passed the Stamp Act to bring in revenue by a duty on legal documents, pamphlets and newspapers. He also fell foul of John Wilkes;* and when the King was seriously ill in 1765 he failed to make acceptable arrangements for a regency.

In July 1764 Richmond recorded a conversation[1] at which he was present, between Grenville and General Conway, on the propriety of officers continuing to hold military commands 'when in settled opposition to the King's measures.' Conway had objected to the Stamp Act, the issue of a general warrant against Wilkes, and the alleged abuse of parliamentary privilege. Grenville was willing to accept occasional adverse speeches in the Commons but forbade systematic opposition in any other place. Richmond claims to have asked him what he

* John Wilkes (1727–97) was an embarrassment to successive ministries for some ten years. He entered the Commons in 1757 and in 1763 he was arrested for a seditious libel against the King in his paper the *North Briton*. He was released on his privilege as an MP and protested against a general warrant issued against all persons associated with the publication. General warrants were declared illegal, and Wilkes and other defendants won substantial damages. He was again condemned for libel, both for his newspaper article and for his obscene *Essay on Woman*, which the Earl of Sandwich read to the House of Lords. Withdrawing to Paris, he was outlawed for non-appearance in answer to the charge and served a prison sentence on his return. He was elected for Middlesex in 1768 but the Commons declared him ineligible. He was three times re-elected and was three times refused his seat, although on the third occasion he had defeated a government candidate by 1143 votes to 296. He was eventually re-admitted to the Commons in 1774 and was instrumental in establishing the right to report parliamentary debates. In later years he verged upon respectability, became Lord Mayor of London and helped to suppress the Gordon Riots.

would define as opposition that was not parliamentary opposition. 'I believe you would compound for a man's disapproving of all your measures if he would but vote in Parliament for you.' This indeed was, and is, a universal political truth, and Conway was dismissed from his military offices.

The King would sooner have the devil in his closet than Grenville, and was anxious to be rid of him. Whig hopes of succeeding him were imperilled by Pitt, who had been in heavy consultations at Buckingham House and had his own conditions for taking office. In June 1765, when the Grenville government was doomed, Richmond assured Henry Fox[2] that for himself he would only come in at the King's bidding, not Pitt's: 'I have nothing to ask, and wish for no favours, but from the King, and those I do wish for from him are only such as to enable me better to adjust and support him, for I sincerely pity his situation.' Pitt's suspected intrigues were disturbing. 'I suppose he will endeavour to take this opportunity, when all parties are broke, to unite them by *douceurs* to support him, for he knows that his great *schemes* cannot be put in execution if he has any opposition to deal with.'

These 'great schemes' amounted to the disruption of family combinations, but George was not ready, or Pitt, already gout-racked, was not ready, or conditions were pitched too high. The consultations immediately were fruitless although they may have cleared the way for future understanding, and responsibility for ministry-making fell upon the King's uncle the Duke of Cumberland, his modest military laurels tarnished by losing Hanover to the French, but of weight and consequence at Court. Under his patronage Rockingham took office in July 1765 as First Lord in a ministry which lasted for just over a year, and to Cumberland, using Albemarle as an intermediary, Richmond applied for a government post.[3]

Cumberland's recent conduct, wrote Richmond, 'raises if possible my admiration for him,' and so 'it now becomes my duty to beg of your Lordship to assure H.R.H. that the utmost of my ambition is to show my attachment to the King on this occasion, and particularly to support an administration formed under HRH's auspices.' He assured Albemarle that his only wish was 'to be in that situation where I can be most useful. I flatter myself that your Lordship and my friends will not suspect me of seeking anything for myself . . . And if 'tis thought that my silent support can be of most use to the King's measures, I am sure I shall be satisfied. But if in the present crisis, when so violent an opposition is to be expected that even some of our friends go off, and most of them are only shy and doubtful, my taking a more active part can be of use, I am ready to do it.'

This letter has been criticised as an unpleasant mixture of the pushing and the obsequious, but royal dukes expected to be addressed in a subservient tone and it was not unreasonable for Richmond to give notice that he was ready to serve when others were 'shy and doubtful' and uncertain whose side to take. He could not have said much less or said it much differently.

He was to be disappointed. He had so far made little political impact and possibly Caroline had been right in thinking that the light-hearted and somewhat irresponsible behaviour of himself and the Duchess in London Society had given him the wrong sort of reputation. After first being considered for such minor posts as Constable of the Tower or Groom of the Stole, he was appointed Ambassador Extraordinary and Minister Plenipotentiary to Versailles, with Lord George as his secretary. As he told Henry Fox, he was not enthusiastic about the appointment. Having Lord George at his side . . .

> . . . gives me much greater pleasure than my going for there are drawbacks to that. But upon the whole 'tis all mighty well. I have laid in my claim to coming home in January . . . for I cannot give up England entirely and I am very curious indeed to see at least part of next session. My brother is indeed a younger secretary than I am an ambassador and neither of us *rompu dans les affaires*, but with the help of a good private secretary I hope we shall do. George you know likes France and is liked there, and that is a good thing.

He would have preferred to be nearer the action and to make his mark in the House of Lords, but here nonetheless was an opportunity if he could make something of it. He was a descendant of Henri Quatre, he had property in France, he might establish a closer understanding between two nations recently at war.

His mission did not start auspiciously. Even before he reached Paris he complained that the fortifications in Dunkirk had not been dismantled as stipulated in the peace treaty, and in spite of his protests little action was taken. He did, however, have the opportunity to make a shrewd survey of the fortifications which would be of value to him in the future. He was more successful in handling the financial settlements which were due to English merchants who had suffered during the war, but otherwise he achieved very little. The Ambassador and his secretary, with their ladies, joined a tight little social clique with a few English residents and associated only with the most distinguished Parisian hostesses. Horace Walpole, who was in France between September 1765 and the following April, met the Richmonds at the play or at supper on no fewer than seven occasions during the first half of November, and was present when the Duke paid £500 for some of the Sèvres porcelain that is still at Goodwood.[4] (At about this time, either during his embassy or on a trip to Aubigny, Richmond also acquired the huge Gobelins tapestries, depicting the adventures of Don Quixote, which are a spectacular adornment of the Tapestry Drawing-Room.) But in spite of the beguiling gaieties of Paris the Duke was anxious to be home and in February he crossed the Channel in a fishing-boat, leaving the Duchess to await calmer winds and Lord George to take over his ambassadorial duties.

Reports of their behaviour reached Caroline, inevitably. 'I hear from all quarters that they treated the French with the utmost contempt and incivility; and

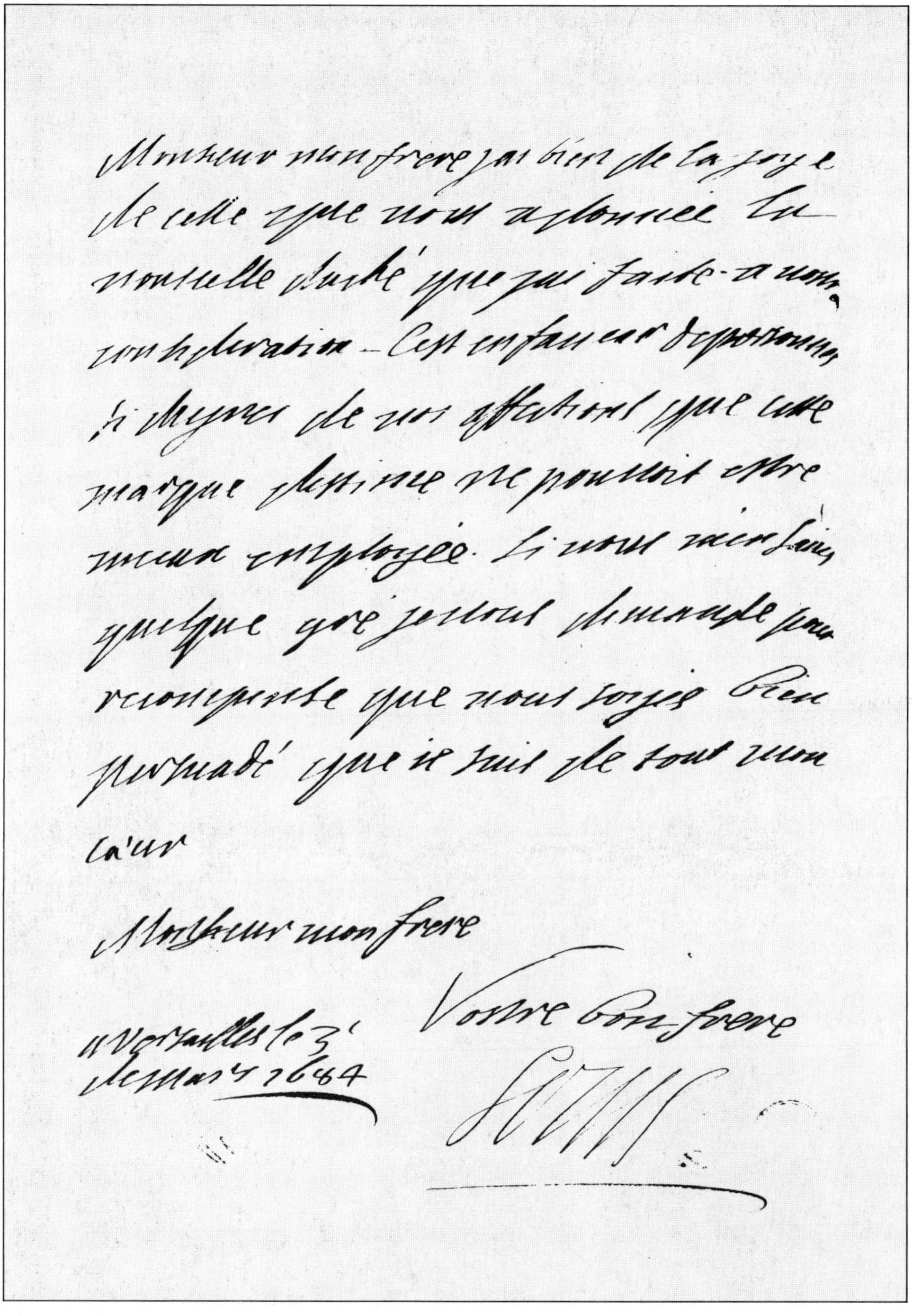

Monsieur mon frere j'ai bien de la joye
de celle que vous a donnee la
nouvelle duché que j'ai faite a vostre
consideration. C'est en faveur de personnes
si dignes de vos affections que cette
marque d'estime ne pouvoit estre
mieux employee. Si vous m'en faites
quelque gré je vous demande pour
recompense que vous soyez bien
persuadé que je suis de tout mon
cœur

Monsieur mon frere

Vostre bon frere
Louis

A Versailles le 3e
de mars 1684

52 (ABOVE) Letter from Louis XIV to King Charles II (*'Roy de la Grande bretagne monsieur mon frère'*), in which he speaks of the new duchy of Aubigny.

53 (RIGHT) The Château of Aubigny, now the village *Mairie*.

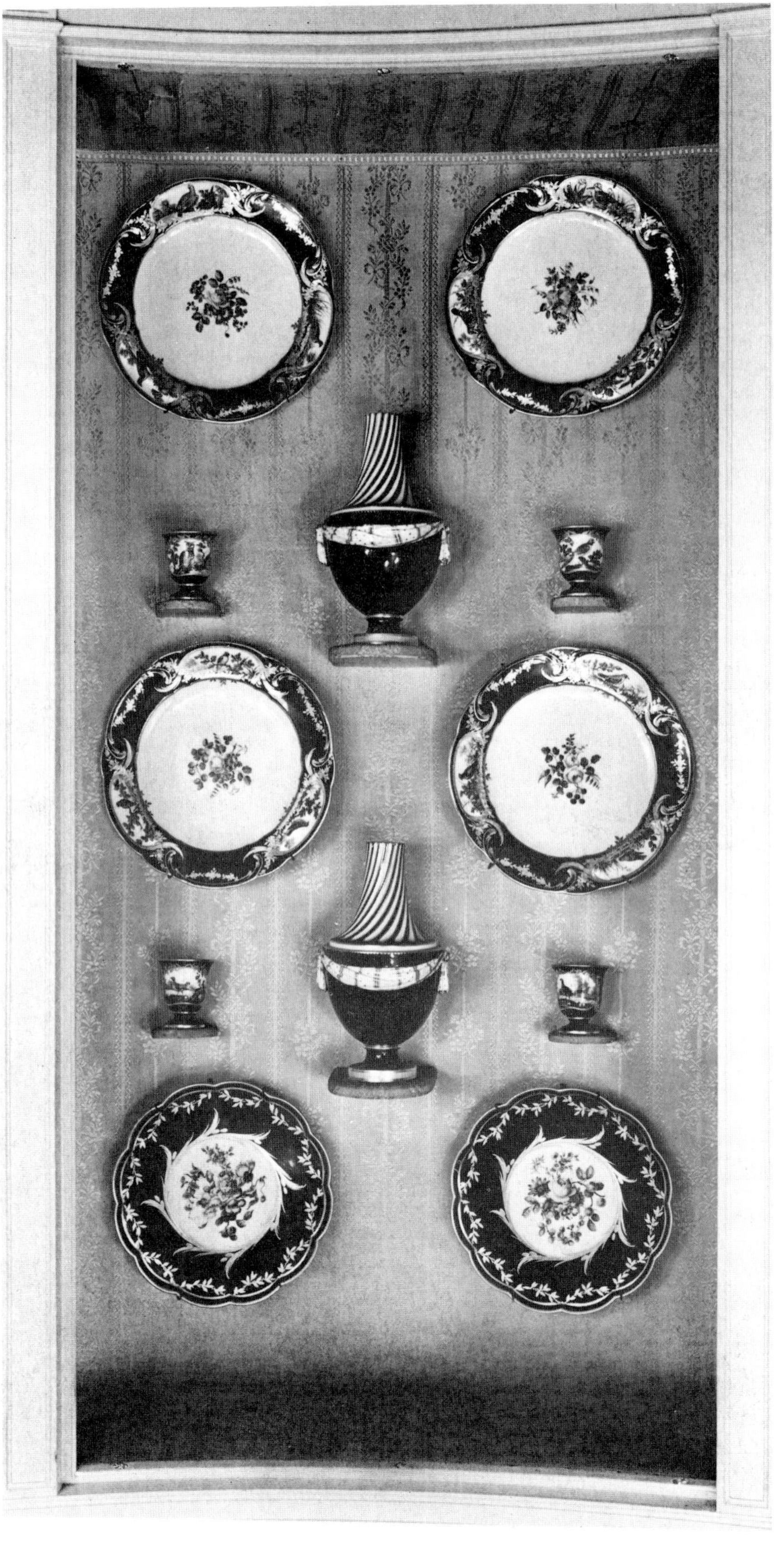

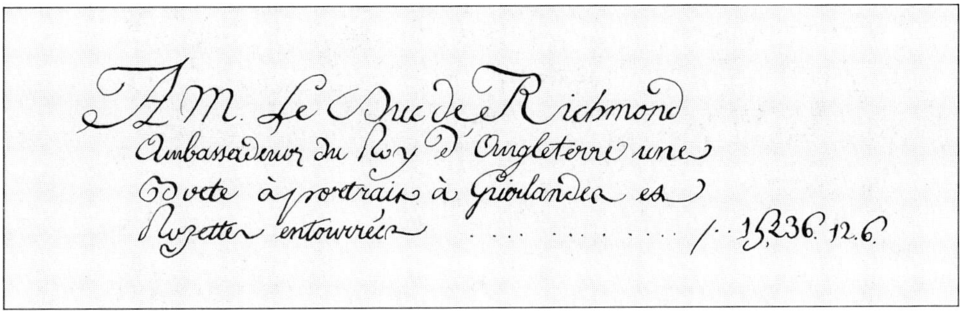

A M. Le Duc de Richmond
Ambassadeur du Roy d'Angleterre une
Boete à portrait à Guirlandes et
Rozettes entourées . . . . l. 15,236. 12. 6.

54 (LEFT) Sèvres porcelain in the Yellow Drawing Room at Goodwood. The plates decorated with bird and flower motifs (top and centre) are in *bleu du Roi* (a particularly deep shade of blue). Also shown are some small sorbet cups with (bottom row) the *tazzas* on which they sat.

55 (ABOVE) Extract from the Day Book (12 September 1766) of a Parisian craftsman recording an order from the Duke of Richmond for a bejewelled portrait box.

56 (BELOW) One of the four Gobelins tapestries bought by the third Duke when he was Ambassador at Versailles. They all depict the adventures of Don Quixote. The tapestries were ordered by Louis XV for the Château of Marly. The Duke was able to buy them because Louis ordered more than he needed.

that contempt of their own set of people is their fault in this country as well as France. They have no desire to please, and of consequence do not.' When the Richmonds had left, the conduct of Lord and Lady George was even more insulting. 'She lives all morning in the stable with the grooms and horses and dogs,' and after dinner 'she goes to the play with a pack of Englishmen in her English night-gown, her queer cap, and no powder; the play half over before she gets there.' Caroline's information service never failed her when Lady George was to be aspersed. She had been told that they took all their meals and played cards in a single room 'which has exactly the air of a coffee-house,' and if Lord George visits a French family, his lady 'calls him a nasty beast for going near those nasty beasts; when he returns, tells him she is sure he must stink, and such-like *douceurs*.'

In London the Rockinghams were already floundering. True, their incumbency would excite Macaulay to wonders of self-parody. In his essay on Chatham (1844) he wrote that:

> They were men worthy to have charged by the side of Hampden at Chalgrove, or to have exchanged the last embrace with Russell on the scaffold at Lincoln's Inn Fields. They carried into politics the same high principles of virtue which regulated their private dealings, nor would they stoop to promote even the noblest and most salutary ends by means which honour and probity condemn. Such men ... we hold in honour as the second founders of the Whig party, as the restorers of its pristine health and energy.

Whig mythology says that their ministry failed because George III and Bute intrigued against them and inspired their fall. In fact, the King had appointed them to govern and gave his word to stand by them so long as they seemed capable of it. But Cumberland's influential patronage was lost to them when he died in October 1765, worn out at forty-four by exertions that had not all been military; and over all was the impending shadow of the elder Pitt (created Earl of Chatham in July 1766).

Conway was an ineffectual leader of the Commons and he and Grafton,* the other Secretary, were both aware that no durable ministry could be formed without Pitt; Newcastle, Lord Privy Seal, no longer had much influence but was congenitally disposed to interfere; Dowdeswell at the Exchequer was a sound appointment but many Tories saw him as a renegade; and Lord Chancellor Northington and Egmont** at the Admiralty were survivors from the previous administration and kept the King informed of the ministry's difficulties. Followers of Bute were driven from office, the Bedfords and the Grenvilles would only co-operate on their own high-handed terms and it became impossible for the

---

* Augustus Fitzroy, third Duke (1735–1811), descended from Charles II and Lady Castlemaine: Secretary 1765–6; First Lord 1766–70; Privy Seal 1771–5 and 1782.

** John Perceval, second Earl of Egmont. First Lord of the Admiralty 1763–6. A settlement on West Falkland was named after him in 1765.

King to sustain a government unable to command adequate support in the Commons.

Rockingham passed a resolution condemning general warrants and repealed Bute's cider tax, which supposedly was not only causing the fruit to rot on the trees but was depopulating the West Country.[5] He also faced the consequences of Grenville's Stamp Act, which had led to a trade boycott in New England and therefore was unpopular with English merchants. He repealed this but passed a Declaratory Act asserting the sovereignty of the British Parliament and its right to legislate for the Colonies. This was felt by some to be a feeble and illogical gesture and it divided the Rockingham party in years to come; but it embodied the principle held by Chatham and later accepted by Burke that Parliament's undisputed supremacy was not diminished by the granting of certain exemptions such as permitting colonial assemblies to vote their own taxes.

Richmond was prominent in this struggle. He had always disliked the Stamp Act and his speech in the Lords, where repeal was carried by 30 votes, caused Burke to predict that he would become 'a considerable man.' When Grafton resigned at the end of April because no overtures were being made to Pitt to strengthen the ministry, Richmond took his place as Secretary, but only after at least two other men had refused it and Rockingham had been insistent with the King, who questioned his experience and ability. When the ministry was removed only seven weeks later, Newcastle, who had opposed the appointment, remarked that 'the King has never once failed to express his own disapprobation of the Duke'; and Walpole, who through Conway had actively supported it, feared that it had been 'a mighty ingredient towards the fall of that administration.' This was quite unfair. Rockingham's government was doomed before Richmond was given office in it:[6] it was just a matter of waiting for Pitt.

In these few weeks of midsummer Richmond had in fact tried to stiffen Rockingham's curiously complacent leadership and persuade him to broaden the ministry's base. A fragmentary journal;[7] often undated, which Richmond kept at this period, described some of their discussions. He wanted to fill as many posts as possible with their firm friends, whereas Rockingham thought that some posts should be left vacant so that they should have 'enough to go to market with' in seeking other connections, for example the Bedfords, because '£8000 a year would be sufficient to buy most parties.' Richmond replied that 'by waiting and giving time the King will have time to settle something else. If he is now unprepared, it is just time to push and acquire the power we want . . . But if we do nothing we shall at last be turned out and what is worst of all, with the reputation of simpletons who could not keep the game when they had it.' Although in general he was mistrustful of Bute and his followers, he suggested a ministerial reshuffle to allow James Stuart Mackenzie, Bute's brother, to be reappointed as Lord Privy Seal for Scotland, an office of considerable patronage from which he had been dismissed by Grenville: whereupon 'Lord Rockingham bounced off his seat and the Duke of Newcastle put on his hat to go away, both exclaiming, "Good God, would you have us join my Lord Bute?"'

Richmond felt that his friend Conway was too weak to bind the Commons and left everything to Rockingham, and of Rockingham himself he wrote:

> The true state of the case is that Lord Rockingham's disposition is always to defer, and by too fine-spun schemes to bring about what he wishes. He loses many opportunities by being always too late and while he is talking and scheming perhaps to prevent a thing, it is done . . . And another great fault he has is thinking that because he acts honestly and fairly, as he certainly does, it will produce a like return. I believe he also flatters himself he is in favour with the King, and altho' there has been lately some things happen'd which to a degree have opened his eyes, yet I believe he still thinks the King likes him and the present Administration.

The end came when Rockingham tried to use the royal finances as a bargaining counter. Cumberland's death had released his annual allowance of £25,000 and the King wished the bulk of this to be shared between his three younger brothers. Rockingham agreed, but seems to have thought that if he did not put it through Parliament before the end of the summer session, his retention in office would be assured at least for the time being. George refused to be dictated to by 'a few weak boys' and instructed Northington to negotiate with Pitt. Pitt had already been sounded out by Conway on behalf of the Rockinghams and had made it clear that he would not come in without some of his friends, and this would require the removal of some of the present ministers. 'He asked Conway if I would like to return to an embassy,' Richmond wrote in his journal, and if such proposals were unacceptable, it would 'drive him to take other assistances.'

Pitt had a strangely reverential attitude to royalty – a courtier observed that in the King's presence he bowed so low 'that his great nose showed between his legs' – and he refused all overtures that had not the King's direct authority. In July, George sent in his own hand a letter to Pitt, then in Somerset, asking him to lead a non-party government on the broadest possible base. A fever briefly delayed the moment when he could 'lay myself at your royal feet,' but within a few days the Rockinghams, Burke complained, were 'swept off at a stroke.'

'The D of R has been hurt at his successor [Lord Shelburne replaced him as Secretary],' Walpole wrote to Henry Fox at the end of the month, 'but has behaved sensibly and nobly, and very differently from two or three of his friends. As it is my great object not to have him dissatisfied, I have laboured to the utmost and flatter myself I have a prospect of succeeding.' 'You act like a true friend,' Fox replied, 'for what medium can there be between the D of R seeming content and going into opposition (perhaps with the base Bedfords)? I don't wonder that he is hurt at his successor, but such behaviour as you prompt him to . . . cannot fail to please him, and that soon we should wish to see him in; and that his parts and birth entitle him to. Marshal Turenne said that if he could not have swallowed many *couleuvres* [non-venomous snakes], he had never been the great man he was. Shelburne is a *couleuvre*, and of the most distasteful sort, but I hope his Grace won't let it have the satisfaction of choking him.'[8]

It was often the practice in those days for a dismissed or retiring minister to ask or be granted some favour, and Fox now hoped that Richmond would take this opportunity of requesting his long-coveted earldom:

Lady Caroline is exceedingly desirous of gaining, and gaining by her brother's help, an earldom for me, or if the Duke of Richmond had rather ask it and the King, which is probable enough, had rather give the patent to her, I shall like it full as well . . . What I wish, my dear Mr. Walpole, is that the D of R would ask it as a parting request, and if it is granted, surely he will go out with a better grace than if he has nothing; Lady Caroline writes to him, and is more eager about it than I ever thought I should see her about anything of this nature.

The rhinoceros hide of Henry Fox protected him from any sense of shame. It is true that blatant soliciting for peerages brought constant embarrassment to chief ministers, and that promotions within the peerage were especially delicate as one titled person might suddenly leap-frog another,[9] but Fox here is hoping to appropriate for his own benefit the 'parting request' for which Richmond might have personal uses and he is also disguising his own ambition as Caroline's. Born into high rank, Caroline was not much concerned about further distinctions, certainly not to the extent of petitioning Pitt or Grafton or the King. If an earldom would gratify her husband, she would be pleased for his sake, but she had eloped with a commoner and it is unlikely that she had any great ambition to become a countess.

Richmond for some reason would not co-operate, or maybe his refusal was urged by Duchess Mary, who had endured more than enough of Caroline's disparagement. Walpole called on Richmond twice within a day and he was not at home. 'However, as I found the Duchess, I spoke to her alone, as I could more freely even than to the Duke. I found by her that it would be impossible to persuade him to ask any favour now; and indeed I suspected so before, for Mr. Conway and I have thought of and been trying everything that we thought could please him, and nothing has gone down at all.' Nor would it when his sister Sarah caused a major family crisis.

10

More Family Affairs

SUFFOLK WAS UNKIND TO SARAH'S HEALTH. Before she had long been married, Fox found her looking 'like halfpenny ale,' and Louisa wondered whether her lassitude was due less to the climate than to reports that had come to Ireland of 'Mr. Bunbury's coldness and reservedness.' But in the winter of 1766–7 the Bunburys went to France, accompanied by Lord Carlisle, a young nobleman who did not conceal his love for Sarah. Caroline heard that in Paris 'all our youth and fashion have had their heads turned by her', even though 'she is not considered outstandingly beautiful.' In a coquettish way she enjoyed the flattery and admiration, having received so little from her undemonstrative husband, but probably she did not allow any man to get too close to her. The banishment of Lady Susan had warned her of the penalties that awaited open scandal, and although the most persistent of her French admirers, the Duc de Lauzun, boasted that when he visited her at Barton she eased his torments and gratified all his desires, he was notorious for his inventions.

It was otherwise with Lord William Gordon, whom Sarah met some time in the following winter. He was of an aspect later to be known as 'Byronic', with red hair and an interestingly romantic pallor, but he was as unbalanced as his younger brother, Lord George, who in 1780 promoted a bloody riot in London. Sarah was overwhelmed by William, and when he came to stay at Barton she was immediately with child. Whatever his faults, Bunbury was too civilised a man to play the aggrieved cuckold. As a hurt dog aroused his pity, so did a hurt wife. He was unusually kind and attentive to Sarah, who was in low spirits during her pregnancy. A daughter, Louisa, who would always bear the name of Bunbury, was born at Richmond House in December 1768 and was christened in the chapel where Sarah had been married, with Lord Holland* himself as godfather.

All might have been well if Sarah had been able to contain her feelings. Her sisters were shocked, but in this family loyalty was paramount. Bunbury was sad but not disinclined to the role of putative parent; Caroline praised his 'extreme perfect behaviour,' which Sarah 'acknowledges and does justice to.' But a couple

* Henry Fox became the first Lord Holland in 1763.

of months later Sarah left Barton and joined Gordon at Knole, the home of the disreputable Duke of Dorset. Louisa's gentle but heartfelt reproaches brought her briefly back to Holland House but within a week she was gone again, 'distracted with her passion,' Caroline wrote to Emily, but also with 'her sense of guilt, which she says had made her so very wretched for these many months past.' Sarah could be a sinner but not a hypocrite. She could not bring up another man's child in the house of a husband whose very kindness was suffocating.

Caroline and 'her angel sister Louisa' would forgive her if she would renounce Gordon and 'lead a life of penitence,' but 'such a life at her age I fear she is not equal to. Her youth and strong passions might lead her into other scrapes.' It might therefore be better if she were to marry Gordon, in the hope that other children would provide a bond strong enough to hold them together. On the other hand, divorce would be a lengthy business (in the event it took eight years, was very expensive, and required a parliamentary statute* which King George, with what feelings we do not know, had to sign) and Gordon was unpredictable. 'God knows, he is such a strange man,' Caroline observed. 'I dare say he will either destroy himself or be shut up before it's long.'

The lovers were lent a house in Berwickshire and in a rainy Scottish summer infatuation died. The baby was difficult with the usual ailments and Sarah, cut off from those who cared for her, knew that she could not marry a man of such uncertain temper who would not be a builder of nests. Gordon had been obliged to resign his Guards commission and no financial help was forthcoming from his angry father. He solved the problem by walking out on Sarah and his child, accompanied by a large dog, and presently he was reported to be in Rome.**

Sarah could only go home. Her sensibility forbade her to return to Barton, and at Holland House, where she was so well known, she would be an embarrassment. At Carton or Castletown she would be welcome and in Ireland the scandal would more quickly be forgotten. But home was Goodwood.

Her elopement had been very disturbing to Richmond, especially as his Duchess was suspected – and the sisters were sure of it – of having connived at it. It will be remembered that the second Duke had arranged for his younger daughters to be brought up by Caroline and Emily until they came of age or married, and Richmond therefore had no direct responsibility for Sarah; but now, without hesitation, he brought her to Goodwood, which was to be her home for more than eleven years. This had its embarrassments. Although society was lax

---

* Until 1857 divorce could only be obtained by private statute and, even if undefended, cost about £800.

** The Lennox and Gordon families were soon to be united in happier circumstances. In 1789 Charles Lennox, the future fourth Duke, married a daughter of the fourth Duke of Gordon. When the fifth Duke of Gordon died without heirs in 1836, the title became extinct and his Scottish estates passed to the fifth Duke of Richmond. Forty years later Queen Victoria revived the dukedom and conferred it, with the earldom of Kinrara, on the sixth Duke of Richmond for his public services.

in its attitude to liaisons and romantic entanglements, most of which were unconcealed, Sarah and her child had to be kept out of sight when guests were invited to Goodwood: an inconvenience that was eased when in due course Richmond built her a little home of her own about a mile from the main house. Seemingly elopement was the sin that could not be forgiven. It implied the choice of a mate contrary to the family's wishes and carried out in defiance of them. The pride of the whole clan was offended.

Richmond gave Sarah more than a home: his gentleness and consideration brought her peace of mind – or, in rougher terms, it rebuilt a devastated area. Louisa was at Goodwood during 1770, a few months after Sarah's arrival, and she found that 'he always does her good. He has her mind so at heart, and is so capable of talking to her in just the right way, that I do think it is the most fortunate thing for her – poor soul! – being under his protection.' Sarah had caused him public shame and yet this 'best of brothers' showed her a patient understanding that is at odds with his public reputation as a man often hasty and overbearing. 'Family' perhaps demanded this. He had decided that the ranks must close and be seen to have closed. One suspects also the influence of the Duchess. Although the incomplete records give little direct evidence of it, he seems always to have been a better, kinder and happier man when he was in her company.

Sarah's divorce was not completed until 1776, after Bunbury had visited her. She told Louisa that she 'never felt satisfied not to have received his pardon ... but his extreme delicacy in avoiding to give the least hint about my conduct ... did at last restore my spirits in some degree ... He contrived to convince me he looked upon me as his friend and one whose friendship he was pleased with. I cannot describe to you how light my heart has felt since this meeting.' His tenderness brought her to tears and although 'we parted the best of friends in the world, it is very true that every mark of his forgiveness is like a dagger to my heart.' Poor foolish Bunbury, after all the expense of the divorce and the pain of his humiliation, had even said that he was ready to remarry her, but Sarah was wise enough not to try her fortunes once more with a man who was so much happier with horses.

Sarah's presence at Goodwood is rewarding for the illumination it gives on Richmond in his home, on his relationship with the Duchess, his sexual indiscretions, his health, his views on education, his politics and his reaction when Emily, of all people, brought further disgrace upon the family. As Louisa Bunbury grew up she was not the only 'little orphan' at Goodwood, and the sisters were assured, as they had long suspected, that there were other women in Richmond's life. There was Madame de Cambis, daughter of a prince and married to a viscount, *'qu'il aime avec passion'*. Sarah had met her and 'think her very pleasing, and quite a proper age for him, for I did not at all approve of his flirtation here with a little dab of a miss 20 years younger than himself, and he allows it was very ridiculous.' These attachments were quite open and the family could only treat them with affectionate indulgence. Madame de Cambis had been to Goodwood, where she was well liked, and the sisters had also met her at Aubigny. Nor was she Richmond's only *divertissement* in France. When in 1776 he was going to Paris to do homage for the Aubigny inheritance Sarah told Emily that as he had not been well, they must 'make a petition to all his French ladies from us of his family, who humbly beg they will send him home to bed early. For though we spare him willingly to them (*vu que* they have taste enough to like him) for a little while, we expect he should be nursed up and sent home at least as well as he goes.'

It was Louisa who asked the Duchess what she thought of these recreations. 'As to my brother's flirting, she don't mind it one bit, provided 'tis with what she reckons creditable and genteel. She is vastly comical upon that subject, for jealousy is not in question, but her pride is and she is discomposed if she thinks he likes anything frippery and vulgar. Now for my part, 'twould be the same whether kitchen-maid or empress, provided I could imagine that I was not the first object, but she is very sure of that with him, and therefore don't mind his flirting, and since she don't, I am very glad he diverts himself, poor soul.'

In the extraordinary understanding that existed between them, the Duchess was sure of her man and could afford to be 'vastly comical' about his back-slidings. He might amuse himself with decent, intelligent girls, but the malkins, who made him look a fool, were not acceptable. Malkins, however, there were, for Richmond seems to have lacked restraint and discrimination. Louisa told Emily of 'the death of a poor little girl that he and the Duchess had taken into the house, whom perhaps he may have told you of. There was a mystery about where she came from, but my brother and the Duchess were kind to her.' According to Sarah, this was not the only one.

Although herself not much interested in politics, except when she grew indignant about the injuries done to America and Ireland, Sarah had too often seen her brother return from London bruised, frustrated and unhappy. She made a penetrating comment in a letter to Lady Susan O'Brien: 'I won't name my brother's politics to you because I really do not understand them, but in my poor opinion ... he will try to be so very right that he will be very wrong.' She was referring to a dogmatic habit of mind that all the family encountered at some time, and his colleagues quite frequently. Richmond could be so firmly convinced of the rightness of his own opinions (even if he would later change them) that he would overstate his case and grow so heated in his own defence that he came to regard other men's disagreement as a personal slight. More than once he spoiled a good case by excessive vehemence.

This worried his family because of its effect upon his health. To judge from the bulletins that the sisters distributed when they met him, he was never really well;

57 Duchess Mary in a brown woollen riding habit.
The picture was painted for the third Duke
by Sir Joshua Reynolds in about 1760.

and even with allowance for feminine exaggeration, he was seldom a wholly fit or eupeptic man. His health as a child caused anxiety to parents who had already lost two sons.[1] In 1742, thanking Newcastle for kind enquiries, his father reported that 'despite two convulsion fits' he appeared to be out of danger and was taking 'common nourishment', although still refusing medicine. Next year his father, then campaigning abroad, heard that the boy had again been ill. 'I own I am a good deal uneasy about him, for I find the Duchess is exceedingly so.'

Yet, apart from juvenile convulsions, it is hard to discover what ailed him. Gout and a troubled liver are mentioned in the correspondence, but the household accounts show that by the standards of his time he was frugal in food and drink. This was a man of great physical energy, active all his life in soldiering, farming on his estate, building, yachting and hunting. When he died at the age of seventy-one he was hoping that a son would shortly be born to him. Only a few months before his death Sarah was happy to find him as sprightly as a lad fifty years younger.

His own account of his condition was different. Ill-health was his continuing explanation of his failure to attend to politics as zealously as his friends expected of him. As one example from many, in a letter from Goodwood to Walpole in 1775 he wrote:[2] 'But, my dear Sir, recollect that to be very active in any business one must be very healthy. I am not often so here, but never in London, and to attempt politics without health is sailing in a very leaky boat.' Probably he was what the Elizabethans called 'humorous', subject to fluctuations of health induced by the dominant 'humour' of the blood or constitution. His was one of the melancholic or atrabilious kind, so that depression made him physically ill. Louisa on a visit in 1772 was perceptive on this. 'What he says himself I believe is the case, that there is some humour about him that sometimes wastes itself in pain, or else falls upon his nerves . . . There are symptoms of several complaints which altogether make a very bad jumble. Anything of business seems to wear him to death. He often seems to have no pleasure in the things that amused him.' It is Hamlet's case exactly. Possibly, too, Richmond was inclined to indulge himself when he had an audience. Sarah left Goodwood when she married again in 1781, but on a visit some years later she found her brother in an orgy of self-medication. His troubles, she thought, were 'all on account of his own mismanagement. Only think what he does! He gets wet, he takes laudanum; he takes salts, he takes emetics!'

Fortunately she was also at hand to nurse him through the shock of Emily's strange misbehaviour in 1774. Soon after the loss of her eldest son George, Emily had planned to engage a tutor to instruct her growing family and she wrote to Rousseau, who was then in London, offering 'an elegant retreat' if he would take the post. She admired his *Émile* in which, to the horror of the French establishment, he had given his views on the upbringing of children. Caroline, predictably, did not agree, although some of the proceedings in the Fox nursery were more disorderly than anything envisaged by Rousseau. 'Examine his principles and they are certainly bad and hurtful . . . Upon reflection I think his writing very dangerous, very destructive of all principles hitherto held sacred, both moral and religious.'

She need not have worried, because Rousseau did not reply to the invitation. Emily appointed instead William Ogilvie, a young Scot who had failed in running a school in his homeland and failed again as a tutor in Dublin. Sarah thought he was 'very ugly and has a disagreeable manner,' but the Leinster children seem to have accepted him, partly for his obvious adoration of their mother.

James Leinster died in 1773 and within a year Emily, aged forty-three and nine years his senior, married Ogilvie: the ceremony supposedly hastened because a malicious son-in-law was declaring that they were already lovers. Dublin society was so shocked that it was eleven years before Emily settled again in Ireland. She insisted on the title of Dowager Duchess of Leinster, but from duke's wife to dominie's wife was a long, downward and humiliating path; to marry so soon after the death of an honoured and devoted husband was in itself unseemly; and Ogilvie, who lacked outward graces, came socially and culturally from a different world. But he did not fail in his conjugal duties. Emily bore him three daughters, raising her total production to twenty-two.

Burke had heard the news some weeks before the marriage took place and concluded that it 'must be extremely mortifying to the Duke.' He wished he could be present 'to contribute if possible to dissipate his melancholy.' This was left to Sarah, who told Emily of his reaction: initially a four-page letter of cautious rebuke which she persuaded him not to post. 'Advice after twenty-five is absurd,' she thought, and his view was coloured by 'his abominable strong prejudice against the Scotch in general.' In fact he had only suggested that 'in the common view of things any inequality between husband and wife generally tends to make them less happy.' His practical response, as nearly always in crises affecting the family, was forthright and generous. He installed Emily and her younger children at Aubigny, visited her regularly and arranged the visits to Paris, London and Goodwood that should compensate her for the social life at Carton and the charming and talented husband she had lost. Ogilvie, too, brought her the companionship she needed. She stayed with him until her death, all passion spent, and he outlived her by fourteen years. Nonetheless 1774 was a sad time for the Lennox family as this was the year when Henry Fox and Caroline died.

SARAH HAD MORE THAN ONCE COMMENTED on Richmond's enthusiasm in giving instruction to the young. This was the didactic mode that was part of his character, and her own daughter and other little girls to be found at Goodwood were fortunate in it. He would throw aside his cares and devote himself for hours with patience and animation. Sarah thus was present during the odd episode of Walker King which, although not particularly significant in itself, reveals a different attitude to Richmond from the one which Burke adopted when addressing him personally. Walker King* was a young man of about twenty-two, lately elected to a Fellowship at Corpus Christi College, Oxford, and in the summer of 1774 Richmond engaged him to teach him classics. This was accompanied by an informal arrangement that he should act as tutor to Charles Lennox, the Duke's nephew and presumed heir, then aged ten, but nothing had been settled about salary or terms of employment. King might be expected, for instance, to accompany his pupil abroad.

Burke had long anticipated Scott Fitzgerald's discovery that the rich are different because they are rich. This was always his difficulty when trying to make his patrician leaders give full attention to their political duties as he felt they should. The rich have their own priorities. If, instead of coming to London, they choose to stay at home to hunt or hold a house party or supervise the harvest, they are not to be gainsaid.** He therefore wrote on at least three occasions to King, advising him to be wary of accepting the post,[3] especially as Richmond appeared to have been casual or dilatory in putting it on a permanent basis:

> I am sure that his Grace partakes of the nature of all persons who are slow to decide. It will be as difficult for him to disengage himself clearly from a connexion with you as it will be for him clearly and distinctly to form one . . . To be long upon trial is not a very reputable situation . . . The Duke of Richmond is a very considerate man; but persons of that rank, who have an assured fortune and situation, independently of the opinions of mankind, never feel thoroughly how much the fortune of a young man circumstanced as you are depends upon every breath of rumour or every light construction given to your affairs.

King therefore had to decide whether he fancied 'gliding insensibly from a visitor to the Duke into a tutor to his nephew, and thence to terms proper for you.'

Burke felt that he should not. 'It was a scheme of amusement which he proposed. I did not promise myself much from that scheme either to his Grace or to you. It diverted him for the moment . . . but, as I told you, the Duke's ideas of

* He later became Bishop of Rochester.

** These absences were a constant annoyance to Burke. In 1772 Richmond wrote: 'I would wish not to stir from hence till after Christmas, as I have engaged a large party to come here on the first of December and stay a month to fox-hunt.' Burke complained to Rockingham about a similar defection by Cavendish: 'To act with any sort of effect, the principal of your friends ought to be called to town a full week before the meeting [of a parliamentary session]. Lord John ought not to be allowed to plead any sort of excuse. He ought to be allowed a certain decent and reasonable portion of fox-hunting, to put him in wind for the parliamentary race he is to run; but anything more is intolerable.' (Trevelyan, p. 471.)

education are not those that are current in the world; and where humour and peculiarity intervene, one has nothing certain to go upon.' As Richmond had not taken the opportunity to offer a permanent engagement, but now was only proposing to retain King until another tutor had been provided, Burke advised King to leave as soon as politeness allowed and to take no money for the time he had spent at Goodwood:

> If the sum offered is considerable, it will look like a sort of compensation for not having employed you; and this sort of smart money is not very reputable. If it be small, small payment indicates slight service, even in the estimate of him who accepts such reward. . . .
>
> All this arises from the peculiarity I have mentioned, and such peculiarities exist in the wisest and best minds; and an abler or a better than that of the Duke of Richmond I do not know. It is human infirmity and nothing more.

When King wrote to Richmond refusing an employment which perhaps he had never been explicitly offered, he was promised full charge of his pupil at an allowance of £200 a year, but he still refused. Oxford, as Burke had reminded him, 'is a great mart for talents' and he preferred to secure his position there rather than risk the proclaimed peculiarities and infirmities of Goodwood, and it is baffling not to know exactly what Burke had in mind.

King and the Duke evidently remained on good terms. Some years later, when they were returning from military manoeuvres in the West Country, Richmond confided his proposals for parliamentary reform; but King promptly disclosed them to Burke.

11

'Les Enfants Perdus'

THE TROUBLES OF THE PITT-GRAFTON MINISTRY (1766–70) began when Pitt immediately accepted a peerage and went to the Lords as Earl of Chatham. He had been offered a peerage before, and no man better deserved it, but his enemies hinted that 'the Great Commoner' had taken the bribe of a title to become a 'King's Friend'. His promotion weakened the ministry's authority in the Commons, and he was already a sick man. The simplicities of contemporary medicine concluded that poison from the gout that had racked his body for years had ascended to the brain and brought about serious mental derangement. Whatever the cause, he suffered progressively from a psychotic disorder that left him, even in the lucid intervals, passionate, inconsistent and unpredictable. Junius* saw him as 'a lunatic brandishing a crutch.'

Chatham's dislike of the Whig family groupings meant that few leading members of the Rockingham, Grenville or Bedford parties could expect high office in his government. Conway stayed on as Secretary but Dowdeswell declined all offers and the few of Rockingham's friends who held minor posts resigned in November 1766 after Chatham had high-handedly removed Lord Edgecumbe from his position as Treasurer of the Household. The other Secretary was the Earl of Shelburne,** an Irishman of uncertain allegiances but always loyal to Chatham; and the eloquent but erratic Charles Townshend was at the Exchequer. Realising that Bute himself was no longer to be feared, Chatham took in some former Bute adherents, but it was not a strong ministerial team and the opposition might have embarrassed it more effectively if they had not been divided among themselves. They gained a meretricious little triumph when in 1767 Dowdeswell, the squire from Worcestershire, talked the Commons into accepting the essentially Tory measure of reducing the land tax from 4*s*. to 3*s*.: the Crown's first defeat on a money bill since the 'exclusion' crisis in the days of

* *The Letters of Junius*, attacking the government, appeared in *The Public Advertiser* between 1769 and 1771. At the time many people thought they were written by Burke, but vitriolic satire was not his style and they are usually attributed to Sir Philip Francis, the man who later sabotaged the work of Warren Hastings in India.
** Wiliam Petty, second Earl (1737–1805); opposed American taxation; Secretary 1766–8; Home Secretary 1782; First Lord 1782–3; negotiated the peace treaties 1783; first Marquis of Lansdowne 1784.

Charles II. Having been at the Exchequer under Rockingham, Dowdeswell knew well enough that the government could not afford the lost revenue, but his success showed what the opposition could achieve if they applied concerted pressure.

In December 1766 Richmond outfaced Chatham during a debate on a corn embargo which the government had imposed. Chatham had been addressing the House in a somewhat hectoring manner when Richmond told him that they 'were not to be browbeaten by an insolent minister.' Chatham had little taste for this sort of confrontation and it was several months before he appeared again in the Lords. But Richmond's political commitment was wavering. He was distracted by Sarah's elopement with Lord William Gordon, and a difference of opinion about Wilkes, who displayed that 'there is in the people a spirit of liberty,' caused an estrangement from Henry Fox and his son Charles, who thought that the authority of Parliament should be upheld in the face of popular riot. Richmond also was cut off from the main body of Rockingham influence, which was concentrated in the north. Inferior roads made Sussex 'as retired as Lincolnshire'* and he did not attend the race meetings at York or Doncaster where the Rockinghams took the opportunity of having political discussions. Nor, since his enthusiasm for racing developed only late in his life, did he join them when they came south for Ascot or Newmarket. Likewise, although they had open invitations, they seldom visited him for the hunting at Goodwood.

For their part the Rockinghams blamed Richmond for the collapse during the summer of 1767 of negotiations with Bedford's 'Bloomsbury gang'. In this typical piece of horse-trading the Bedfords' price for an alliance was a hard line against the Americans and the dismissal of Conway, who was holding to the Secretary's office from a soldierly sense of duty rather than any liking for the job. Neither price would Richmond pay, and he could not understand Rockingham's reluctance to seek some accommodation with the Butist remnant. In a long and frantic letter to Rockingham in October[1] Richmond urged him to stand by Grafton and Conway, if necessary with Butist support, rather than trust the Bedfords and Grenvilles.

> If the support of Lord Bute's friends, which you would have if you joined the present ministers, frightens you, I suppose you mean never to come in but when you have them in opposition to you. If so, I would ask your Lordship if you think you can ever come in but by force? How long may you think to bring that about? Whether, when brought about, you will not have the King at heart your enemy and hating you? . . .

Richmond's last question, 'a very material one,' was this: 'Will you be most

* Gibbon would have endorsed this. When visiting Lord Sheffield at Fletching he crossed Sussex on rutted roads 'that would disgrace the approach to an Indian wigwam.'

likely to carry with you your friends in the City, and those who are attached to you from principle and opinion, when you join with the Bedfords and Grenvilles, or with the Duke of Grafton and Conway?' These views were prompted by his sincere regard for Rockingham, 'and I would beg you would keep them to yourself... for although I am not ashamed of my opinion, I do not care it should lie on your table, as I have sometimes seen you leave papers of more consequence than this.'

By the end of the year Charles Townshend was dead and the Bedfords had joined the ministry. Townshend had succeeded Henry Fox at the richly rewarding Pay Office and had continued to occupy it under Rockingham. At the Exchequer his official emolument was much reduced but he recouped himself with a profit of £7000 from speculations in East India Company stock, in defiance of his own government's policy of restraining unauthorised dividend increases.[2] He planned to raise money from the Americans by means of taxes disguised as duties imposed for the regulation of trade. This was a scheme proposed by Samuel Touchet, a failed financier who – not the last of his kind – had been co-opted as a ministerial adviser. Before the storm broke, Townshend suddenly died.

With Chatham virtually isolated from politics, or apt to speak against his own government when he did appear, Grafton had to strengthen his ministry by the usual method of buying in a slice of the opposition so long as the price was right. With Bedford himself reluctant to take part, as his eyesight was failing, followers like Gower, Rigby and Weymouth were not a significant acquisition. Chatham formally resigned in October 1768 and Shelburne followed his master; discontent mounted in America, the electors of Middlesex refused to be disfranchised, the attacks of Junius and other pseudonymous tribunes of the people grew more virulent, and weary of a struggle he had not the resources or the inclination to fight any longer, Grafton resigned in January 1770 to enjoy the superior consolations of Euripides and his mistress Nancy Parsons.

Richmond had become increasingly despondent. An article in the *Sussex Daily Advertiser*[3] in June 1769 commiserated with him on 'all the fatiguing trips your Grace has made through every sign in the political hemisphere,' but this was unfair: he was unsettled because the opposition had no coherent policy. 'He seemed greatly at a loss for what you meant to pursue,' Burke told Rockingham, 'but was extremely willing to take a warm and vigorous part with your Lordship in case you could come to settle some distinct plan of political and parliamentary conduct.' He must, however, be presented with 'a certain object ... He has an anxious and busy mind. Work must be cut out for him.'

During 1768 Richmond was offered the pocket borough of Haslemere, which would not have cost him much in travel or heavy expenditure in libations to the electorate, but he declared that he could not afford the purchase price and that he was 'not particularly desirous of that sort of interest.' It was, in fact, the sort of ballast that he needed, and a block of territory south of Guildford, together with Haslemere's two members,* would have added to his political weight. In the following year he did not attend Parliament during the spring although he was often in London, and from August to November he was abroad. He met Madame du Deffand in Paris and discussed with her his difficulties in registering the ownership of his Aubigny land. In March he had explained to Rockingham his present lack of enthusiasm. Although 'the times require every exertion of public spirit . . . as I know that I could not be of the least service, and should suffer most exceedingly, I trust I shall be forgiven staying away. You will do me the justice to say that I have not hitherto spared myself, and you have seen to how little purpose . . . Indeed, my dear Lord, I must for some time at least indulge myself in my present disposition which I will give no name to. I hope that time will wear it out.'[4]

When in France, however, he still had thoughts of the party's difficulties at home, and in correspondence with Burke he discussed the expedient of promoting county petitions to the Crown in protest against the government. In a letter from Paris in September[5] he feared that the Sussex gentry were too supine to act on their own and he was reluctant to stir them up. 'I could plainly see that there was discontent enough, if it was encouraged enough to do the business of a Petition, but I must have stirred it up and in so doing I should have appear'd factious.' The people would in due time 'feel and resent the illegal and oppressive measures that are pursuing,' and it would be better to await a spontaneous outburst of discontent. Walpole, also in France at this time, recalled (*Memoirs*, III 390) that Richmond 'told me with satisfaction that his friends had resisted an example so inconsistent with the principles of liberty as appealing to the Crown against the House of Commons.'

Such constitutional scruples did not help the Rockinghams when King George chose a new minister after Grafton's resignation. Rockingham hoped for a substantial office, if not the Treasury itself, and Richmond would have come in with him, but the King appointed Lord North, a good-humoured man and an able debater who had followed Townshend at the Exchequer. Although they could not at the time have believed it, Rockingham, Burke, Richmond and their close associates were destined to stay in the wilderness for twelve more years. Chatham was still a mighty presence, but intermittent and unpredictable. Grenville died in 1770 and Bedford the following year, succeeded by a six-year-old grandson. The opportunity was there for strong, co-ordinated

---

* Until the Reform Act of 1832, boroughs that had once been places of importance still had the privilege of having two members regardless of their present size. Haslemere, where voting rights were vested in all freeholders, had about one hundred electors.

leadership based on something more nourishing than Burke's *Discontents*. In Chatham's view this pamphlet 'had done great harm' in encouraging the defeatist view that North's administration was packed with 'King's Friends' sunk in bribery and corruption. In 1771 Burke was still talking about 'the Bute faction' and Richmond reported to Rockingham a friendly discussion with Chatham on opposition policy.[6]

> My principles were, that the Court had adopted a system destructive of the constitution, viz. to have the minister depending solely on the will of the Crown, and not on the opinion of the public, for his situation, weight and consequence; that this idea had been started by Lord Bolingbroke to the late P. of Wales, improved by Lord Bath [Pulteney], the Princess and Lord Bute. That it arose from the Whigs and Sir Rob. Walpole and the Pelhams' time having perhaps carried things with too high a hand in the Closet; that the means of effectuating their system was to break all party . . . That I took this to be the true source of all the evil and confusion that had happened; and therefore to remedy it, the only way was to reunite in party, to hold steadily together and by acting on true Whig principles to recover the weight and party of the Whigs.

Chatham was not impressed.

With such notions the Whigs truly were 'Lost Children'. Walpole, forsaking his usual urbanity, would describe North's Whig opponents as 'the most timid set of time-serving triflers that ever existed . . . You might as soon light a fire with a wet dish-clout.'

Richmond himself had strong constructive ideas on four particular issues: America, the East India Company, Ireland, and parliamentary reform; and in this book, which is about Richmond rather than the politics of the period except in so far as he responded to them, it will do him greater justice if his ideas are referred to separately in a later chapter, regardless of chronological sequence. This chapter will rather confine itself to lesser matters in which he had some part.

It needs to be said, first, that Lord North was not a fool and his administration did not lurch from one disaster to another in the manner depicted in Whig legend. North's quiet wit and personal amiability kept his colleagues happy and could even soothe his enemies. His ministry lasted because it was acceptable to the King, the placemen had no cause to disturb it and, until the American war was lost, it had the support of the independent gentry. This was the constitutional balance which George had been seeking for the first ten years of his reign. Measures were not merely rubber-stamped. Fluctuations in the voting at divisions reflected some freedom of opinion. Gibbon, who was not a political imbecile, admitted privately that he usually voted with the government, although disagreeing with some of its policies, because the times were too serious for wise men to rock the boat.[7] Gibbon knew better than anyone what happens to empires where the centre does not hold. He enjoyed the gladiatorial clash of debate wherein 'every operation of peace and war, every principle of justice or policy,

58 Caricatures by James Sayers, published in 1782.
(FROM LEFT TO RIGHT) Lord North, the third Duke of Richmond,
Lord Shelburne, Edmund Burke.

every question of authority and freedom, was attacked and defended.' Most sessions were more humdrum than this, but the opposition could mount an effective performance when the issues were large enough and they could agree among themselves. What discouraged them was to go on winning moral victories in the debates while so seldom making a serious dent in ministerial majorities.

With Rockingham himself seldom to be heard, Richmond was the group's principal speaker in the Lords and he found an opportunity in a dispute about the ownership of the Falkland Islands. In March 1770 a Spanish expedition from Montevideo removed the small English garrison from Port Egmont on West

Falkland. Before this news reached England, Richmond had pressed for 'the augmentation of seamen' and strengthening of the Navy against possible enemy action, especially 'the formidable Spanish fleet that seemed to threaten Jamaica.' An operation against a handful of settlers at Port Egmont was not quite in this class, but it justified the opposition's prescience.* North's government acted firmly to this threat, demanding redress for an attack on territory under British

* Richmond's letter to Burke on the matter (*Correspondence*, I, 142–3) ends characteristically: 'The farm is smiling, amidst the frowns and gloomy aspect of politics. After all it is the best trade to be in. Tho' one can do less good, one is liable to do less mischief . . . I wish you could come and see my sainfoin improvements on a hill not worth half a crown, now worth a pound an acre.'

sovereignty. The Duc de Choiseul, who had been rebuilding France's army and navy for a war of revenge on Britain (and incidentally fortifying Martinique by methods which won Richmond's admiration), decided that the time was come to meet force with force. The hawkish Count d'Andrada in Spain supported him in threatening that British action to recover the Falklands would be resisted. The scent of battle was like incense to Chatham, who spoke of leading a united ministry to fight the war and win it, but when at the end of the year Choiseul was dismissed and Spain decided not to go it alone, the threat suddenly disappeared. North insisted that the settlement at Port Egmont be restored, and he privately promised that the question of sovereignty would be open to negotiation, although he did not say when this should take place.

Choiseul's fall can have been no surprise to Richmond, because he had predicted it. When writing to Burke from Paris in September 1769 he had reported the rise of Madame du Barry as Louis XV's new mistress, with Choiseul and his followers so violently against her that 'all the women of that party have been turned out from the King's private suppers' for having shown her insufficient attention.[8] In consequence Choiseul must fall.

This analysis was not wholly correct because, although Richmond could not have known it at the time, it was Choiseul's belligerence that brought him down. Louis XV had been led into too many unsuccessful wars to risk an engagement in the South Atlantic, and in 1770 he turned to ministers who promised peace and retrenchment. Richmond, however, made the further comment that Choiseul had 'put the army on so high a footing that it is at this day the best in Europe ... Whoever his successor may be will certainly follow his plan in this respect.' He understood that the French navy was 'not on a very respectable footing' and their finances were 'as bad as ever. They have given over their plan of paying their debts and I believe find resources very difficult.'

12

Public Business

RICHMOND SELDOM HAD MUCH RESPITE from family concerns and in 1771 he had come to the aid of his brother George, then with his regiment in Minorca. There the commanding officers had formed the practice of forcing their men to buy wine from them, selling it, according to Burke's account of the episode,[1] at an exorbitant profit. On behalf of his men Lord George complained to the Governor, General Mostyn, and increasingly heated letters were exchanged between them until Lord George's friends prevailed upon him to 'write a letter to the Governor in which he disclaims any intention of behaving disrespectfully to any person the King appointed to command in that island. As this letter conveyed no personal compliment to the Governor but went solely to the office, Mostyn affected to consider it an aggravation of the first offence' and he ordered a court martial, for disrespect to a superior officer. The court sentenced Lord George to write a letter apologising for his fault, this letter to be published in Orders; it was later remitted to an oral apology which would not be published.

'However, the D. of R. thinks that his brother is not only blameless but meritorious; that he ought not to submit to the sentence, but rather to resign his regiment, and that he will take care that he shall not be a loser by that resignation. The Duke's letter is handsome and full of spirit.' No doubt it was: *nemo me impune lacessit*, nor my brother either. Lord George did not resign, his friends pointing out that the alteration of the court's original sentence sufficiently protected his honour. Not long afterwards the unlucky Mostyn went to law with a Portuguese vintner, lost his case and had to pay heavy damages.

In 1771, especially during the early months when Rockingham was absent looking after a sick wife and he was leader of the party, Richmond was active in public business. He 'is very attentive to any method of keeping us together, and of connecting us with the high and mighty allies,' Burke assured Rockingham. He had frequent discussions with 'that great being' (Chatham) and 'soothes and manages him, as far as I can judge, in a very firm and very conciliatory manner.' The opposition, who claimed to believe that North had capitulated to Spain in the Falklands dispute, divided the House 157 to 275 on a motion formally thanking the Crown upon the settlement, but their inability to sustain their efforts was shown in their disagreements about a jury bill. When Woodfall, publisher of *The Public Advertiser*, was tried for libel, Lord Mansfield instructed the jury that they were to determine only the fact of publication and not the criminality of the libel. Dowdeswell proposed a measure to remove this limitation of a jury's duties, but Chatham, although agreeing with the principle, argued that as Mansfield had already acted illegally, all that was needed was a declaratory act stating that he had done so. Dowdeswell's measure therefore was unnecessary. Chatham's view prevailed, and it was withdrawn; and so, although the opposition mostly believed that juries ought to assess the criminality of a libel and the damages to be paid, this did not become law until Charles Fox procured it in 1792.

During the same session Richmond failed to persuade the Lords to expunge a resolution that they had no right to interfere with the Commons' decision on the Middlesex election. They were, he said, 'as contemptible as the Lords of Charles I' and 'regardless of their dignity and honour.' Their resolution was 'by law unconstitutional, in precedent not only unauthorised but contradicted, in tendency ruinous, in the time and manner of obtaining it unfair and surreptitious.'[72] In May he urged 'a general union of all the discontented parties, upon a full explanation of our principles,' but such a union was an empty hope when in 1772 a bill to relieve Dissenters from their legal obligation to subscribe to the Thirty-nine Articles was defeated in the Lords, with Richmond the only member of the Rockingham party to support it. As he told Rockingham (who had not even attended the debate), the Dissenters were a powerful body and could be useful allies: 'their religious principles and our political ones are so very similar and most probably will generally make us act together.'[73]

From November 1772 until the following April, and again for a few months in 1776, the Rockinghams tried to organise a mass secession of the opposition groups. Against a government buttressed by the Crown's malignant influence, honest men could not prevail and there was no point in their attending Parliament. The idea of secession was always in the air, but proclaiming one's impotence is not good politics and the gesture was never a success. Chatham's followers did not support it, nor did all of Rockingham's own friends.

Burke's letters give a useful insight into Richmond's character as it appeared at this time to a zealous Whig who – probably acting on instructions from the party's northern citadel – was determined that the Duke should remain in public life in spite of its discouragements. Of his reservations about the Duke's private humours we know from the advice he was later to give to Walker King, and he made another revealing assessment in the letter to Charles O'Hara describing Lord George's quarrel with the Governor of Minorca. Richmond's brother, he wrote, 'has got into difficulties by being too like himself, very full of rectitude, zealous against abuses, a little teizing in his disposition, and of little management with the world.' Lord George's management problems were largely to do with

61 (RIGHT) Lady George with her husband's Regiment (the 25th Foot) in Minorca. She is wearing the coat and hat of an officer of the Regiment, with a white waistcoat and scarlet skirt. On the horizon are the fortifications of the capital, Mahon.

59 Batoni's portrait of Lord George Lennox, painted during a visit to Rome with his brother in 1755.

60 Lady George Lennox, by Romney.

62 (ABOVE) The Duke and Duchess of Leinster walking by an ornamental lake at Carton, their estate in County Kildare.

his wife, but Burke finds certain similarities of character between the brothers. They are high-minded but impulsive, and apt to overstate their case. To 'teize' meant to rouse and drive the game, rather like a beater, and he seems to suggest that they would pursue their causes, or anyone who had offended them, more vigorously than was prudent.

These were remarks made to a third person, and Burke had to be more circumspect in his personal addresses. During 1772 he and Richmond were very close. He was received at Goodwood more than once and was treated there to a course in experimental farming. They must have held personal and political discussions also, because in November[4] Richmond communicated 'a reflection that I have made. You know I pass in the world for very obstinate, wrong-headed, and tenacious of my opinions. Now (as is not uncommon in such cases) I think I am the reverse; I do not mean to say that I always judge right, but I do think that upon some very material questions I did judge more right than those whose opinions were follow'd and I do think that far from being tenacious I do give up my opinion to that of my friends much too often.'

He goes on to explain why he will not go to London for a meeting before Parliament assembles:

You know how little weight my opinion is with our friends in the lump (for I exclude particular friends) . . . You say the party is an object of too much importance to be let go to pieces. Indeed, Burke, you have more merit than any man in keeping us together, but I believe our greatest bond is the pride of the individuals, which unfortunately, tho' it keeps us from breaking, hinders us from acting like men of sense. The Marquis manages us better than any man can, but he will never make us what we ought to be, the thing is not practicable.

Burke drafted an immediate reply[5] whose ramifications cannot be brought into coherent order. His discourse covers the whole field of the party's activities and the contribution that wealthy men like Richmond should make to them, and he is insistent that Richmond should not feel that he is undervalued. 'Whatever others may have imagined, I never thought your Grace too tenacious of your opinion. If you had rather leaned to that extreme, I should not have esteemed you the less for it. I have seen so many woeful examples of the effect of levity . . .' What some may have regarded as 'an obstinate and intractable disposition' was in reality 'your steady attachment to your principles,' and detractors 'know nothing of your compliance and practicability in carrying on business among your friends.'

Richmond should not suppose that his friends do not appreciate his character and his services:

. . . there can be but one opinion of your conduct and abilities. With regard to others, your Grace is very sensible that you have not made your court to the world by forming to yourself a flattering exterior, but . . . if your Grace does not, everyone else does remark how much you grow on the public by the exertion of real talents and substantial virtue

63 (LEFT) View of Molecombe in the nineteenth century. The third Duke built this house on the Goodwood estate for his sister Sarah after her ostracism from Society.

64 AND 65 (LEFT) 'Miss Bunbury' (Sarah Bunbury's daughter Louise), and (OPPOSITE) 'Miss Lennox' (Lord George's daughter, Mary). These two pastel sketches are from a series of portraits of members of the Charlton Hunt.

66 (BELOW) Lord George Lennox with the 25th Regiment of Foot in Minorca, *c.* 1770. Lord George is on the far right, attended by a Sergeant Major.

. . . One thing, and but one, I see against it, which is that your Grace dissipates your mind with too great a variety of minute pursuits, all of which from the natural vehemence of your temper you follow almost with equal passion . . . But though it is right to have reserves of employment, still some one object must be kept principal; greatly and eminently so; and the other masses and figures must preserve their due subordination to make out the grand composition of an important life . . . Your public business with all its discouragements and mortifications ought to be so much principal figures with you that the rest in comparison of it should be next to nothing; and even in that principal figure of public life it will be necessary to avoid the exquisiteness of an over-attention to smaller parts and to over-precision and to a spirit of detail.

After reviewing earlier incidents in the party's affairs Burke ended with the passage quoted on the first page of this book: 'You, if you are what you ought to be, are the great oaks that shade a country and perpetuate your benefits from generation to generation.' He appears to be urging Richmond to concentrate his energies on one principal object – his public life in the service of Whig policies. Activity in other pursuits 'should be next to nothing.' But to use Burke's own metaphor against him, a spreading oak does not cover only a single patch of ground. It protects equally all the interests nurtured by the great patrician families, and Richmond would have achieved less in his life if he had been just a 'Whitehall man'.

Burke did, nonetheless, act as a tonic when party fortunes were low, Rockingham was complaining again of his 'little illnesses' and saying that as a worn-out horse benefits from winter soiling, so do tired statesmen, and

Richmond himself was talking of resignation. Ill-health had been the theme when in 1774[6] Burke reminded Richmond that he had 'tolerable corroborants' for weakness of the stomach, and petty ailments should not distress him when . . .

> . . . your constitution of mind is such that you must have a pursuit, and in that which you have chosen you have obtained a very splendid reputation . . . If on casting up the account you find your power in the State not equal to your services to the public, you have notwithstanding an high rank in your country which Kings cannot take from you, and a fortune fully equal to your station though not – it would be hard to find one – to the personal dignity of your mind. My dear Lord, the whole mass of this taken together is not to be called unhappiness, nor ought it to drive you from the public service. Private life has sorrows of its own for which public employment is not the worst of medicines . . . Your birth will not suffer you to be private. It requires as much struggle to put yourself into private life as to put me into public. Pardon a slight comparison, but it is as hard to sink a cork as to buoy up a lump of lead.

Even in his deepest disillusion Richmond knew that his birth would not allow him to be merely a private man, but he had a contrary and rather curious view of the sources of his authority. 'The grand principle' of George III's system, he suggested to Rockingham,[7] was 'to make the King govern by his own power and the weight of his influence, instead of governing by that party or set of men who had most personal influence in the country.' Such men were 'obliged to consult the good of the people and court them as deriving their power from them.' This is a peculiar view of the development of the English constitution, but Richmond declared that royal corruption was steadily destroying the character of the nation 'as the falling water will perforate the stone.'

The defection of Charles James Fox to the Whig opposition was of little comfort to his uncle. He had held two minor positions in North's ministry, resigning from one in 1772 and being dismissed from the other two years later, and he had as yet no great reputation for liberalism, having spoken against the rights of the Middlesex electors and of juries in libel cases. Upon his going into opposition Gibbon wrote: 'Charles Fox is commenced patriot and is already attempting to pronounce the words "country," "liberty," and "corruption," with what success time will discover.'

Fox's character has always been a problem to historians because the warmth and affection shown by most of his contemporaries, even those who despised his politics, are not to be explained by his public or private behaviour. Those who have not experienced the magnetism of a living personality can only judge by the records, wherein Fox's recommendations are very few. He must have glowed with a bonhomous charm and generosity of impulse that dismayed rebuke and left it tongue-tied. Effrontery, if it be brazen enough, assumes a winning air of childlike simplicity that conceals the underlying opportunism and treachery. Even his speeches, much applauded in that golden age of oratory, must have been delivered with an impish confidence that disguised the speciousness of their content.

His love of the classics and his astonishing memory for apt quotation in part redeem him, but he was amoral and unscrupulous and his financial improvidence, mostly due to gambling, was disagreeable. 'The Jerusalem chamber' was his cynical name for the room at his house where the money-lenders gathered with little expectation of being paid. When he was a teenager and 'the comfort of my life in every respect,' his mother's fear was that 'indolence may get the better of his superior genius, which won't satisfy my vanity. I shall not be content with his being only an amiable, sensible, agreeable man.' If by indolence she meant a lack of consistent application, Lady Caroline was partly right, but Shelburne put most of the blame for Fox's erratic development on the father: 'He educated his children without the least regard to morality, and with such extravagant vulgar indulgence that the great change which has taken place among our youth has been dated from the time of his son's going to Eton.'[8]

For Richmond the young man's arrival among the opposition was an embarrassment. With his father dead and his large inheritance mostly owing to his creditors, Fox needed gainful employment, or at least the prospect of it. He began to cultivate the great northern houses of Rockingham, Portland, and the Cavendishes in an ingratiating style for which Richmond never had any inclination. Any success he might achieve there would be at the expense of Richmond's own influence with them.

North's government, meanwhile, was battling through heavy seas with still some instinct for survival, and this was not just due to the King's support. The work of this government has for so long been shrouded in historical myths that just appraisal is difficult. With his pop eyes and languid manner, North was not an inspirational leader, but he was not greedy or overtly ambitious and he had some skill in holding his ministry together and winning parliamentary support. In finance he was able and honest, and here his reputation has been salvaged: he initiated reforms which the younger Pitt later brought to full effect.[9] In some other areas the ministry did well enough. Their Regulating Act (1773) was a sensible interim solution when a merchant company's territorial acquisitions had made them responsible for the administration of millions of natives in India. The religious provisions of the Quebec Act (1774) ensured the loyalty of most Canadians during the American war. Although they were doubtless alarmed by the massing of Irish volunteers and the possibility of a French landing, in 1778 they relieved generations of Irish discontent by granting trading concessions.

If the series of coercive measures that pushed the American Colonists into war proved to be a mistake, it had the support of the majority of Englishmen who had no wish to see the colonies independent and were confident that a short, sharp lesson would restore them to their proper allegiance. But such confidence was misplaced, and once war had broken out, North could not reasonably expect to win it even before European powers joined in. Remote by six months and 3000 miles, against irregular troops familiar with the terrain, it was logistically the most difficult war Britain had so far undertaken. The administrative machinery for an enterprise on this scale simply did not exist, and the combined effects of economy and corruption had been weakening the Forces ever since 1763.[10] The ministry were fortunate when Warren Hastings stood fast in India and Sir Gilbert Elliot held on to Gibraltar but they were not well served by their generals in the field: Howe complacent and dilatory, Burgoyne reckless, Clinton petulantly quarrelsome. But if this war went badly, so too would the younger Pitt's operations in the 1790s, although he was campaigning nearer home with support from European coalitions.

Under the pressure of military failure North's government slowly disintegrated and their opponents found a new drive and purpose. The Whigs could make detailed objections instead of nourishing themselves on their sense of superior virtue. Richmond found a proper focus for his energies, as Burke had hoped in a note to the physician Richard Brocklesby, a friend of the Duke, written in 1777.[11] (Richmond had been in France to confirm at last his title to Aubigny, and although Louis XIV had given the property to the Duchess of Portsmouth in 1673, possession was only now registered with the French *Parlement.*) 'Assure his Grace that I most heartily rejoice in the great object for which he went abroad. Would to God he had had as much success in the still greater objects which he was pursuing at home! However, he has done all for his country which could be done by any man ... in the example he has shown of resolution, disinterestedness and public spirit. I wish his repose may recruit, not rust, his great abilities.' Burke this time did not have to worry about the Duke's application to 'one principal object'. Although not yet accepting their total independence, he wanted the Colonists to be left in peace to organise their own economic and financial affairs. A Society lady thought that he and Walpole would rejoice together at 'one of the King's armies being rendered useless' by Burgoyne's surrender at Saratoga (1777).[12] Unlike Fox, who would rejoice in British defeats by revolutionary France, Richmond did not rate patriotism lower than personal ambition. He did not welcome national humiliation, but the Colonists were men of British stock and tradition, and if Saratoga would end the war, most sensible men would be glad of it.

In sniping at ministerial failures, the opposition found particular targets in Lord Sandwich at the Admiralty and Lord George Germain, who as Colonial Secretary directed the land operations. John Montagu, fourth Earl of Sandwich, has left his name to islands and a convenience food. He was the 'Jemmy Twitcher' who in Parliament had betrayed his friend Wilkes, a fellow-celebrant in young men's orgies at Medmenham. He was a rake* and a gambler, but he was First Lord of the Admiralty in three different ministries and he came of a seagoing family. His grandfather, an Admiralty colleague of Pepys, had been killed in action and he presently had a brother and two sons at sea. A recent historian has said that he 'understood more about the Navy and its administration than any civilian who had presided at the Board since James II,'[13] working long hours at his desk to master his duties and give prompt answers to every official query. He even made some progress in overcoming a serious weakness in the Navy, lack of suitable oak. 'Heart of oak are our ships,' and although in the late seventeenth century mahogany had begun to replace oak in the manufacture of furniture, so much matured oak had been consumed in the ship-building enthusiasm of the Interregnum and Charles II that there was a grave shortage.

Germain was the revised name of Lord George Sackville who had failed to pursue the retreating French at Minden. He was a bold deviser of military strategies, one of which went astray at Saratoga, but he was let down by departmental and regimental rivalries and the shortcomings of the men in the field. Neither he nor Sandwich could grasp the huge administrative complexities of the war or the lack of a proper chain of command and supervision.[14] The services were riddled with peculation and incompetence and also with the favouritism found at every level of eighteenth-century politics. After 1778 naval organisation did improve, with Sandwich's appointment of the ruthlessly efficient Charles Middleton, the future Lord Barham, as comptroller, but Richmond and other opposition critics may often have been correct in their allegations that at a given place or time there were not as many troops or ships as ministers said there were. With communications so slow and erratic, the ministers themselves did not always know.

In retrospect, the court-martialling of Admiral Keppel in 1779, with the furore that it aroused, was perhaps the incident that finally turned public opinion the opposition's way. It sometimes happens in history that particular events are decisive beyond their intrinsic importance: as when, for instance, the Whigs' hounding of Sacheverell in 1709–10 led to the fall of Marlborough. Richmond was actively concerned because Augustus Keppel was a brother of the third Earl of Albemarle and therefore 'family'. He was an experienced seaman who had sailed round the world with Anson in 1740 and had fought in numerous engagements in two major wars. Richmond had suspected what might happen when in 1776 he said[15] that he could wish his cousin no joy in . . .

---

* Contemporary opinion, strangely erratic in sexual judgments, was disturbed when he kept both wife and mistress, with their respective children, under the same roof at his country house at Hinchingbrooke (once the home of Oliver Cromwell). His mistress was Martha Ray, a young actress half his age, and he was heart-broken when in 1779 she was shot outside a London theatre by a demented clergyman who had been in love with her.

... having a fleet to command prepared by the Earl of Sandwich ... to risk your reputation and the fate of your country upon ... No man can be surprised that you should suspect a Minister, whom you have constantly opposed, of not giving you all the help he might do to a friend. If he has a bad fleet to send out, 'tis doing Lord Sandwich no injustice to suppose he would be glad to put it under the command of a man whom he does not love, and yet whose name will justify the choice to the nation ... I would determine not to trust Lord Sandwich for a piece of rope-yarn.'

The capitulation at Saratoga brought France and Spain into the war, assisted by a league of defensive Scandinavians, and for many Englishmen this clarified the issue. Fighting the old enemy dispersed all scruples about the justice of the Colonists' cause, and even Chatham's wandering thoughts found a firmer anchorage. 'France is still the object of my mind,' he had said, 'whenever thought calls me back to a world infatuated, bewitched.' The government might still save themselves by a crushing victory over the French and they looked to Keppel, now in command of the Grand Fleet, to provide it.

The King went personally to Portsmouth to speed him on his way and in July 1778, in the so-called battle of Ushant, he met the French out in the Atlantic. It was to be an engagement crucial to the government's credit and morale, but nothing happened. The French slipped home to Brest and not a ship was lost on either side. Sir Hugh Palliser, Keppel's third-in-command, accused him of misconduct, and Keppel, to clear his name, demanded a court martial. The charge of misconduct rested on the Fighting Instructions,[16] a code evolved in Cromwellian days to prescribe the tactics to be followed in naval actions. With commanders like Blake and Prince Rupert the options were flexible, but gradually, as admirals grew old and grey in service,* the regulations contracted and hardened into the rigid principle that a fleet must be kept together and on no account must 'the line' be broken. If an enemy ship tried to slink away, it was improper to break formation and pursue it. Adventurous spirits might disregard the rules, like Hawke in the Quiberon shoals, but it was for breaking the line that Admiral Mathews was cashiered after a battle off Toulon in 1744 while Lestock, his disobedient second-in-command, was acquitted, and Byng – whose impossible instructions were to defend Gibraltar and at the same time to relieve Minorca – was shot on his own quarter-deck in 1756: not so much *pour encourager les autres* as to save the face of Newcastle's government.** Admiral Graves's obsessive adherence to the regulations prevented his relieving Cornwallis at Yorktown in the final surrender in America.

The Fighting Instructions persisted until romantics like Rodney and Nelson

---

* When a French invasion was expected during the 'Forty-five rebellion the defence of the Channel was entrusted to Admiral Norris, aged eighty-four.

** Keppel had been a member of the court which condemned him.

showed them to be obsolete. At sea they were difficult to enforce because the commander's intentions could be communicated only by a crude form of signalling or, on occasion, by oral messages blown away on the wind. Nelson preferred to break the enemy line and have a mêlée in which individual enemy ships were gripped in a pincers movement, and the new short-range cannon devised by Sir Charles Douglas, a fighting seaman, was aimed at the hull to force surrender. During the heyday of the Fighting Instructions the enemy hardly ever lost a ship. At Trafalgar they lost 18 out of 33.

Sea battles between wooden ships sailing under canvas on a wide ocean are not easy to analyse, and it was usual to hold a commission of enquiry when things were thought to have gone wrong. Sandwich had this to say about captains who muddled or misunderstood their orders: 'There is no set of men that understands these matters so ill as sea officers; for it scarcely ever happens that after an action they do not call in the whole world to hear what complaints they have to make of each other, and the decision of the world generally is that all sides are in some degree to blame.'

This was in effect the decision of the court martial, which was held in Portsmouth and lasted for five weeks: Keppel, and Palliser, who was charged with insubordination, were both acquitted. (Louisa Conolly was one of the few who had a positive view of the action: it must have been a victory for Keppel 'because the French ran away.') Keppel's defence was that Palliser had ignored, or not received, his instructions to detach and pursue the departing French, but the real significance of the trial was political. Opposition leaders took lodgings in the town and turned it into a demonstration against the government. Keppel was a Whig and Palliser, formerly Governor of Newfoundland, had been appointed by Sandwich in the hope of bolder enterprise and better results and therefore was a 'creature' of the ministry. Richmond had no doubt that the government were trying to save face by throwing the blame on Keppel. After the trial further demonstrations were staged in London, with Palliser's house ransacked, ministers assaulted, and Keppel granted the Freedom of the City. Keppel and Admiral Howe refused to serve again until the ministers were changed and Barrington, who had commanded in the West Indies and captured St Lucia, would only accept a subordinate position. The government had to bring back Sir Francis Geary, whose successes had been won in the 1740s, and Sir Charles Hardy, who had managed to lose a convoy in the Atlantic some thirty-five years previously and had been in secluded retirement as Governor of Greenwich Hospital.

Later in 1779 Richmond kept up the attack with a detailed criticism of 'ignorance and mismanagement in the naval department.'[17] Hardy was disregarding his orders despite the King's urgent requests for action, but Richmond laid the blame on inefficient administration. D'Orvilliers should have been prevented from taking his fleet into Spanish waters; conflicting orders from Sandwich had

67 (ABOVE) Admiral Augustus Keppel, who faced a court martial following the sea battle off Ushant in 1778.

68 (RIGHT) Extract from a letter written in 1780 by Richmond to Admiral Jervis (later Earl St Vincent) on the nation's failure to prepare against attack by the French.

Importance with the first Ships from the Westward.

Our Enemies seem to have so decided a Superiority every where that they must be more ignorant than even our own Minister if they do not avail themselves of their Force. Their wonderfully inactive Conduct has long been our only Security, but I cannot flatter myself that it is always to last, and I fear it is moraly impossible, but that e'er long we shall receive some fatal Blow. and the only Preparations we are making at Home is to disgust our navy by the Promotion of Sr H. Palliser to Greenwich Hospital. This & the hanging miserable pickpockets has taken up all our attention. A Dissolution of Parl^t is also talked of, which will occupy our minds for a few Months longer, but we seem never to think of avoiding or of bearing the blow that is preparing for us. It is vexatious for a man of feeling to see his Country, lately so great, so soon reduced to what there is scarce a name to express. it will be happy for us if such Exertions as Yours may promote a better Spirit in a better age. I am My Dear Sir ever Your prevented Hardy from offering battle, and instead he had been three months at Spithead awaiting repairs and reinforcements that did not arrive; after that Hardy sat in Torbay while the French stood dangerously off Plymouth. Things were not better in the West Indies, where the Frenchman D'Estaing would have been in difficulties if Byron and Arbuthnot had co-operated; with resolute and organised action we should have recovered Dominica, Grenada and St Kitts. It appeared that Sandwich preferred to have his fleets following the enemy instead of trying to prevent their sailing in the first place.

Probably Admiral Hardy, never a headstrong advocate of 'Seek and Destroy' policies, was more than content with the sedentary role thus enforced upon him, and it is unlikely that Richmond had access to any precise information of what was happening in the Caribbean. (In 1805 even Nelson found this difficult.) The address is a classic example of an opposition spokesman having enough bits of partial information to create a distorted picture, but it was effective in its purpose of harassing an administration that was losing confidence in itself as well as the confidence of the nation.

Richmond harassed it again in its plans for raising local troops and local money by questionable methods. Counties were asked to provide money by voluntary subscription, but the outcome was confusing because they were allowed to decide how their money was to be spent and they made different choices – additional militia, bounties to seamen, an increase in regular enlistments, local bodies of horse and foot. Burke thought that under the appearance of being voluntary the system laid 'more unequal burdens on men than could be done by almost any compulsory tax,' and at a meeting in Sussex[18] he praised Richmond for resisting it. This meeting asserted the superiority of the civil over the military power and objected to the government's proposals. The King was so angry at the lack of co-operation that he contemplated depriving Richmond of his Lieutenancy.

As Lord Lieutenant the Duke was responsible for leading the militia, but Sussex was apathetic, preferring to pay fines for default rather than to enlist and train a corps, and it was not until the prospect of French invasion in 1778 that anything was done. Richmond did not ask for men from the regular army, as here, too, there was a shortage in Sussex, and in the Lords in 1779 he helped to defeat a government scheme to double the size of the militia by a ballot. He said that the proposal had already caused rioting and that the militia was becoming too like the Army. Local patriotism was the foundation of militia morale and local knowledge of their usefulness. They should be employed in digging earthworks, at which the Americans excelled, and he recommended that men should be enlisted for eighteen months only and, if chosen by ballot, not enlisted until the enemy landed.[19]

Recalcitrant Sussex had a militia nonetheless, although it might not have greatly inconvenienced the French if they had landed. The Thrales and Fanny Burney were in Brighton when a detachment was quartered there, 'but since their duties were not too onerous, the officers could be seen at most hours of the day on the Steine, strolling beside the lady visitors, while the ranks entertained their maids in some less fashionable spot.' When a parade was called, 'the whole of the company, so drunk that the men could not stand upright, was giggling uncontrollably,' and Captain Fuller explained to the ladies that they were unaccustomed to having sixpence in their pockets and had just been paid their arrears. A day or two later Fuller had just cut off the men's hair. '... "The Duke of Richmond ordered that it should be done, and the fellows swore they would not submit to it, so I was forced to be the operator myself ... But it went much against them. Some said they would sooner be run through the body, and others that the Duke should as soon have their heads." That the men resented the Duke's orders is not surprising; at that date it could only have been a personal whim.'[20] The Duke's unguarded whims were sometimes as unwelcome to his peers as to the licentious soldiery. When he taunted Chancellor Thurlow with the lowliness of his birth, he was reminded that his own presence in the Lords was due to his being 'the accident of an accident.'

The growing strength of the opposition against a wilting ministry had justified the passive policies of Rockingham which to Richmond had often seemed an abdication of leadership. All through the decade, while American relations deteriorated, Rockingham had promised that the day would come when the English people would realise how badly they were governed and bestir themselves and turn to honest men. As early as 1769 during the London demonstrations on behalf of Wilkes, young men of reforming mind – lawyers, writers, merchants – had formed the Society of Supporters of the Bill of Rights, committed to changes in the law and the representative system. Gradually such groups had begun to proliferate, in the counties as well as in the towns, and whatever scruples the Whig leaders may once have had about 'factious' behaviour, they fostered these local associations and the petitions they were preparing against the government and, by implication, against the King.

These manoeuvres did not have universal support. In December 1820 the aged Earl of Sheffield wrote to Lord Egremont at Petworth[21] agreeing with his proposal for 'a general declaration of support and attachment to the Monarchical Government and the Person of the King.' He felt this to be necessary on account of the radical and republican agitation following the scandals disclosed in George IV's divorce proceedings against Queen Caroline. This was promoted by 'the factious opportunists who are so ready to take possession of the Government, and who have no other object than to destroy Government,' and it reminded Sheffield of his own part in organising a protest 'against a petition to the House of Commons promoted by the Duke of Richmond at Lewes on the

20th January 1780.' Besides refuting 'certain unfounded allegations' in the petition, the protest particularly objected to appointing . . .

> . . . Committees of Correspondence with the declared purpose of forming general associations apparently tending to overrule the Legislature, to introduce measures inconsistent with, and subversive of, our present excellent Constitution, and leading to confusion and anarchy.
>
> All the noblemen and considerable men in the county who had not committed themselves with the Duke of Richmond signed the protest, and perhaps there never was so large a signature of gentlemen, magistrates, clergy, etc. I have now before me the Sussex newspapers containing the protest and signatures. There are 9 peers, 5 baronets, 65 esquires, 72 clergymen, 180 gentlemen and upwards of 500 yeomen and free-holders, . . .

and there would have been more if Richmond and his adherents had not 'counteracted as much as they possibly could.'

So with Richmond hawking his petition and Sheffield promoting his protest, Sussex had become unwontedly lively. Conservative resistance there was probably stronger than in most areas because elsewhere the profusion of associations, correspondence committees and petitions was embarrassing the government. They could not have done it without the failure in America, but the Rockinghams had widened the basis of their national appeal. They wooed the merchants by promising to make peace with the Americans and to re-establish commercial ties as soon as possible, and at the same time they exploited the traditional 'Country' interest in the reduction of government expenditure by promising Household reforms that would limit the number of placemen and sinecures. They would appease Grattan in Ireland and they would reform Parliament, too, although not on the extravagant scale proposed by Richmond.

In 1779 Richmond himself moved reform of the Civil List as being 'lavish and wasteful to a shameful degree,' and although this was inevitably defeated, in the following year North made tentative overtures to Rockingham. The Bedfords, tell-tale straws in any wind, were ready to desert and the government had to be strengthened. Rockingham made certain conditions, including the appointment of Richmond as Secretary, that the King would not accept, and North soldiered on for another unhappy year, his frequent offers of resignation as frequently refused. At last, in March 1782, he insisted on going, and King George, after a discouraging survey of the alternatives, turned to Rockingham because he had nowhere else to go.

13

'I Prize Liberty'

When in 1752 Richmond said in a letter to the Duke of Newcastle, 'I prize liberty beyond anything,' it was a bold assertion by a youth of seventeen so far little acquainted with the world's restraints, but – Sir George Savile being the only possible exception – he was more consistent than any Whig leader in defending legal and natural rights wherever they were challenged: on America, on Wilkes and the rights of electors, on the reporting of parliamentary debates, on the East India Company's charter, on relief for Catholics and Dissenters, on the need to extend the parliamentary franchise to those who had been deprived of it. Often, it is true, his motive was to oppose a government that he considered to be corrupt and tyrannous, but always underlying his actions was a disinterested belief in liberty for its own sake. It was the guiding principle of his public life.

He did not at first think that the American Colonists should be independent, and he only accepted it as inevitable after their refusal to be defeated had encouraged France and Spain to join them. No 'wind of change' was as yet blowing through Europe to suggest that colonial territories had any case for being in full control of their own affairs. Most of the opposition – Rockingham certainly – had no theoretical interest in the Americans' attitude and were disturbed by it only in so far as it became a threat to Britain. If the war had gone the other way, they would have found objections to the method of conquest but they would have acquiesced in the reassertion of the rights of the imperial power. Richmond was among the few who sensed from the start that the Colonists had rights of their own, and a character of their own. Burke felt this sometimes, Chatham also, but each, for different reasons, found sustained argument elusive. Burke would say that the issue was whether it was in Britain's interest to be generous to the Colonists and leave them happy rather than to tax them and leave them unhappy. Neither Burke nor Chatham was willing to surrender full imperial power. The quarrel was due to the misguided policy of an oppressive administration, and a change of government would soon settle it. Richmond, without ceasing to criticise the government, took a broader approach, and when he said in 1775 that colonial resistance to the Prohibitory Act, forbidding New England trade and fisheries, was not *treason*, he was taking a different view of imperial relationships.

He would still have said this if he had been better informed of colonial motives and behaviour, but there was a lack of comprehension on both sides of the Atlantic. The British were not aiming to enslave America when they tightened the laws against smuggling and imposed a small contribution to defence against the Red Indians after the Seven Years War had removed the very real threat of French expansion from Canada. The various Acts of Trade restricted colonial manufactures and shipping but guaranteed a preferential market for raw materials and goods useful to Britain. These Acts, extending the policy of the long-established Navigation Laws, were loosely applied and not much resented. A more serious grievance was the Proclamation of 1763 which sought to avoid frontier conflicts by creating an Indian Reserve to the west of the Appalachians; and this was aggravated when the Quebec Act (1774) extended the province of Quebec southward into the hinterland between the Mississippi, the Ohio and the Great Lakes, bringing with it the French seigneurial tradition and, to the fury of Puritan New England, toleration of the French Catholic religion. This attempt to confine America to the narrow eastern seaboard was Britain's greatest mistake because it failed to recognise the land-hunger – with its accompanying speculation – of a maturing people who wanted to expand to the west.* At bottom the Colonists did not want to be protected from the Indians, they wanted to go out and seize their land: as was evident in the rapine and genocide that followed not long after the Declaration of Independence had asserted the 'inalienable rights' of all God's creatures. The covered wagon would be the *Mayflower* of the future: different transport and different motives, but the same greedy, questing spirit.

The constitutional argument turned on the right of the British Parliament to impose external taxes, as distinct from trading regulations, without the consent of those who would pay them, and this was used as a pretext for resistance by radicals who had other ends in view. 'Sons of Liberty' formed themselves in the American cities to defy the jackbooted King George, and they spread into the rural areas. To relieve their debts they printed paper money (which the British government had always forbidden), ignored the Proclamation of 1763, abolished entails and primogeniture and in some states disestablished the Church. Aristocratic planters such as George Washington,** who wished to retain the British connection and had no taste for urban agitators like Christopher Gadsden or Samuel Adams, could not control the violence so unexpectedly unleashed. In 1773, to relieve the East India Company's financial difficulties, Lord North

---

* The most significant clause of the treaty that ended the war amended the Quebec Act by extending the boundary of the United States to the rivers and the lakes.

** In 1789 Washington became the first President of the new union and worked to establish it as an aristocratic republic purged of radical ideas. Tom Paine, the stay-maker from Thetford who did more than anyone to unite the Colonists against Britain, denounced Washington as hypocrite, apostate and traitor. To less elegant extremists he was a hyena and a crocodile. The language of demagogy does not change: *Mutato nomine de te Fabula narratur.*

69 (right)
'The Blessings of Peace', 1783 satirical print showing the negotiating parties: in America, Benjamin Franklin with the Kings of France and Spain; in England, the politicians, including (LEFT) Charles Fox ('Keep Peace on any Terms'), and the Duke of Richmond ('I have made 10,000 savings in Sand Bags and Wheelbarrows').

70 (BELOW)
Washington's troops attacking the British garrison at Trenton, New Jersey in December 1776.

31. Lord Cholmondeley	37 Earl of Coventry	43. Duke of Devonshire	46 The late Earl of Chatham (Decd)	51 Duke of Richmond
32. Lord Camden	38 Earl of Effingham	44 Duke of Portland	47. Earl of Shelburne	52. Marq of Rockingham (Decd)
33. Richd. Brocklesby M.D	39 Hon. Wm. Pitt	45 His Royal Hs. ye D. of Cumberland (Decd)	48 Earl Temple (Decd)	53. Earl Spencer Decd
34. Duke of Grafton	40 Ld. Visct. Mahon		49. Earl of Radnor	54. Earl Fitzwilliam
35. Duke of Manchester (Decd)	41 Hon. Jas. Pitt (Decd)		50. Lord De Ferrers.	55 Earl of Besborough
36. Ld. Visct. Courtney (Decd)	42 Present Earl of Chatham			

permitted them to carry their surplus tea to America in their own ships at a duty of threepence instead of the usual shilling. It undercut the smugglers as well as the legitimate importers who had paid London prices; but for the ordinary American consumer it meant a saving of ninepence. This was felt by some to be despotically cheap, and Sons of Liberty in fancy dress poured some 300 chests of tea into Boston harbour, at a cost of £10,000. The government responded by closing the port of Boston and passing other coercive measures, known in America as the Intolerable Acts, which fixed on the state of Massachusetts as the main focus of rebellion. Intransigence on both sides had made a peaceful solution almost impossible.

From the first, Richmond had supported the Colonists' case, respecting the authority of Parliament but recommending that taxation and defence be left to the colonial assemblies – who in fact would have been unlikely to vote large sums for British troops to protect them from the Red menace. In 1770 he moved eighteen resolutions relating to 'the late disorders in America.'[1] These were directed mainly at threats to dissolve the colonial assemblies if they would not accept certain propositions sent to them in the King's name. Richmond said that ministers were highly improper in implicating the King in parliamentary decisions and giving the impression that he might intervene personally to grant relief from taxation. 'To pledge the faith of the Crown' in matters of taxation was an insult to the King's honour and a breach of parliamentary privilege. In his penultimate resolution Richmond spoke of the nature of the Colonists' resistance: when did resistance become rebellion and when did rebellion become treason?

Burke delivered his two great orations, on American Taxation in April 1774 and on Conciliation with America in the following March. The government, he said, were allowing their sense of dignity to blind them to the necessity of changing their policy, 'but what dignity is derived from absurdity is more than I ever could discern.' He sought to persuade the Commons that the Americans would have 'no interest contrary to the grandeur and glory of England when they are not oppressed by the weight of it.' His famous peroration to the second speech spoke of the 'ties which, though light as air, are as strong as links of iron,' but it is doubtful whether his eloquence had much impact. The playwright Sheridan, regarded by contemporaries as the greatest orator of the age, once remarked to Samuel Rogers, 'When posterity read the speeches of Burke, they will hardly be able to believe that, during his lifetime, he was not considered as a first-rate speaker, not even as a second-rate one.'*

In the summer of 1775 news arrived of the early clashes at Lexington and

* Rogers himself thought that as a speaker Burke's 'manner was hurried, and he always seemed to be in a passion.'

71 (LEFT) The collapse of the Earl of Chatham in the House of Lords on 7 April 1778. He had risen to reply to the third Duke of Richmond's motion for the recall of British troops from America. This reconstruction of the scene by John Singleton Copley was painted in the following year. The key, part of which is shown below, was made at a later date.

Bunker's Hill, and with war now seeming inevitable, public opinion was on the government's side and shared their confidence in an easy victory. Dr Johnson had no doubts of the justice of this: 'Sir, they are a race of convicts and ought to be thankful for anything we allow them short of hanging.' It was the general view that the handful of malcontents who had been roaring like lions would come as lambs to the slaughter. Writing to Rockingham in June, Burke was very despondent. The party could not look to the merchants to join them in opposition as 'they all, or the greatest number of them, begin to snuff the cadaverous *haut goût* of lucrative war,' and the party could only 'spin out of our bowels, under the frowns of the court and the hisses of the people, the little slender thread of a peevish and captious opposition, unworthy of our cause and ourselves, and without credit, concurrence or popularity in the nation.'

Burke, whose feelings for his native country stemmed from an irrational 'dearness of instinct', considered that Ireland held 'the balance of the Empire and perhaps its fate for ever, in her hands.' If her Parliament would suspend all extraordinary grants and supplies for troops to be employed outside the kingdom, 'they would preserve the whole Empire from ruinous war, and with a saving rather than expense prevent this infatuated country from establishing a plan which tends to its own ruin by enslaving all its dependencies.' In September Burke appealed to Richmond[2] to help by using his influence with 'the first Peer and first Commoner of that kingdom', William Leinster and Thomas Conolly.

Richmond was not disposed to risk setting the Irish against Britain when America was in rebellion, but in the autumn the Rockinghams made a last effort to compose the quarrel by accepting Chatham's doctrine that the right to legislate did not necessarily imply the right to tax. Burke moved a bill to recognise that, just as Edward I, without diminishing his sovereignty, had agreed not to tax his people without their consent, so Parliament, as the supreme legislative authority, should grant to the Americans the privilege of assessing their own taxes, aids and customs duties. The bill was defeated, but the opposition, in a rare spirit of comparative harmony, mustered 105 votes in the Commons against 210.[3]

North's Prohibitory Act, which suppressed coastal trading and gave English ships special rights of search and seizure, was denounced by the opposition as a violation of the Bill of Rights.[4] Richmond's argument, criticised by the Chathamite Lord Lyttelton, was that although the Colonists were resisting the mother country, they were not in a state of rebellion. 'I say the present bill is cruel, oppressive and tyrannic. I contend that the resistance made by the colonists is in consequence of other acts equally cruel, oppressive and tyrannic. Such a resistance is neither treason nor rebellion but is perfectly justifiable in every possible and moral sense.' This was the clearest and firmest statement made by any English statesman before the formal declaration of war, but having spoken on the second reading he did not attend the third. As this was in December he probably had a hunting party, but in one of his abrupt switches of mood he had become 'very languid about the American business.' He had passed through a similar psychological trough earlier in the year when he had lamented to Burke that the people would not care whether America was won or lost until they felt the effect in their purses and their bellies. 'In our present state we are not fit to govern ourselves, much less distant provinces ... I believe our meridian is past, and we must submit to our political as to our natural old age, weakness and infirmity.' Rockingham, too, had fallen inactive, awaiting the inevitable catastrophe that would arouse the nation from its complacent torpor. Even Burke was relatively subdued during 1776 and party morale was only sustained by Fox. Dowdeswell's death in the previous year had given Fox the opportunity to become their chief spokesman in the Commons, and his more flamboyant style of leadership was a stimulus to flagging spirits.

According to an anecdote, undated and from a not wholly reliable source, Richmond was still capable of a characteristic gesture. At some time during the war, presumably during a naval review, he 'sailed in a yacht through the fleet, when the King was there, with American colours at his mast-head.'[5] Meanwhile he had the benefit of Sarah's determined opinions on the dispute. First, 'the Bostonians, being chiefly Presbyterians and from the north of Ireland, are daily proved to be very, very bad people, being quarrelsome, discontented, hypocritical, enthusiastical, lying people.' Her knowledge of history was dubious but her opinion was not uncommon. On the other hand:

> ... I hate the King should conquer too, because he sits there at his ease in Windsor and fancies he has nothing to do but to *order* to conquer such a place as America. He will grow so insolent about it that it will provoke me beyond all patience, and were it not for the blood ... I should wish him to have a complete mortification in having Ireland whisked away from him whilst his troops are sailing, and so have him obliged to give up America and look like a fool without Ireland.

Sarah was anxious for the welfare of General Howe, who was Conolly's brother-in-law, and also for some of Emily's sons who were in the action. Then there was George Napier, son of the sixth Lord Napier of Merchiston, a young officer whom she had met, with his pleasant little Scottish wife and their three small children, when his regiment was quartered at Chichester.

A short domestic interlude may be appropriate here because this was the man whom she would marry.

When Napier was posted to America, his family fell ill in New York of the dreaded yellow fever. His wife and two of the children died and he caught the disease himself. He had to sell his commission to pay the medical expenses and he returned to England with his surviving child and no prospects. He had not even the money to buy himself back into the Army.

Sarah married him at Goodwood in August 1781, he twenty-nine, she thirty-six: in defiance of Richmond's coolness (he mistrusted Scotsmen), a flood of sisterly doubt and admonition and more practical warnings from Lady Susan O'Brien. 'It is the very nature of passion to destroy,' Susan wrote and Sarah already knew. Lack of means 'is an additional and never-ceasing plague,' as Susan had discovered with a loving but improvident husband. So she wondered why Sarah should think of leaving Goodwood where, with a brother's care, she had gradually erased the past. 'There was a propriety in your retreat, and a dignity annexed to the idea of one great passion, tho' unfortunately placed, that gratified your friends and silenced your enemies.'

'Till I was 36,' Sarah was to tell Susan, 'I find I never knew what real happiness was, which from my marriage with Mr Napier is much greater than I had any idea of as existing in human life.' In eleven years, with one miscarriage to interrupt the sequence, she bore him five sons and three daughters. Very few families, at any time, have produced sons of such talent and distinction. The three eldest fought with Moore and Wellington in Spain: Charles, later conqueror of Sind; George, later Governor of the Cape; and William, author of the epic *History of the Peninsular War*. Richard, denied an active life by sharing his mother's weak eyesight, was a mathematician who became a Fellow of All Souls; and Henry a naval captain, wrote a six-volume history of mediaeval Florence – and also married one of Richmond's illegitimate daughters.

In the late summer of 1776 Howe's capture of New York and defeat of Washington at Brooklyn caused Richmond and his party to hope that the ministry would use this as the basis for negotiation rather than for further military success. Both expectations were disappointed. Although Howe pushed Washington up the Hudson, across New Jersey and beyond the Delaware, he dispersed his troops too widely, moved too slowly, and failed to force a decisive engagement. Washington restored languishing colonial morale by turning on his pursuers and defeating them at Trenton. Burke did not know of this when in January he told Rockingham that it was now evident that the rebels 'cannot look standing armies in the face', and in effect he suggested that the opposition had become too weak to look the ministry in the face. He proposed a mass secession lest by their presence in Parliament they might seem to be giving 'silent assent' to policies of which they disapproved. He also prepared a lengthy address to the King and another to the Americans, assuring these 'brethren' that they were not at war with the real British nation. Neither was sent. In the endless outpouring of words Burke found balm for his bruises; but as Richmond remarked of the speech on Conciliation, 'there may be a season for poetry, but in the present awful moment the grave sober language of truth and cool reason is much better timed.'

Richmond disliked the scheme for secession, which had not been 'steadily pursued'. In February 1777 he advised Rockingham[6] that a better way would be 'attendance and opposition upon great questions in a melancholy, desponding way' or enquiries about the expense of the war. 'I have so very bad an opinion of my countrymen that I believe nothing will move us but being obliged to *pay*. Injustice, rapine, murder, desolation, loss of liberty, all these we can inflict, or suffer our fellow-subjects to endure, but when we are to pay, we shall grumble.' By the summer he was certain that America could not be defeated.[7] 'This war has already destroyed 30,000 Americans and 10,000 English, it has cost us fifteen million and will cost us as many more ... though we should make peace to-morrow ... We cannot be in a worse way than we are at present. Some of the misfortunes which our present measures tend to will be a less evil as they may teach us to stop in time and prevent the remainder ... The disposition the nation will then be in will determine whether more or less good can be done.'

Before Parliament met in the autumn he tried to persuade Rockingham to move the repeal of the Declaratory Act. 'The passing it was a weakness, necessary I grant in the moment, but it is a most dangerous weapon in other hands, would now be useless to ours, and had therefore better be broken.' Rockingham would not agree. He was uncomfortably aware that his party were open to criticism as the original appeasers by their repeal of the Stamp Act and he dare not repeal the balancing measure that asserted Parliament's ultimate supremacy. The surrender at Saratoga in October, however, convinced him, as it convinced Richmond and Fox and others of his party, that American independence must be accepted and the war brought to an end before France came in. At the end of the year Richmond demanded a full enquiry.[8] He was especially critical of Sandwich, who had been 'atrociously culpable' in his misuse of the lavish grants Parliament had made for the Navy. 'What money can accomplish all men know. What it has effected in the navy department remains to be discovered.' A successful peace was still as remote as when the war had started and he demanded a complete list of the military and naval forces involved and of all losses and casualties.

Richmond was supported by Chatham, who said that his complaints had not gone far enough. Were there ships available to protect Gibraltar and Minorca or ships in The Downs to counter threats from the Dutch? In closing the debate Richmond said:

> The sincere wish of my soul is for peace – peace with America and the remains of the empire. A firm alliance with America would be a favourable compact indeed. Should this unhappy war continue, the ruin of both countries will be inevitable. England will most assuredly fall. Too late shall we find that by desolating America we have only hastened the destruction of this country.

In the following March (1788) Richmond was drafting a protest against a further extension of the war. He discussed it with Walpole, who said, 'it ought to be drawn in the plainest and simplest words, not in figure and metaphor (I meant not by Burke), which few would understand and fewer be struck by ... I concluded it was drawn by Burke, and would not half answer the purpose.'

This draft may not have been completed or circulated before, in March, Richmond moved an address for the recall of troops from America and in April, for the ending of the war. It had been the government's object, he said in the second of the two debates,[9] 'to enslave America and to exercise a degree of tyranny over that extensive continent entirely repugnant to the spirit of the British constitution.' The war was in its scope unparalleled in history, and indeed every nation had 'confessed their admiration of the lunatic scheme. The acts of madmen create admiration as well as the acts of the sensible.' Britain had never sent out a greater or more respectable force, with 48,616 men in the land forces and 22,337 in the armed vessels. From the losses sustained during 1777 it was estimated that 12,000 reinforcements would now be needed to keep up the numbers, but no more men could be spared from the defence of Britain herself and the Mediterranean bases.

The war so far had cost £26 million and more would have to be borrowed. 'As the principal foundation of credit is a confidence in government, we have much to apprehend under ministers who have justly forfeited the good opinion of the nation.' The ministers had been grossly misled about American resources and morale, and Richmond moved that the King be advised to withdraw the troops and seek to reconcile Britain with the Americans 'on such terms as may preserve their goodwill, on the preservation of which the future greatness of this nation may depend.' With France and Spain now arming for war, self-preservation must be the paramount concern.

Richmond closed with routine observations on the Glorious Revolution and its betrayal by ministers who had 'tarnished the lustre of the Crown.' Replying for the government, the Bedfordian Lord Weymouth said that as control of the armed forces was an undoubted prerogative of the Crown, the proposed address was 'a direct invasion of the executive power.' Moreover, the colonies would be unlikely to agree to conciliation if it were made evident that Britain now 'despaired of conquest,' and it would be highly imprudent to indicate to the French that we were too weak to resist attack: although in fact the forces were much stronger and more numerous than Richmond had allowed.

The Whigs had expected that Chatham, who had usually urged conciliation and had criticised the conduct of the war, would support their motion, but opposition unity was always a fragile concept and – for the last time – he had altered his stance. Frail and tottering but trying to speak with his old authority, Chatham said that if Britain, which had survived attacks from the Danes, the

Saxons, the Normans and the Spanish Armada, were now 'to fall prostrate before the House of Bourbon, this nation is no longer what it was.' If peace could not be preserved with honour, war was the only course, and so long as he could raise himself on his crutches and lift his hand, he would reject pusillanimous proposals for yielding sovereignty to America.

Confronted with an adversary where he had expected an ally, Richmond transferred some of the blame to George III. He applauded Chatham's great achievements in former years but said that in his day the country's armies and finances had been in a flourishing condition because 'the influence of the Crown had not yet got to the alarming height it has since arrived at.' He challenged Weymouth's argument about the constitutional impropriety of the proposed address on the ground that ministers were servants of the public as well as of the King; and although the King was 'the first magistrate,' nevertheless he was no more than this. 'If Parliament and the people disapprove of ministers' conduct, it is the duty, as it ought to be the wish, of the King to dismiss them.'

The session ended dramatically. Chatham rose to reply; 'frail and emaciated . . . he looked like a dying man but also like a being of a superior species.' He collapsed with a stroke from which he never recovered, and the House adjourned after Richmond had spoken briefly of his great abilities and integrity.

On the American dispute Richmond had conducted himself as a patriot and a statesman who saw from the start how it was likely to develop, and had striven to limit the harm it would do to Britain. He lived to see the Americans become firm allies after they had ceased to be subjects. With only intermittent help from his political friends he fought an entrenched and often contemptuous government, and with his combative nature it is little wonder that fatigued and overstretched nerves sometimes led him into follies such as the unfortunate incident with Lord Francis Rawdon. Richmond was always looking for opportunities to attack ministers and their servants and on this occasion he did not verify his facts.

Rawdon was a brave soldier who fought with some success in America until his health broke down and he had to return home.* He was known as a stern disciplinarian who treated all Americans as rebels and boasted of putting a price on their heads if they were captured. In February 1782, when the fighting was over and North was about to resign, Richmond asked for an enquiry into Rawdon's alleged responsibility for the execution at Charlestown of a certain American officer, Colonel Isaac Hayne. He said that the procedure had been inhumanely bungled and demanded that the papers should be laid before the House as 'the whole transaction was a piece of unwarrantable cruelty . . . neither supported by prudence, justice or martial law.'[10]

When these charges were made Rawdon was absent in Ireland and he

* Later, as Lord Moira, he was a distinguished Indian administrator.

demanded an apology, saying that if this were not forthcoming he would welcome a duel. Richmond replied that he had not intended to impugn Lord Rawdon's honour, but as so far no specific statement had been offered, he had nothing to add. He was still dissatisfied when Rawdon merely objected to 'the general cast of the proceedings.' He was willing to refer the matter to the Lord Chancellor or any other unprejudiced peer, 'but the Duke of Richmond cannot suffer himself to be dictated to by any man, and such expressions can only serve to make it impossible for the Duke of Richmond to give Lord Rawdon the reasonable satisfaction he is otherwise desirous of doing.' Rawdon answered with an ultimatum. It was immaterial whether or not a slight had been intended: Rawdon himself was the only man able to decide whether his honour had been stained. He enclosed the text of the apology he required, which would admit that the matter had been raised on unreliable authority and that no imputation had been intended against his justice and humanity. Richmond had to back down completely and convey his 'unqualified acquiescence.'

An article in *The London Magazine* for September 1779 commended Richmond's attitude in the colonial quarrel, wherein he showed his manly eloquence and patriotic zeal. 'In his person he is tall and comely, wears his own hair but is rather bald. He has a musical voice, an easy and genteel address, but has a warmth in his temper which sometimes exceeds moderation and injures a delicate constitution.' A fuller assessment, also referring to his style as a speaker, appeared in another article whose source is not available, although the familiar sentiments in its opening lines show that it was obviously Whig.[11] Richmond's attitude, the unknown writer says, was founded on unyielding opposition 'to the introduction of a nefarious Court system; a system of simple favouritism, by which everything in Cabinet, Parliament and elsewhere is to be conducted and tried by the test of private opinion, in contra-distinction to, and in defiance of, public opinion.'

Richmond had surveyed the American question in terms of justice, expediency and practicability. On its justice, the writer continued:

> . . . he shewed that the claim, pushed to the length of unconditional submission, . . . was unjust, despotic and oppressive, and led both in form and essence to arbitrary power; for where no line was to be drawn, either in respect of taxation or chartered rights, but the option lay with one party to act according to their own discretion, and no right of restraint, refusal or control lay with the other, *that*, in his opinion, was the only true and substantial definition of arbitrary power.

On the expediency of British policy, he had spoken of France's ancient enmity and her determination to avenge her recent humiliations, and against this 'our only sure bulwark, the navy, did not consist of more than the guard-ships, and they not above half-manned; to which he added this very alarming circumstance, that the whole military force then within the kingdom did not amount to quite

8000 men.' The third point, the practicability of succeeding in an attempt to establish a government founded on conquest, 'he treated with all possible ridicule.' The entire wealth of Britain would be insufficient for such an undertaking, and even if it succeeded, the expense of maintaining a military occupation would be intolerable. The outcome would be a semi-depopulated territory along a coastline occupied by a few 'subjugated spiritless slaves.'

The article goes on to praise the way in which the arguments were presented: judicious selection of relevant material, alertness in detecting falsehoods and evasions in ministerial answers, ability to gather and organise facts, 'his energy on some occasions and his coolness and recollection on others.' The delivery, however, was not so impressive, and criticism from such a warm admirer is significant. Although Richmond was 'a most useful speaker and formidable antagonist ... his tedious, unmarked manner of speaking, his slow costive delivery, his frequent pauses and want of recollection, leave him far behind several, as a public speaker, who are destined to follow him on the same side. In fine, it is his matter, and his sincerity, not his oratory, that renders him at present so valuable to the English nation, so prized by his party, so detested by the Junto, so feared by the ostensible ministers and so obnoxious to the others.'

Finally, his opposition 'has been uniform; never languid; it is not mixed with indolence, inattention and a certain tone of pliability, a certain air of political charity, a certain trimming, lukewarm disposition.'

Some of this is questionable: Richmond himself would not have denied occasional languor and inattention, and the writer – perhaps an early 'lobby correspondent' – may not have known him very well. But in spite of its bias this is a revealing estimate of the character he presented to an intelligent contemporary observer. As a summary of his views on the American question, and of his parliamentary speaking also, it seems to be basically just. Burke remarked that '... all that is necessary for the triumph of evil is that good men shall do nothing.' In Richmond he recognised a good man who at least tried to do something.

14

The East India Company

THE VAST ADDITIONAL WEALTH AND INFLUENCE acquired by the East India Company during the Seven Years War (1756–63) could hardly escape the government's attention: the wealth because, if diverted to the Exchequer, it would help to pay the National Debt; the influence because it raised doubts about the propriety of a merchant company maintaining native armies commanded by British officers, undertaking administrative duties not contemplated in its charter and exercising manifest corruption through involvement in the rivalries and confusions of India's tribal politics. In Bengal alone, with its twenty-five million inhabitants, the Company kept an army of 30,000 and collected an annual £4 million in revenue. It was disingenuous to claim that they were merely the administrators of territory that was under the sovereignty of the Mogul Emperor.[1]

Taking his stand on the Company's chartered rights, Richmond was ready in the early 1770s to try to prevent the operation of a statute that brought its affairs partly under ministerial control. Chatham's proposal to annexe all the Company's territory and revenues, returning an agreed sum to finance their administrative work, would have violated their charter, and Charles Townshend proposed instead that they should pay an annual £400,000 to the Crown and limit their dividend to ten per cent. The Company agreed to this to ward off the more drastic intervention that continued to be threatened. On several occasions since the granting of the first charter in 1600 they had made grants or loans to the government for the protection of their monopolist privileges against interlopers and foreign competition, and the new arrangement might be held to formalise existing practice. But everyone realised that sooner or later India must become an imperial possession governed by men on the spot who would be responsible to the supreme authority of Parliament. The problem was how and when this should be done without conferring excessive power on the ministry in office. Rockingham felt that it would be a severe trial of men's virtues. 'The lucrative offices and appointments relative to the E. I. Company's affairs will naturally fall into the patronage of the Crown. Such addition to all the appointments of the Crown – in army, navy and revenue, Church, etc. – must be felt when already what the Crown possesses in patronage has nearly over-balanced the boasted equipoise of this constitution.'[2]

Meanwhile the government had a direct interest in maintaining the Company's financial stability, and this was at risk when Hyder Ali was rebelling in Mysore and the French were likely to support him with an expedition from Mauritius. A famine in Bengal followed, and when in spite of falling revenues the General Court of Proprietors raised their dividend, the government had to act. The unfortunate expedient of allowing cheap tea into America was only a temporary palliative. North acted efficiently, holding a thorough enquiry, and in the Regulating Act of 1773 introducing a compromise system of 'dual control'. The Governor of Bengal was created Governor-General with authority over the presidencies of Bombay and Madras; he was to be assisted (or possibly supervised) by a council of four members appointed by the Crown; and a judicial court was set up to hear complaints against the Company and their agents. The Act also provided that the twenty-four Directors elected annually by the General Court should hold office for four years, six retiring annually in rotation. This measure was designed to ensure greater consistency in Company policy.

The Whig opposition viewed this with great suspicion. Not even Charles I had been vested with such wealth and authority. Since in the first instance the Regulating Act was to be operative for five years only, the ministers might be planning even more acquisitive measures to follow it. On the other hand, the Whigs had allies in greedy and vociferous Proprietors who opposed the Act in their own interest, and the opposition were embarrassed. The preservation of civil liberties was traditional Whig orthodoxy; and if the chartered rights of the East India Company were disturbed, other corporations, notably the Whiggish City of London, would expect protection.

Richmond's holding of £500 in East India stock was immaterial, although it would be used against him. As soon as he learned that the Company's affairs were under enquiry he saw this as the first step towards the loss of its independence. As was his habit when he engaged his mind on a clear objective, he worked rapidly to gather information and to try to rally the opposition to reject the Regulating Act. In this he was unsuccessful, and he was one of only five peers to vote against it. The Indian problem could not be ignored, and except to men who were fanatical about Crown influence and suspected it in everything that North thought or said or did, the Act seemed a sensible compromise deserving a chance to prove itself. Richmond could be represented as the champion of an admittedly corrupt company in which he was a shareholder.

Defeat of any kind produced varying reactions. Sometimes Richmond became resigned and apathetic, sometimes he was provoked to further resistance. On this occasion he tried to sabotage the Regulating Act by making it unworkable.[3] As it had left intact most of the Company's administrative procedures, the General Court had formally to approve the Directors' advice on its implementation; and Richmond aimed to persuade the Directors to recommend an alternative scheme

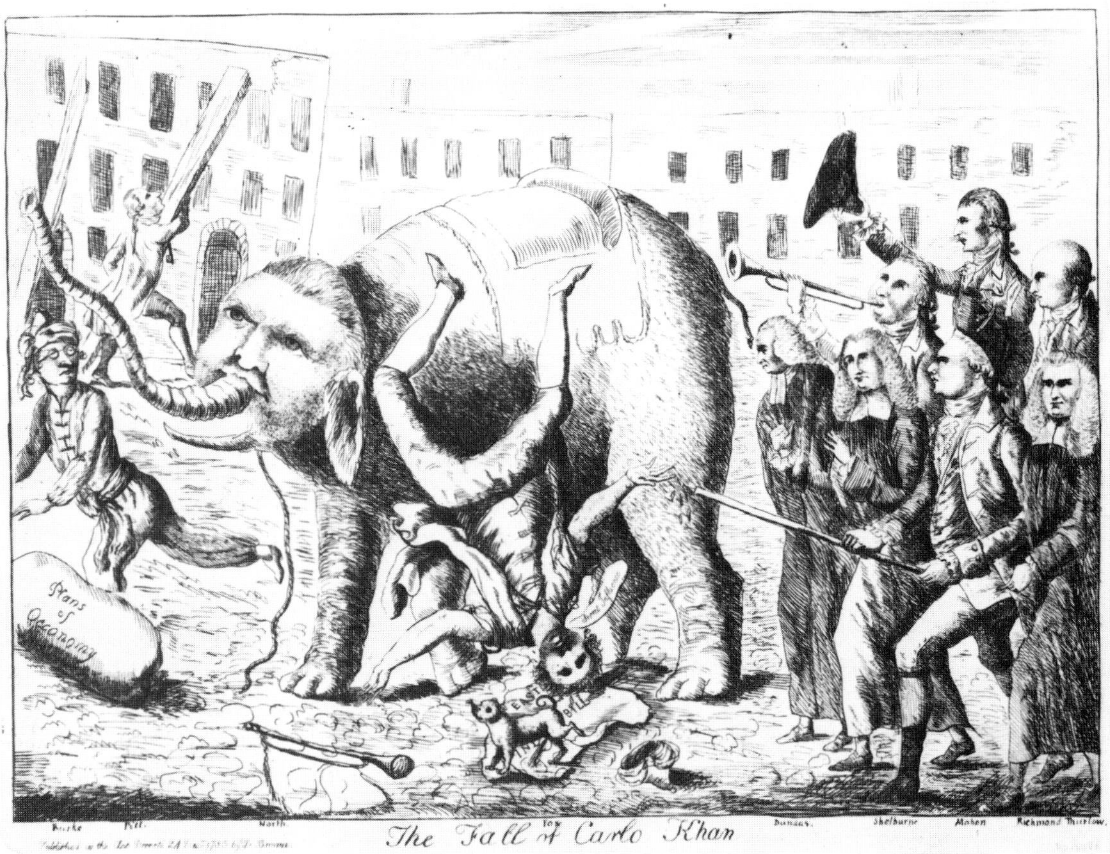

73 A cartoon (1783) by James Sayers, depicting Charles Fox as Carlo Khan falling from the back of an elephant (Lord North) with Burke, regaled in oriental garb, trotting ahead.

drawn up by himself – or perhaps in his name – but he could be quick and ingenious when he wished. The scheme failed, possibly on its own demerits as a programme devised by an angry man in a hurry; but its failure was assured by a small clause in the Regulating Act that raised the minimum investment conferring a vote in the General Court from £500 to £1000. This disfranchised 1600 stock-holders unless they could find more money. Government supporters bought stock at the new price and went to the General Court of Proprietors to reject Richmond's scheme and to defeat his candidates in the ballot for the new list of Directors.

Richmond was disappointed, because he had canvassed energetically and had allowed himself to become optimistic. He had tried also to make Rockingham realise the importance of his campaign. 'I think that the whole of the Company's independency rests upon the choice of the next Directors. If the ministry, who are making their friends buy in, carry their Directors at the next election, all is over. But if we carry ours, I shall not despair of baffling every attempt of the ministry (powerful as they are) to get the patronage of the Company.' He was so urgent for success that in December 1773 he was ready to leave Goodwood despite the presence of 'a large party of friends come to fox hunt and stay a month.'

He was downcast in defeat. The outcome, he told Rockingham in Feburary, would be 'decisive as to the Company and (but that is of infinitely less importance) of your humble servant as a political man,' and failure was the more galling because at one time, until the government played the superior cards they had dealt themselves, he had stirred the Court into rejecting any change in the Company's consititution. It proved, Richmond wrote to Walpole in May 1775,[4] that 'one often does real harm with the best intentions': by rallying the Company in their own defence he had caused the government to act more forcefully.

If I had not united the Company against the ministers, they would have been content to thieve a little by connivance, and the resources of the constitution might have been left to have been more fortunately exercised – so it might be with the state if I, or any man, had it in his power to unite the country against the ministry. They would overturn the constitution, and the army would be to the nation what Parliament has been to the India Company, an engine of violence and oppression . . . But, alas, what prospect is there that any man can bring this country to its senses? Indeed I fear it is quite labour in vain to attempt it, and particularly for me who lie under so many disadvantages.

Richmond's manoeuvres are suspect in the light of a letter to Burke written in December 1772,[5] only a few months before he tried to influence the Company's policy. Here he says that:

. . . we shall not act wisely to be over-eager in taking a part. We have been much too ready in taking up the cudgels for every body the ministers please to attack, and the consequence of our readiness has been that people think we attack only for the sake of opposition and to get ourselves into place . . . Now, in my opinion, the only way to cure this stupefaction is to lie by, and let people fight their own battles a little . . . Indeed I would not enter into action again till I was lugged out by those who now leave us to ourselves.

He did not need much lugging. What he writes about opposition tactics is true: the opposition did not always choose their battlefields sensibly. But he cannot have been, in this case, so ill-informed and tactically imprudent that he did not know that in the new year he would put all his energies into the Indian struggle after he had re-fuelled himself with the Christmas hunting. The letter's closing sentences are almost a stereotype.

> You laugh at me for staying a fox-hunting. I would give that up, or anything else, to do real public good; but to do none I am unwilling to break up a party of my friends and neighbours, which is met and will stay here some time; and I might add that my health is not in a good condition; for only going to Uppark [Lord Tankerville's mansion a few miles away at Harting] in this easterly wind has made me quite ill.

Unless the wind changed, what would hunting do for this delicate condition?

The Regulating Act was not an instrument of oppression, and Richmond's labours in this issue have an air of rather murky intrigue. With allies within the Company who were far from disinterested he tried to abort an Act of Parliament lawfully passed against relatively little opposition. The Company's charter was obsolete in the altered circumstances, and in this case Richmond would seem to have been moved by his almost pathological hatred of the government rather than by any elevated principle of justice or freedom. That he did not himself see it that way is at least a tribute to the integrity of his purpose to protect the Company's chartered rights, but he would not always be consistent in Indian affairs. In 1783 Fox and Burke conceived a scheme giving Parliament much more authority over India than North had done. Richmond disliked this also, but in the following year he acquiesced in Pitt's India Act which again increased the powers of the central government.

15

Ireland and Parliamentary Reform

By the beginning of the 1780s a strong independence movement had grown up in Ireland under the leadership of Henry Grattan, the Irish parliamentarian and protagonist in the cause of Roman Catholic Emancipation. As with America, Richmond was opposed to independence and wanted the traditional connection with England to be preserved. Thus although the Anglo-Protestant ascendancy in Dublin was selfish and unjust, its power should be reduced by constitutional means. Local associations to achieve this were to be encouraged, and if England's difficulties during the American war spurred them to become increasingly active, that was no more than England deserved. Richmond could not foresee the tragedy of Lord Edward Fitzgerald,* the most grievous blow suffered by the Lennox family in his lifetime, but he begged his friends in Ireland not to let the Irish do their work by violence. Concessions extracted by force, with the help of French invaders or demagogues imported from America, would result in permanent separation.

In 1780 Richmond's brother-in-law Thomas Conolly withdrew from the English Parliament to devote his wealth and influence to the Irish cause. Richmond praised his efforts[1] to:

> . . . secure to yourselves those benefits which I will say God and Nature has given you, and to free yourselves from those shackles which were preserved, not from any real good to England, but merely to enable an English ministry to corrupt an Irish Parliament, and to enrich their own dependants while at the same time endeavouring to preserve the connection between the two countries. My opinion is that a connection is necessary for our mutual safety. I confess that that which is established is founded upon absurdity and injustice . . . but still a *connection* is necessary. I would not put down that which does not exist before I erected another to stand in its place. Whenever a better bond of union can be framed and meet with the concurrence of the two kingdoms, I think it ought to be adopted; and the more liberal it is the more likely it is to be of general benefit and to last.

Richmond added a warning that while it was proper for established leaders like Conolly and William Leinster to be at the head of local associations, the purpose

---

* See Chapter 21.

should be 'to lead them to good and to prevent them from doing mischief.' In the hands of men who had 'no good public views' the result would be violence and civil war and the dissolution of ancient links between the two countries.

This summarises his unvarying attitude to the Irish question. Speaking in the Lords in the previous year on Rockingham's motion to relieve 'the distressed state of Ireland,'[2] he had discounted the complaints of manufacturers from Manchester and Liverpool that the reduction of Irish import duties was ruining their trade. He said that 'all local distinctions were the creatures of prejudice and selfishness ... A great, a loyal and a brave people were not to be ruined because Manchester thought this or that, or this or that country were alarmed.' His own wish was for a 'union of hearts, hands, of affections and interests.'

In 1782 the Rockingham ministry granted independence to the Irish Parliament, but it was hedged with qualifications that left much administrative authority with the Crown and with the Lord Lieutenant as its representative. It did not concede full 'ministerial responsibility,' so that decisions by the legislature might be modified or ignored by the executive. In practice the Dublin ascendancy continued, and Roman Catholics and Ulster Presbyterians were not allowed to vote. A choice had still to be made between union, with Irish representatives elected to the English Parliament, or independence leading to separation.

Richmond was steadfast for union. In his letter to Colonel Sharman in 1783, mainly about parliamentary reform, he hoped that 'the mutually essential connection between Great Britain and Ireland may soon be settled on some liberal and fair footing.' The existing system was ...

> ... founded on constraint and dependence incompatible with the condition of free men. Ireland has an indisputable right to dissolve it whenever she chooses to do so. But surely, if we do not mean a total separation, it would be right to agree upon some new terms by which we are to continue connected ... It is for the interest of the two islands to be incorporated and form one and the same kingdom.

Although he was always in favour of freedom of conscience, Richmond did not wish the Catholics to receive any political concessions until legislative union had been accomplished. He feared that otherwise the Catholics, being the most numerous element of the population, would dominate the Irish Parliament and demand separation. When the Act of Union was passed in 1800, George III refused to emancipate the Catholics because this would violate the oaths that he took at his coronation. By that time Richmond was out of office and, apart from occasional stirrings of ambition or duty, was fulfilling his threat to retire from public business.

A small pendant to the Irish story illustrates the ingenuity and suppleness of his mind. In 1773 North's government were considering a proposal to levy a tax on absentee landlords who drew revenues from Irish properties which they seldom or never visited or tried to develop for the benefit of their tenants. The proposal was eventually rejected by the Irish Parliament, but while it was under discussion at Westminster most of the Rockingham party argued against it. Rockingham and the Cavendishes had extensive Irish estates. Richmond had intellectual doubts which he expressed in a letter to his leader.[3] 'I cannot wonder at the Irish, who in every instance are so unjustly treated by this country, endeavouring to catch at any means of recovering some part of the money which so regularly goes out of their country and which this country will not allow them the fair chances of commerce to recover. This is in fact a tax upon England to assist Ireland.' But it was 'partial and unjust upon the individuals on whom it falls. As such I think we ought not to consent to it as Englishmen.'

This was the dilemma:

> The landlord might truly say, Why am I not allowed the free enjoyment of my full profits of my estate because I live in England, is that a crime? The Irish trader and even landed man may say also, Why am I not allowed the free enjoyment of the full profits of my trade and the produce of my land because I live in Ireland, is that a crime? ... Notwithstanding that I think the Irish very excusable in wishing this tax, I think the English would be very inexcusable to suffer it. I am not among brothers for retaliating injuries. I am for having the original redressed and ... I am not for obtaining justice by multiplying injuries.

Although he had worked himself to the conclusion that he disapproved of the tax, he then proceeded, at some length, to give Rockingham his reasons for not attending the Privy Council to say so or attending any party meeting to organise opposition to it.

Drifts in population and the emergence of large industrial towns were emphasising the need for constitutional change. Blackstone's* *mystique* of an ideal and unalterable constitution was challenged in 1776 in the crabbed prose of Jeremy Bentham, and with the American war producing higher taxes and few successes, men were readier to listen to Whig complaints of the Crown's influence in Parliament. This was a very small part of the problem, as was to be proved by the negligible advantages of Burke's 'economical reform' when at last he achieved it, but motions for reducing patronage were brought in the Commons and, although as yet unsuccessful, gained increasing support.

Outside Parliament, a campaign for reform was led by the Reverend Christopher Wyvill, an incumbent in Essex but a landowner in Yorkshire, where he organised a county association in the Rockingham heartland. Associations sprang up in several counties, London recovered its Wilkesite enthusiasm, Fox spoke on public platforms wherever he could find them, and petitions recommended different kinds of reform. Wyvill largely spoke for landed gentry who

---

* Sir William Blackstone, author of Commentaries on the Laws of England (1765–9).

wanted increased representation for the men of the shires, but reformers covered the whole political spectrum. They included John Cartwright, a naval man who had served for many years in Newfoundland and who acquired his 'majority' from a command in the militia; academics under the wing of Shelburne, such as John Jebb, a Cambridge don who had placed a Unitarian construction on the Greek testament; Richard Price, a dissenting minister who in his support of the Americans had become a close friend of Benjamin Franklin; and Joseph Priestley, a scientist and philosopher; Sir George Savile; James Burgh, a headmaster of Stoke Newington who died in 1775 but was posthumously active through his political pamphlets; and Thomas Hollis (1720–74), a young firebrand who set out the programme to be adopted by the Chartists. Thus when Richmond introduced his own plan for parliamentary reform he was riding a swelling tide. He may also have reflected how difficult it would be to secure agreement in such diverse company.

His own motion in 1779 for a reduction in the Civil List, recently increased to £900,000 a year, contained the suggestion that if the King would 'add true lustre to his crown' by graciously consenting to reduce it, after such an example there was no peer who 'would not cheerfully relinquish such a part of his public emoluments as His Majesty might think proper to recommend.'

He knew well enough that minor changes of this kind were only cosmetic and already he had revealed to Walker King what was really in his mind: annual parliaments elected by universal male suffrage and the division of the country into electoral districts of about 1000 voters. In this way the conduct of ministers would be controlled and the independence of Parliament assured. King was sceptical of this further evidence of the Duke's 'humours' and told Burke of the objections he had put forward.[4] (The letter was written from Lord George's home at West Stoke, where King after all may have been giving some instruction to young Charles.) On their way home from Exeter, where the Sussex militia had been stationed in the autumn of 1779, Richmond had treated him to 'a dish of politics . . . instead of a supper,' and King supposed that the 'cookery' would not be to Burke's taste. To lay some specific principles before county associations would give them grounds for protest: 'It is a sort of appeal to their judgment that flatters their vanity and gives them, together with a strong desire of proselytising, all the ardour of self-consequence.' But King objected that Richmond's ideas would 'strike pretty deeply at the power of the Crown,' which would not only 'set the whole power of the Court for ever against him' but might alienate many men who already were 'alarmed at what they call the levelling and republican principles of Opposition.' King pointed out also that the abolition of the existing franchise would 'by depriving them of their existing rights, set the whole body of freeholders and electors against him.'

Richmond heard King 'with great patience' and said that if 'his friends' did not agree with his proposals, he had no intention of putting himself at the head of a

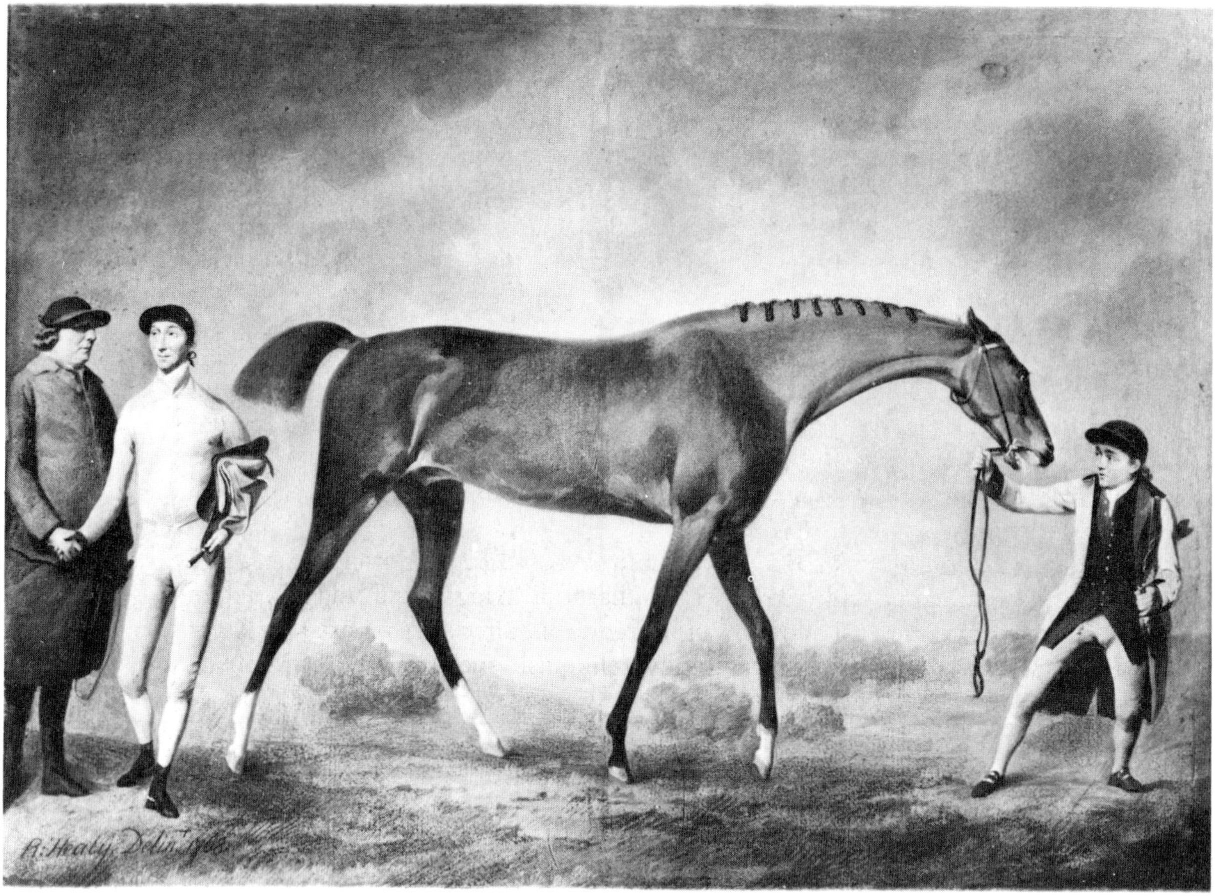

74 AND 75 Two sketches of members of the family in Ireland by Robert Healy: (ABOVE) A racehorse held by a groom with Tom Conolly of Castletown in racing colours, and his trainer. (OPPOSITE) The Duke of Leinster skating with friends and Lady Louisa's dog Hibou.

party and appealing to a wider public. If men 'whose opinions and judgment he valued much higher than his own' disliked his scheme, he had no doubt that it was 'defective and faulty.' He would leave it before the public and hope for a change of circumstances that would make it more acceptable to his friends. 'In the meantime, as a man whose political sentiments did not entirely agree with those of any party, he should retire.'

There were, of course, no immediately conceivable circumstances in which his friends would surrender a substantial part of their inheritance. Richmond himself had little personal patronage, and after 1780 even his limited hold on Chichester was weakening. But the Rockingham Whigs were an aristocratic party jealous of

their patronage and they would not extend the vote to the uncertain multitude or change the eccentric but traditional franchise in the boroughs.

When Richmond presented his bill in June 1780, the proceedings on the first day were overwhelmed by the agitations of a noisy assembly outside the House, protesting not against the bill but against an earlier measure by Savile giving religious relief to Roman Catholics.[5] The Lords Hillsborough and Townshend were deprived of the bags in which they carried their wigs; the Bishop of Lincoln had to escape in disguise over the rooftops; the Duke of Northumberland lost his watch and his purse. As Richmond tried to speak he was interrupted by a report that the Duke of Bolton had been dragged from his coach and a suggestion that the robed peers, preceded by the mace, should go to his rescue. The parliamentary report says that 'it is hardly possible to conceive a more grotesque appearance than the House exhibited . . . while the skies resounded with huzzas and shoutings in the Palace-yard.' Members asked why the military had not been warned of the riot in order to quell it, and Richmond could only outline his 'Declaration of the Rights of Englishmen.'

In a calmer atmosphere on the following day he spoke for an hour and a half and made three concrete demands: a vote for every adult male not disqualified by law; the division of England, Scotland and Wales into 558 equal constituencies (not the one thousand he had suggested to Walker King); and annual elections. Whereas every commoner had the right to vote for his representative, at present only one in six possessed it. Boroughs, which were 'the very sink of corruption and enabled the ministry to buy and sell the dignity and honour of the nation,' would be absorbed into the new electoral districts. These proposals would require the alteration of long-established laws, but here Richmond made a distinction between statute law and the ancient principles of the constitution. The laws of Parliament were not necessarily consonant with the spirit and intentions of the Anglo-Saxon founders, and over the years thousands of Englishmen had lost their natural rights. It was not clear what 'natural rights' Richmond supposed serfs and villeins to have enjoyed at the rural gemot, and this point was made by Lord Stormont: 'The noble Duke wishes to restore to all the subjects a right of voting, but is he sure that they ever possessed it?'

Richmond's plan was rejected without a division. It was a cruel irony that it should have been brought before the Lords just when the sovereign people were rioting for a week. The Protestant Association, led by Lord George Gordon, were petitioning against concessions to Catholics, and the disturbance was more vicious than anything seen before in London. The rioting for Wilkes had been relatively good-humoured, with indignities inflicted on obdurate individuals and damage done to the property of those who could afford it. Gordon's mob set fire to buildings indiscriminately, but concentrated their destructive passion on prisons, chapels, churches, wine-shops and distilleries. The troops were called out and some three hundred people were killed.

The Westminster Magazine[6] made the comment that 'if men are apt to blame Lord George for the measure of assembling 40,000 men to present the petition, they should consider that his Lordship in this only followed the example of all the other Patriots who pretended to a knowledge of the corruption and venality of Parliament. He used the same language as Mr. Fox.' Richmond knew, however, how much the rioting had damaged his cause. Ten days later he was seeking to refresh his spirits in camp with his soldiers at Dorking, and in assuring Rockingham that on no account would he support the repeal of Savile's Act, he went on to say that he despaired of England:[7]

I never should despair of it against any combination of foreign foes, but *I do despair* seeing the enemies it has at home. . . . If the nation can so tamely bear all it has borne, and the evident loss of their own liberty, without stirring, and will submit to being led by Scotch fanatics, and to the tune of the bagpipe,* – set Newgate loose and burn London, turning against the best friends of liberty – such a nation *cannot* be saved.

Burke believed that the riots had strengthened the hand of the government as few other events at that time could have done, and Richmond agreed that 'a general stupidity and indolence seems to have seized the nation; its character is lost.'[8] This was not only Gordon's doing. 'The few who are capable of any exertion are split into miserable little palliating politics, unable to act together, un-united upon any system . . . I am sure individuals will never agree while those they have just confidence in differ.'

Perhaps because it was overshadowed by the riots, Richmond's parliamentary scheme attracted little attention at the time and he seems to have been content with putting his views on record. According to Wyvill, he later told the House of Lords[9] that he had introduced it 'not that Parliament might be reformed but that the close of the American war might be accelerated,' though it is hard to see why it should have that effect and certainly when the war was over he did not give up his plans. When, early in 1782 he urged Rockingham to 'keep back and be very coy' with overtures from the Court, he meant that Rockingham should not accept conditions that would prevent him from carrying out his policies. In an anxious letter to Rockingham in May, when the Whigs were now in office, he indicated that these policies included a promise to himself that a committee would be set up to consider parliamentary reform: 'You know it was *my bargain*.'

He did not want to tie the new ministry to any particular measure, he only asked to have the committee. 'I trust to them for the measure, and am only content for *some* plan being adopted . . . If I am wanted I have the best right to insist on the terms which appear to me essential to *enable* me to serve you well . . . I believe no man can say with greater truth than I that he should prefer a retired life. I am daily sacrificing my health and the comforts of life for the public and should be happy to retire.' So if he were to give up so much, 'those who call upon me should first make up their minds to the terms on which alone I can serve them with credit . . . and those opinions clearly are that unless some essential parliament reform takes place, all we do will be undone.' Rockingham did not live to fulfil the bargain.

Richmond's ideas took firmer shape when he was one of six reformers consulted by Colonel Sharman, a leader of the Irish Volunteers, on their ideas for political development in Ireland. His reply showed the essentially conservative and aristocratic nature of proposals that had alarmed his political associates.

---

* Cf. Lord Halifax, 'The angry buzz of a multitude is one of the bloodiest noises in the world.'

He wrote predictably that the right of every British subject to be 'governed only by laws to which he has consented by himself or his representative was the essential of freedom, founded on the eternal principles of justice and freedom, and our unalienable birthright.' This was the conventional rhetoric of every public platform, and Richmond revealed more of his true feelings when he discussed objections that had been made to his proposals.

It is feared by some that the influence of power and riches will give to the aristocracy so great a lead in these elections as to place the whole government in their hands. Others again dread that when paupers and the lowest orders of the people shall have an equal vote with the first commoner in the kingdom, we shall fall into all the confusion of a democratic republic . . . The contrariety of these two apprehensions might of itself be a sufficient proof that neither extreme will take place . . .

It is true that men of superior fortunes will have a superior degree of weight and influence, and I think that as education and knowledge generally attend property, those who possess them ought to have weight and influence with the more ignorant. But the essential difference will be that altho' the people may be led, they cannot be driven . . . The equal rights of men to security from oppression, and to the enjoyment of life and liberty, strike me as perfectly compatible with their unequal shares of industry, labour and genius, which are the origin of inequality of fortune. The protection of property appears to me one of the essential ends of society.

The last sentence contains Oliver Cromwell's message to the Levellers in his army who thought they had been fighting for social justice. Elsewhere Plato is evident in the élitism, Thomas Hobbes in the surrender of personal rights to a protective government. Richmond thought that secret balloting at elections would be 'a cloak for bribery and a school for lying and deceit.' A public declaration of his choice was consistent with the spirit of 'a British or Irish free man, that all his actions should be open and avowed, and that he should not be ashamed of declaring in the face of his country whom he wished to entrust with his interests.' This is naïve. Might not a voter be bribed or intimidated when making this public affirmation? How many servants or tenants on the Goodwood estate would have publicly voted for a candidate unfriendly to His Grace's interests?

Being more succinct than his troubled parliamentary performance, the letter to Sharman was produced as a pamphlet and reprinted several times, even as late as 1859. It did not, however, become a text-book for the Chartists,* who realised that despite its eye-catching appeal to man's universal rights, it did not assist their more determined purposes. Without secret balloting, payment of MPs and abolition of the property qualification required of Commons' members, most eighteenth-century theories of reform were inadequate.

* In the 1830s, supporters of a people's charter which called for, among other measures, universal manhood suffrage and the payment of MPs.

When Prime Minister, Pitt proposed in 1785 a modest scheme to abolish thirty-six rotten boroughs, transfer their members to the counties, London and Westminster (not to the new industrial towns), and slightly widen the right to vote in boroughs. This reflected the soberly progressive mood of Pitt's ministry in the 1780s, and although it fell short of Richmond's larger notions, he was in the Cabinet and could be grateful that something was being attempted. The measure was defeated, its opponents including Burke, North and Fox. Burke by his situation was unavoidably a lackey of the borough-mongers, and Fox plausibly objected to the compensation of the 'owners' of the extinguished boroughs: the franchise, he said, was a trust, not a commodity of the market-place.

In 1790 Charles Grey alleged that 306 members of the Commons were returned from pocket boroughs, but realistic prospects of reform disappeared with the French Revolution, and Richmond denounced those who continued to support it. When in 1792 he spoke in favour of a proclamation against seditious writings, the Earl of Lauderdale, an exuberant Foxite and supporter of the new policies in France, accused him of 'apostasy' in the cause of reform, and there was nearly a duel.* In the following year, John Cartwright made a personal appeal to him to intercede on behalf of two Scottish agitators sentenced to transportation for revolutionary activities. Then in 1794 the defence cited him to appear at the trial for treason of Thomas Hardy, founder of the London Corresponding Society, and Horne Tooke,** a parson in Brentford and expert promoter of disaffection. Pitt also was summoned, partly on the grounds that he had been present, with Wilkes and Richmond, at a meeting in 1782 at the Thatched House Tavern in St James's at which parliamentary reform had been discussed. At the trial the letter to Sharman was read, and the accused argued that it was hardly treasonable to support policies which had been advocated by two members of the present government. Defended by Sir Thomas Erskine, who earlier had persuaded a jury that Lord George Gordon had not acted treasonably, the defendants were acquitted.

Richmond has been called 'the radical Duke', but he wanted to preserve society, not to change it, and he was never radical or democratic in the way of the followers of Wilkes or the new 'philosophers' thrown up by the French Revolution. He detested mob violence as a threat to a stable society and had no more love for Burke's 'swinish multitude' than Burke himself or for that matter Fox, who never compromised his populist rhetoric by association with needy knife-grinders.*** The natural rights that Richmond defended sometimes

---

* Lauderdale matured with age. He became a staunch Tory and used his proxy to vote against the Reform Act of 1832.

** Until 1782 he was just a Horne. The Tooke was added out of respect for a benefactor from Purley who gave him £8000.

*** See George Canning's poem in *The Anti-Jacobin*, November 1797.

approximated to the prescriptive rights proclaimed by Burke in the *Reflections* (1790) when he saw how the Revolution would develop: they were based on 'one great immutable, pre-existent Law, prior to all our devices and prior to all our contrivances, paramount to all our ideas and all our sensations, antecedent to our very existence ... This divine Natural Law is the source of all true growth and all real political development.'

Richmond was not given to philosophical reflections such as these, nor to the language that expressed them, but he believed with Locke in the natural morality of pre-social man who surrenders some of his personal rights to the magistrate but will rise against him if they are abused. He would make changes where natural growth had been perverted or obstructed, and these changes were restorative. Even in his parliamentary proposals, which in 1780 looked to be extreme, his purpose was to revive what he believed to be the original character of representative institutions. He did not intend to relax the authority of men whose education, wealth and influence fitted them to be the leaders of society. He wanted only to dam the revolutionary river before it swamped the ancient landmarks.

In his own day his parliamentary initiatives were seldom successful. In India he tried to uphold the existing system although he knew it to be obsolete and corrupt; this may not have been one of his better performances, but respect for chartered rights was in itself an honourable principle worth defending against an opportunist government greedy for the Company's wealth and patronage. Though he failed to save the American connection, the sympathy and understanding of men like him helped to attach the Colonists to English constitutional principles. The Irish connection was preserved in form by the Act of Union but it would have been more durable if, as he expected, it had acknowledged the rights of Roman Catholics. If the English parliamentary system had not in due course been adapted to social and economic change, parliamentary institutions would have been overthrown. In his own fashion Richmond tried to lead Britain peacefully into the nineteenth century by strengthening her traditional institutions rather than by uprooting them.

16

Difficult Decisions

'I WAS ABUSED FOR LYING GAZETTES,' Lord North remarked, 'but there are more lies in this one than in all mine. Yesterday his Majesty was *pleased* to appoint the Marquis of Rockingham, Mr. Charles Fox, the Duke of Richmond, &c &c . . .'[1]

Among those whom the King said he was pleased to welcome into his service in March 1782 were Fox and Shelburne as Secretaries, Lord John Cavendish at the Exchequer, Richmond as Master-General of the Ordnance, Thurlow as Chancellor, Burke as Paymaster (his only State appointment), Keppel at the Admiralty, and Grafton, Conway and the lawyer Camden in other posts. It has been said that before taking office Rockingham made the King agree to American independence and Household reform: measures which would have represented an important constitutional innovation. Rockingham certainly intended to adopt these policies and so informed the King, but a recent biographer has found no evidence that he insisted on a prior agreement. It was inherently improbable that after all those years in the wilderness he would have imposed conditions likely to ensure his immediate return to it.[2]

Before Richmond could be confirmed in office certain formalities had to be observed. For some years he and the Duchess had not attended royal *levées* or drawing-rooms, and he explained through Rockingham that no discourtesy had been intended. He wrote a letter to be laid before the King,[3] stating that he 'has for several years been apprehensive that a letter he had the honour of writing his Majesty when the late Lord Granby died, although meant most respectfully, must somehow or other have given offence to the King.' This letter, which the King did not acknowledge, had been written in 1770.[4] It referred to an intimation Richmond had received from Henry Fox in 1763 that George had intended to offer him the command of the Royal Horse Guards (the Blues) on the death of Marshal Ligonier. (Ligonier died in 1770.) But he had 'learnt at the same time of another disposition's having taken place whereby the Blues did not then become vacant,' and with fulsome expressions of loyalty and appreciation of the King's generous intention, he begged to be permitted to relinquish the claim. Twelve years later he recalled the circumstances and declared that he had withdrawn 'from a desire not to stand in the way of any other arrangement his Majesty might wish, and not from any disinclination to serve his Majesty in any situation his Majesty might command; and further to explain to his Majesty that the apprehension of having given some offence is the only reason why he has not presumed to offer himself in his Majesty's presence.' Thus, rather ponderously, protocol was satisfied.

Rockingham's second ministry lasted only a few months, as he died in July, but it had no signs of durability. Several members belonged to Shelburne rather than to Rockingham; Shelburne and Fox were at odds over the peace negotiations and Thurlow regularly reported their divisions to the King. It granted legislative independence to Ireland and expunged from the Commons Journal the resolutions that, until 1774, had prevented Wilkes from taking his seat for Middlesex. Peace with America was a slow business because Fox was treating with the French and Shelburne with the Americans. Here a significant change took place in administrative practice, not imposed by statute but just following the course of events. Hitherto the two Secretaries had been in charge respectively of the northern and southern departments, an obsolete arrangement that led to conflict rather than efficiency. Now Fox became responsible for foreign policy, Shelburne for the home department and the colonies.

Britain's hand in the negotiations was strengthened by Admiral Rodney's victory at Les Saintes in April 1782,which recovered command of the sea and prevented a French attack on Jamaica. Rodney, born in 1719, joined the navy when he was thirteen and he had been in some spectacular actions. But he drank too much;* he was improvident, and from 1775–8 he was in Paris, on half-pay that was in arrears, to escape his creditors. The French Marshal Biron paid his debts and enabled him to return to sea, and after assisting in the relief of Gibraltar he was engaged in the West India station. Off Dominica he cut the French line, capturing seven enemy vessels as well as the French Admiral de Grasse on his flag-ship, and the Fighting Instructions were gone for ever. Just before the battle, Fox in one of his less felicitous interventions, had issued an order for Rodney's recall and his replacement by Admiral Pigot, one of the Navy's more unattractive disciplinarians who had been assaulted by his own men on the *Hermione*, set upon with cutlasses and thrown overboard.[5] The returning hero of Les Saintes was given a barony and a pension.

Rockingham's other cherished design was economical reform, and with a sort of unobtrusive gallantry Burke brought three measures always associated with his name although he actually moved only one of them, the Civil Establishment Act. They disfranchised revenue officers, debarred government contractors from election and removed some sinecures. Shelburne deplored the time wasted on

---

* It is said that the brandy decanter acquired its splayed bottom in order that Rodney's refreshment should not be spilled in rough weather.

'the nonsense of Mr. Burke's bill. It was both framed and carried through without the least regard for *facts*.' The disfranchisement of revenue officers reduced the electorate at Bosinney in Cornwall to one man; the disqualification of contractors affected only seventeen seats; the pruning of sinecures saved only about £72,000. Burke aimed, for instance, to save £12,600 paid to the Lords of Trade, among whom Gibbon received £750 a year for writing his history. Locke, Prior and Addison were among literary men who had preceded him in an institution which Burke described as 'an Academy of *Belles Lettres*.' In 1786 Pitt revived it with the future Lord Liverpool at its head. Another of Burke's economies was to abolish the separate office of Colonial Secretary which had recently been created to handle the increasing volume of business. Its amalgamation with the home department ceased in 1801 when colonial affairs were brought under the new Secretary of State for War. Shelburne, himself an Irishman, detected an overheated Irish imagination in Burke's insistence on producing measures irrelevant to the present needs of government. The real need was for administrative reform to complete the separation of the Crown's personal income from all the salaries and charges that fell under public expenditure. Meanwhile, the State's servants had to be rewarded somehow.

On Rockingham's death (1782) the Whigs indulged again in their habit of disintegration. The King gave the Treasury to Shelburne, whom he saw as a non-party man, but most politicians feared his acerbic tongue and regarded him as dangerously duplicitous in his custom of failing to carry out what he had promised – or, according to him, what he had not promised. Thomas Townshend advanced from Secretary at War to Home Secretary, and Keppel stayed for a short while at the Admiralty. Fox, Burke, Cavendish and most of the Rockingham group resigned, but Richmond did not, despite heavy pressure. He was happy at the Ordnance where he felt he had a job to do, and he had been encouraged to believe that Shelburne was willing to reform Parliament. A lengthy meeting was held at the house of Earl Fitzwilliam, Rockingham's nephew and heir, during which Burke spoke for two hours and Richmond was attacked so violently for wishing to remain in office that 'at length he burst into tears. . . . The Duke is among his old friends in a state of damnation,' Carlisle said in his account of the meeting.

Richmond stood his ground and defended his decision in the Lords.[6] He said he could be more vigilant within the ministry than outside it: he 'had no distrust of Lord Shelburne's intentions but as a Whig he held it to be his duty to keep a watchful eye upon ministers.' Peace with America, 'the most pressing object at present,' had not yet been settled, and also pressing was constitutional reform, wherein he believed that Shelburne would act with vigour. The people knew that 'the influence of the Crown in Parliament was to be diminished . . . It was a mockery and a libel to call the House of Commons a fair representation of the people.' Whether or not something similar to his own bill in 1780 would be adopted, the nation demanded 'some regulation that should remove the House of Commons from obloquy.'

Walpole thought he was right to stay in office. He told Sir Horace Mann,[7] far away in Florence but receptive to the *minutiae* of politics at home, that,

> ... the Duke is grossly abused by the new separatists, as he had been before by the late administration. When a man is traduced by both sides it is no bad symptom of his virtue. If a man sacrifices all parties to his monetary interest, he may be universally despised but he does not provoke. If his change proceeds from conscience, he must be aspersed that his integrity may not shine ... The trifling post of Master of the Ordnance could not be worthy of his ambition or selfishness, and by retaining it he shows that he did not aim at an higher.

Shelburne's splintered ministry did not last for long. His conditions for an American peace were statesmanlike in theory, but he was under attack from Fox and he was discovered to have employed a confidential agent to 'assist', or possibly undermine, the official discussions. Indifferent to high office, he resigned in February 1783, thanking his Maker that he 'remained independent of all parties.' He never held high office again, nor probably wanted to, but as Marquis of Lansdowne he was a detached and acidulous critic of ministerial errors wherever committed. This suited his peculiar temperament and unfulfilled talent. He could avoid making any future commitments and repudiate any that he was accused of having given in the past.

If Richmond had ever hoped or expected to succeed Rockingham as leader of the party, he had prejudiced himself by advocating reforms that struck at the magnates' electoral influence. His failure, and his growing separation from his old friends, were evident when the Duke of Portland became nominal head of the ministry which succeeded Shelburne. He was well connected, mild, muddled and unobjectionable,* and for the sake of peace he agreed to lead the Fox-North coalition that struggled on until the end of 1783. For years these two had been in opposition, on Fox's part crude as well as bitter: North, he said with his refined sense of what was politically appropriate, was 'a lump of deformity and disease,' fit only to be impeached and possibly hanged. Their association in government was the nadir of Whig opposition to George III.

Richmond once more had to decide what to do, and this time he resigned his office in the Cabinet (April 1783). Motions by Pitt – who had refused the Treasury on Shelburne's resignation – to enquire into the redistribution of seats and more frequent elections were defeated, but in September the American war was ended at the Treaty of Versailles. The Colonists gained all that they wanted,

* The Duke of Portland was put between the shafts again in 1807, but by that time he was a Tory, having carried his Whig following to Pitt's side in 1794 and been appointed Home Secretary.

and they knew that for political and economic reasons they needed Britain's continuing friendship. The French, who had overreached themselves and had serious financial difficulties, had to be accommodating. Although minor concessions were made, apart from the surrender of the small island of Tobago the gains which Britain had made from the Bourbon powers during the Seven Years War were substantially preserved. In a debate on the preliminaries of peace in February, Richmond wondered whether sufficient advantage had been taken of Britain's improved bargaining power, and said that he would be happier to support a ministry intending to reform abuses at home.

Fox's India Bill brought about the fall of the coalition. The provisional Indian Regulating Act had to be replaced because the relationship between the Governor-General and his council had broken down. Fox left the details to Burke, who produced a bureaucratic scheme for control of India by a board of parliamentary commissioners who would remain in office despite ministerial changes. Fox described this as 'a good stout blow at the influence of the Crown': public opinion, however, saw it as a scheme to put him in possession of the riches of the Orient.

The bill passed the Commons, and the King, seeing it as an infringement of his prerogative, resolved to defeat it in the Lords. Richmond had no intention of voting for the bill but he took occasion for an attack on the coalition.[8] Portland had denied rumours that the King had made plain his disapproval of the bill and of any peer intending to support it. In that case, 'if the noble Duke meant to take up all unconstitutional interference by the Crown, he would join him; but then the noble duke must leave his present connexions: he must once more act as a Whig.' The present administration had abandoned Whig principles from the start and had acted upon the corrupt system of their opponents. Foreseeing this, Richmond had refused to join them and he gave examples of improper influence: three men of no political views whom he had brought into office dismissed and replaced by three MPs; a former ambassador given a pension of £1000 a year to resign his seat and make way for Sir Thomas Erskine; a noble lord high in the naval administration appointed Ranger of St James's Park in order to buy his influence. Why, Portland asked, did not the noble Duke investigate these transactions and report them to the House as 'dangerous and alarming?'

Richmond was in the plot to destroy the bill. The crux was the bishops' vote and once an ecclesiastical swing was assured the bill was lost and the ministers were at once removed. Pitt became Prime Minister in 1783, 'a kingdom committed to a schoolboy's care,' and was given a solid majority at an election in 1784. Richmond was back at the Ordnance to which he had been appointed Master-General in 1782, and 'his firmness during the memorable contest of 1784 is said to have prevented Mr Pitt from resigning in despair. It was on that occasion George III was reported to have said, "There was no man by whom he has been so much offended, and no one to whom he was so much indebted, as the Duke of Richmond." '[9]

Richmond was now parted from his old friends, most of whom continued in opposition until Burke persuaded them of the democratic danger spreading from revolutionary France. Pitt's policies contained little for a reasonable man to oppose: sound finance and a sinking fund to reduce the debt; quiet administrative reforms that achieved what Burke's efforts had failed to do; attempts to reform the electoral system, abolish the slave trade, establish better trading arrangements with Ireland and France; sensible legislation for the government of India and Canada – though perhaps less sensible for the settlement of Australia: Richmond doubted whether shiploads of convicts to Botany Bay were altogether suitable for the purpose.

Nevertheless, Richmond's actions since Rockingham's death had puzzled his family. Sarah feared that his differences with his nephew Charles were developing into a lasting estrangement. The efforts of Fox and the Cavendishes to persuade him not to serve under Shelburne had 'talk'd his voice quite away and sunk his spirits and health,' she wrote to Lady Susan, 'but, thank God, my brother is allow'd to have acted a most upright, disinterested part; whether it turns out ill or well is another question.' When she asked him why he had not followed his friends into resignation, he answered: 'It may seem very vain to say I think I can be of service in the Ordnance, and no man ought to take a place if he is not of opinion he is fit for it. I own I think I am. I have begun great changes. I meant them for the good of my country and not for my own emolument.'

Sarah praised his determination not to serve in the coalition, but she could not understand his joining Pitt. 'It is vastly beyond my comprehension by what reasoning he can prove that he is of service to the country by being on the opposite side to the Whigs.' But despite the unpopularity it brought him, Richmond was right to believe that he could do valuable work at the Ordnance. Within the department these were the most fruitful years of his public career.

17

The Ordnance

Horace Walpole was wrong to describe the Ordnance as 'a trifling job': it was exacting enough to engage Wellington's experience and resources between 1818 and 1827. The Board was set up in Tudor times, with its headquarters at the Tower of London, to supply munitions to the forces with the growing use of gunpowder. It was reconstituted by Royal Warrant in 1683 and was responsible for ordnance supplies to the Army and the Navy; and as it controlled the engineering and artillery branches, the Master-General was *ex officio* colonel of the Royal Regiment of Artillery and the Corps of Engineers. He was responsible for fortifications and military defence, and until 1828 he had a seat in the Cabinet as its principal military adviser.[1]

The Duke of Richmond's employees at Goodwood would not have been surprised to learn that when in London he would arrive at his office by eight o'clock; and his quick grasp of detail showed itself in the copious records of the Ordnance's daily business. He turned it into the most efficient department in the armed services: more flexible than the Admiralty, which was barnacled with tradition and ancient rivalries, more experienced than the troubled body that was trying to become a War Office. During his twelve-year tenure as Master-General, the Ordnance records reveal more innovation and experimentation in almost all areas of its responsibility, but especially in artillery and small arms, than at any previous or subsequent period.

Just as at Goodwood he had forbidden his servants to accept tips and had raised their wages in compensation, so in 1783 he obtained a Royal Warrant to increase the salaries of surveyors and draughtsmen and to concentrate their energies on their public duties by forbidding them to receive any 'gratuity, fee or reward.' In 1786 another Warrant forbade any Established employee in 'constant pay of the Office at the Tower' to work for anyone else without express permission of the Master-General or Board.

By his personal interest and encouragement Richmond was a creator of the Ordnance Survey, and he sponsored and trained the Royal Horse Artillery in its infant days: lasting achievements for which history has given him only sparing credit, perhaps because their benefits could not be fully appreciated in his lifetime. His immediate concern was for national defence; and in the areas of land and sea artillery and small arms modernisation his great personal interest achieved the most prominent results. To a generation which associates defence with radar, aircraft carriers and fighter pilots there is something antiquated and unreal about forts built to protect docks and harbours, adding rifling to cannon barrels, giving the cavalry breech-loading carbines and strengthening and simplifying the muskets used by the Army and Navy, which Richmond regarded as essential for an island nation always exposed to attack. Britain would have to defend herself when much of her navy would be dispersed in Atlantic and Mediterranean bases. Unfortunately the Duke's enthusiasm for fortifications was to lead to a humiliating parliamentary defeat, brought upon himself because 'he courted persons too little,' and many of his technological innovations in equipment would be stillborn, or aborted, by the limitations of the manufacturing processes and the pressures put upon them by the outbreak of war with France in 1793.

In the Library at Goodwood is a manuscript volume, *Artillery Experiments*, compiled in 1780 when Viscount Townshend was Master of the Ordnance. By analysing the ranges and angles of possible gunfire it was a thoroughgoing effort to assess the vulnerability and realistic defence of Fort Landguard in Suffolk, under enemy attack. Richmond had the volume at home, presumably to study it when making his own plans for the defence of Plymouth and Portsmouth. He had discussed these with Shelburne, and in January 1783 reminded him[2] of the importance of defending the two ports 'not only against a *coup de main* but against a regular siege, that in case any future misfortune should befall our fleets and render such an attempt possible, the total annihilation of our navy may not follow by the destruction of the dockyards.' The cost would be not less than £400,000, but with a garrison of 9000 or 10,000 men at each, 'they should be impregnable against four times that force.' (Richmond claimed later that Shelburne had endorsed the scheme; Shelburne said that he had not.) It was agreed finally that £400,000 should be allocated to the fortifications, to be paid in eight annual instalments of £50,000.

Opposition came in 'A Short Essay' on the most suitable methods of defence by James Glenie, who had served in the Artillery and the Engineers during the American war. He argued that the coast of Great Britain was too extensive to be fortified against invasion and therefore it was wrong to convert our active strength into a stationary force: the prime need was for a navy powerful enough to protect our foreign possessions and commerce. Glenie estimated that the real cost of defending the two dockyards would be £2,336,271, and the work would take forty-seven years to complete and 50,000–60,000 men to defend. The scheme would in any case be counter-productive, since if the dockyards were captured they would be hard to recover.

An anonymous reply in 1785 was inspired by Richmond, if he did not actually write it. He agreed that Britain's coastline was too extensive to be protected against an enemy landing and for that reason he was concentrating on the principal dockyards 'which contain the vitals necessary for the existence of the navy.' He pointed to the 'extravagant schemes' begun during the last war at Dover, Sheerness, Gravesend and other ports, but still not finished. For permanent defence he proposed to supplement the regular soldiers with the militia, which should be sufficient for the purpose.

On expense, the 1783 estimate of between £400,000 and £500,000 might have to be increased in view of the complexity of the engineering works at the two sites. A thorough and detailed investigation would be made to arrive at a more accurate figure, but he rejected Glenie's claim that the final cost would be five times the original estimate. He noted that the French had fortified their main harbours such as Toulon and Brest. However superior an attacking force might be, the invaded country would soon recover once it had time to re-group its forces. Thus the great object during an invasion would be to preserve the dockyards by fortifications until the strength of the country could assemble. In the Commons in 1785 Colonel Isaac Barré, who had held a small post in Rockingham's ministry but was always a Shelburne man, questioned the payment of the second annual instalment of £50,000 and moved that the whole scheme of naval fortifications be re-examined before any more money was voted for it. The scheme itself was not the issue so much as Richmond's personal standing. Barré blamed him for the omission of Shelburne from Pitt's government, and the Whigs treated him as a renegade.

In his *Memoirs* Nicholas Wraxall wrote in the entry for March 1785: 'Among the most unpopular members of Administration might be accounted the Duke of Richmond. His enemies accused him of domestic parsimony, contrasted with profusion of the public money as Master-General of the Ordnance. His kitchen was said to be the coolest apartment in his house, both at Goodwood and in Privy Garden.'[3] The same petty abuse was employed against him in the *The Rolliad*, a series of anti-government satires that began in 1784:

Hail, thou for either talent justly known,
To spend the nation's cash or save thine own.

Richmond was now on the receiving end of the scurrilous lampooning, most of it of low quality, that may have mildly entertained him when Whig satirists directed it at Lord North. The triviality of this charge of parsimony, even if there may have been some truth in it, is its own condemnation. Undoubtedly, however, he was not popular at this time. At the Ordnance he was a hard taskmaster and on occasions he could be overbearing. He ran the Royal Regiment of Artillery as a private army – a royal fief – and complaints about his proceedings were normally met with a 'royal' rebuff. As Hertford had remarked twenty-five years earlier, his pride would bear humbling.

Psychologically, too, it was the wrong time for many of his schemes. The recent war had passed without the threatened invasion, the perils of the French Revolution were as yet unimagined, and English opinion had settled again into its civilian habit – mistrustful of any move to increase the numbers or the expense of armed forces.

On Barré's motion a board of enquiry was set up to examine the fortifications plan and to make a report. Some members sat on the committees for both the Plymouth and Portsmouth dockyards, including Admiral Barrington, Sir Guy Carleton (defender of Quebec), General Howe, and Lord Cornwallis; General Burgoyne, Admiral Hood (Rodney's second-in-command at Les Saintes) and Lord George Lennox were on the committee for Portsmouth. The Duke of Richmond presided over both. Their lengthy report, completed before the end of June, was mostly favourable, but for security reasons some of its conclusions were 'of a nature not proper to be disclosed' for public debate.

The report came before the Commons in February 1786, preceded by an estimate from a board of engineers that the cost would be £760,097. Burgoyne moved that as much of the report as could be made public without danger to security should be laid on the table since 'the House might otherwise unwarily be led to think that the report sanctioned the plan of fortifications more than it really did.' He was more or less accusing Richmond of having doctored it.

Pitt himself introduced Richmond's scheme in the form of a general resolution that it provided effectively for the fortification of Plymouth and Portsmouth on the most economical principles and required the smallest number of troops. It would enable the Navy to defend the Kingdom and the nation's overseas possessions and also to prosecute offensive operations should the need arise. He paid compliments to the noble Duke whose military experience and long study of naval defences had devised the scheme. He would have distinguished himself in the war against America if he had not been politically opposed to it.

It must have seemed like old times to Richmond – except that he was now on the other side of the fence – when the opposition opened a concerted attack. Certain provisos in the report gave them ammunition. Captain John Macbride, an unusually truculent seaman, objected that the defences proposed for Portsmouth were 'founded upon a calculation of a large imaginary force' descending upon it, much larger than an enemy would be likely to muster; Burgoyne and Earl Percy, a land officer, said that their agreement was conditional upon the expense not being greater than the State could afford and the number of troops allotted to Portsmouth being consistent with the general defence of the kingdom; Burgoyne, Percy and three others explained that their general assent depended upon the supposition that the whole British fleet would be absent at the same time, thus

76 Cruikshank cartoon (1793) showing the Duke of Richmond, Master-General of Ordnance, vomiting a cascade of munitions. One side of the banner reads, 'Thou hast done those things . . .' – a reference to the Duke's right to tax coal by sea from Newcastle to London. On the other side are the words, 'And has left undone those things . . .' – implying that he had failed to supply in time heavy artillery for the defence of Dunkirk.

allowing the enemy uninterrupted action. 'How far it is probable that the whole British fleet may be sent on any service requiring so long an absence, at a time when the enemy is prepared to invade this country . . . we must humbly leave to your Majesty's* superior wisdom.'

John Pollexfen Bastard, a militia colonel from Devon, at once moved that fortifications on so extensive a plan were inexpedient.** His argument was partly constitutional, that it was dangerous to allow groups of soldiers to be stationed in separate buildings. Militiamen billeted in private houses retained 'their character of citizens,' which they would lose if they became an isolated body confined in fortresses. Courtenay, another Devonshire man, was alarmed about the threat to property: no man's house or domain would be safe from seizure to provide space for the new constructs. On more dignified grounds he referred to the French philosopher Montesquieu who in his commendation of the English way of life had applauded the people's refusal to build fortifications 'as by such means despotism may be established.' Sheridan agreed with this: troops confined to forts were 'more likely to lend themselves to the active purposes of tyranny.'

Members criticised Richmond personally, alleging that he had made himself president of a board set up for an objective enquiry into matters to which he was party; that he had 'packed' the board by excluding reputable officers expected to be hostile and including others who were indebted to government patronage, or hoped to be; that he had befuddled the board with irrelevant and confusing questions; and that he had tampered with the report before submitting it to the King.

Some of the criticisms were of the plan itself. Barré objected to 'a paltry, narrow, circumscribed plan' of fortifying two dockyards when Chatham, Dover, Sheerness, Harwich, and Yarmouth were equally in need. Courtenay said that a gun battery at Southsea was useless and 'the enemy could penetrate between his two projected forts, and his boasted works would then fall at once.' (Fort Cumberland at Southsea may have been designed by Richmond himself.) Burgoyne said that whereas in the American war not more than 8000 men had been employed at the two dockyards, the number now proposed was 22,000.

The final demolition came from Sheridan in a speech that was 'the subject of much admiration.' He dismissed the scheme on two grounds: that it was in itself 'dangerous and inimical to the constitution' and that by its nature and circumstances the board's report 'did not warrant or authorise the system.' The report demonstrated Richmond's engineering skills in devising 'a fortress of sophistry' and in that sense members would waste time by throwing desultory observations at it. Misgivings from naval officers had been excluded from the published

---

* Formally the board had been commissioned by the King.

** The world may have looked different to Mr Bastard when in 1799 he had to save the Plymouth dockyard from destruction by the men who worked there.

findings, although there were indications that they disapproved. Even the concurrence of the land officers was 'hypothetical and conditional.' The data on which the board had to reach their conclusions 'were founded on a supposition of events so desperate and improbable' that not only the two dockyards but the whole country would be in danger of conquest.

At seven o'clock in the morning the House divided on Pitt's resolution 169–169, and Mr Speaker Cornwall, a barrister, gave his casting vote against it. He would have liked to state his reasons but much time had already been spent.

Some of the opposition's arguments were trivial and specious, but Richmond in his day had put forth such things himself and was sufficiently versed in parliamentary tactics to recognise the irresponsible. The merits or demerits of the scheme cannot be evaluated because 'public safety' suppressed the essential details, but as a peacetime measure it would have cost a lot of money and employed a lot of men. What is significant is that although the resolution was moved by the Prime Minister himself, the independents and the placemen were insufficiently convinced to give it the expected support. Perhaps the opposition had persuaded them that there had been bungling or manipulation in Richmond's handling of the board.

Hastiness and patriotic duty drove him on. The English have periodically had nervous fits about their coastal defences ever since Julius Caesar first penetrated them; the Martello towers and Palmerston's 'follies' still lay in the future. In 1805 Richmond's critics would have slept more comfortably in their beds when Napoleon's flat-bottomed barges were gathering at Boulogne if the Channel ports had been more strongly defended, but he failed in 1786 to persuade the Commons that this was necessary. Probably he was so confident in the correctness of his ideas that he failed to foresee the opposition they would encounter and to organise the government's natural supporters to meet it. On the other hand, if in 1786 the casting vote had gone the other way and he had squeezed home, the annual appropriation would have been challenged in some future year and he would have had to fight his battle again.[4]

Meanwhile worse was to follow. The fortifications plan had to be either withdrawn or amended for Parliament's further consideration. Richmond appears to have assumed that this time there would be no difficulty. He had only to change the minds of a few government men who had voted against it or drifted home during a long night. So in May he authorised the presentation of a virtually identical scheme with only a few trivial amendments that failed to answer the criticisms that had been made. The opposition said that it was an insult to the House to come forward with a measure that had already been rejected, and it was thrown out without a division.

Richmond salvaged something of his scheme by minor improvements at Portsmouth and Plymouth which fell within the regular Ordnance budget but he abandoned his more elaborate ambitions; and Pitt was not the man to enter the lists again on behalf of an ailing lieutenant who did not have the confidence of the Commons.

Perhaps unwisely, Richmond raised the question in the following year when the Lords were debating a commercial treaty with France.[5] He accused Lansdowne (Shelburne) of having accepted the fortifications plan when he was First Lord and sanctioned the expenditure. Lansdowne denied this, saying that it had not been 'a serious consultation' and he would not have approved the proposals without taking expert advice. The Cabinet minutes contained no record of any formal discussion. Not the first victim of Lansdowne's selective memory, Richmond angrily replied that if written evidence was required of all discussion between colleagues, 'there was an end of confidence between man and man.' He added that it had been said that 'fortifications were his hobby-horse . . . His duty would always be his hobby-horse.' The altercation nearly led to a duel, in which event, according to an observer with Whiggish instincts, 'one should be shot and the other hanged.' A spurious argument in the opposition's attack on the fortifications was that the soldiers would be used to impose political tyranny, and Richmond was most unjustly branded as a militarist. In 1792, for instance, Lauderdale evoked memories of James II's host on Hounslow Heath by suggesting that Richmond had been appointed to command a camp at Bagshot in order to 'overcome the people of the metropolis . . . He was the most fit person for that command.'[6]

A newspaper article in 1788[7] had charged him also with hypocrisy and the cultivation of aristocratic power. 'It is a fact that the Duke of Richmond has never yet received a shilling of his salary as Master-General of the Ordnance – but do the public derive the least benefit by this affectation of public spirit in his Grace? Do not the ordinary estimates of the Ordnance contain a yearly demand for his salary? – and as it lies unappropriated, may he not hereafter claim it in a moment of the same caprice that at present prompts him to refute it! – and if not, will not his heirs, when he is gone, put in their claim for it, and receive it accordingly?'

The writer described this 'mock virtue' as an insult to all office-holders not enriched, as Richmond was, by the hereditary coal duty which Charles II had granted to the first Duke. By this he was indirectly indebted to every impoverished person who had to contribute to it:

> It has frequently been a doctrine with his Grace that no person should have an office in the state who was not enabled by an independent fortune to remit the emoluments of office! – but this system, adhered to, would tend to the total exclusion of abilities . . . and make for that aristocratic and petty monarchial power which will ever be the first anxiety of Englishmen to guard against. If his Grace would deserve the thanks of his country, he would apply his salary to some good public purpose: – and no longer make a parade of his forbearance, for which he has at present so little credit.

Lord Sandwich and his kind no doubt found some wry amusement in such innuendos against their old tormentor, but this was (and still is) the currency of politics. Unluckily for his reputation, Richmond's real achievements did not come within the public eye. The capable administration of a busy and important department is not noticed when it goes smoothly, and the importance of his encouragement of land surveying and the horse artillery was not fully realised in his lifetime.

He was unusual, if not unique, among contemporary landowners in employing trained surveyors in the management of his estates.[8] Thomas Yeakell, who had served under him in the army, became a salaried surveyor at Goodwood in 1758, and Richmond sent him to a professor for further mathematical instruction. James Sampson, employed in 1763, was unfortunate: the Goodwood wages book records him as 'run away' in 1766 and hanged in 1768,[9] apparently for arson. His successor was William Gardner, a Sussex man who, like Yeakell, also did some private work. For the Duke they prepared a six-inch map, embracing 72 square miles, of his estates and manors, and in their private practice they undertook a two-inch map of the county of Sussex. Only the southern part had been completed when Richmond brought them into the civil establishment of the Ordnance, Yeakell in 1782, Gardner two years later; and both remained there for the rest of their lives. Thus the conception of an Ordnance Survey did not orginate only with professionals within the department, although Richmond depended on their expertise. It coincided with his interest in the mapping of his own estates and environs, and his concern for the best use of land for defensive purposes was complementary to this. Gardner's first commission at the Ordnance was a six-inch map of the Plymouth area which was available for the board of enquiry. Despite the defeat of the fortifications plan Gardner continued to be employed on military surveys, together with two other Sussex men, Yeakell's son and Thomas Gream.

The director of their work was William Roy (1726–90), who was made a Fellow of the Royal Society in 1761 and a major-general in 1781. He served in the Corps of Engineers under the Duke of Cumberland. After executing a map of Scotland on a scale of 1000 yards to the inch he proposed to incorporate this in a trigonometrical survey of the whole of Britain at one inch to the mile. Although this was rejected as too expensive, in 1763 he was appointed Inspector-General of coasts, under the Board of Ordnance, to prepare plans for their defence. When Richmond became Master-General, Roy had in mind a national survey for general as well as military purposes.

Richmond had a cartographic mind and some knowledge of geodetic techniques and he was excited by Roy's ambitious design, which supported his own ideas on national policy. He made men and equipment available from the Ordnance and in Roy's words assisted the project 'in the most liberal manner

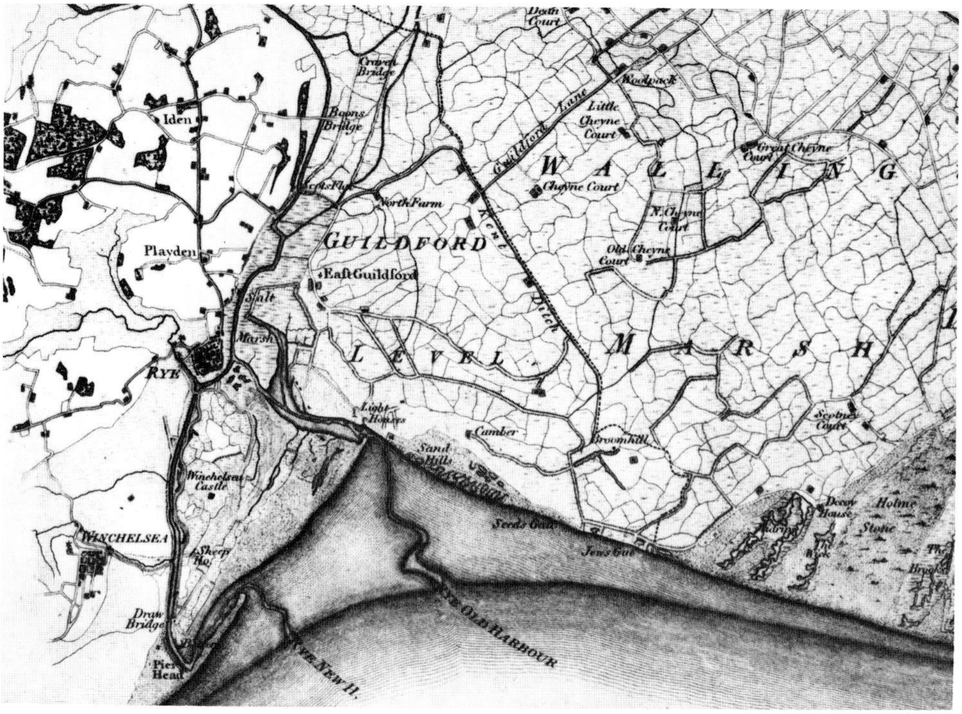

possible.' On Roy's death in 1790 Richmond did not abandon it, as might have happened under less committed leadership, but encouraged the project by his own initiative. He appointed two artillery officers to continue the trigonometrical survey in consultation with Isaac Dalby, a mathematician who had researched a method of connecting the meridians of Greenwich and Paris, and he obtained, as 'a proper instrument for this purpose,' a three-foot theodolite constructed by Jesse Ramsden.

The Ordnance Survey was officially launched in 1791, and in the next five years surveying parties were busy in Surrey, Sussex, Hampshire, the Isle of Wight and Kent. (In the Sussex survey Gardner was on his own ground with a station close to the Trundle at Goodwood.) Gardner also completed the earlier map of Sussex that he had begun with Yeakell, and this was published in 1795 with a dedication to the Duke. In his work on the national survey Gardner checked data for Essex and parts of Suffolk and Hertfordshire, and his one-inch map of Kent, the first publication of the Ordnance Survey, appeared in 1801 a few months after his death.

Richmond's part in this was more than nominal, especially in instituting the collaboration between the military surveyors, of which Roy was one, and draughtsmen of the civil branch like Yeakell and Gardner. In 1800 (and until extinguished as a post-war economy in 1817) the civilians were constituted as the

77 (LEFT) Part of the first Ordnance Survey map of Kent, published in 1801: 'An entirely new and accurate survey . . . done by the Surveying draftsmen of His Majesty's Honourable Board of Ordnance . . .' It shows the fringes of Romney Marsh to the right, and Rye and Winchelsea in the lower left-hand corner.

78 (BELOW) Jesse Ramsden's second great theodolite, made in 1791. This improved version of the original instrument was used on the early trigonometrical surveys carried out by the Ordnance.

Corps of Royal Military Surveyors and Draughtsmen. 'The continuity of cartographic tradition in England is exemplified no less by these appointments of men who had learnt their trade in estate and county surveying than by the affinity of their topographical workmanship in private practice and in public service. By putting in harness together the civilian surveyor and the military engineer the Duke created the national survey of Great Britain, fitly known as the Ordnance Survey.'[10]

For a long time in warfare wheeled guns were brought into action by foot soldiers, and so at the pace of the slowest man. The origin of horse-drawn guns is disputed. Although Gustavus Adolphus has his supporters, Frederick the Great is usually regarded as the innovator. Except for the 'light gallopers,' mere three-pounders, it was not until the middle of the eighteenth century that the wheeled gun become a decisive force on the battlefield. Mobile batteries required a new technique in warfare, and although they were still limited in number, the French revolutionary armies used them devastatingly. The British Army was the last major European force to adopt them.

Their deployment would be the responsibility of the Ordnance Board, and in 1788 Richmond received proposals for a mounted branch of the Royal Artillery. Being himself more interested in static defence, he referred them to a committee. Gestation took longer than usual and it was not until February 1793, the month when the French declared war on Britain, that two troops of horse artillery were created by Royal Warrant. The Duke was not a gunner but he brought 'A' troop to Goodwood under his personal supervision: the horses side by side with hunters in the stables designed by Sir William Chambers, the guns in the park in front of the house. The new unit, coming under the direct command of the Master-General and owing nothing to military tradition, was free of the confining snobbery of the line regiments. Promotion went to ability and flair, not to birth or purchase, and morale among the men training on the Sussex Downs was high. Two more troops were formed before the end of 1793. Part of the new equipment for the Royal Horse Artillery included a six-pounder gun incorporating Richmond's specifications for a standard (interchangeable) gun carriage wheel and an iron axle and a double-barrelled pistol with one rifled barrel and a detachable shoulder stock which would convert the piece into a carbine for longer-range, accurate shooting.

In 1794, after the Duke of York's perennial failure in the Netherlands, Sir Harry Calvert remarked: 'We want artillerymen, drivers, and smiths, a commanding engineer of rank and experience. We want at least two of the four brigades with which his Grace of Richmond is amusing himself in England.' Calvert then was York's aide-de-camp, and York did not like Richmond. This may explain

80 Manoeuvres at the Royal Artillery Barracks, Woolwich, of the 2nd and 4th Batteries of the Royal Artillery in the presence of King George III, 9 July 1788. Watercolour by G. Sandman.

79 (ABOVE) Royal Artillery uniforms, *c.* 1792: (LEFT) Officer, (CENTRE) Gunner. (Watercolours by E. Dayes). (RIGHT) 'Present Arms, First Motion': a Royal Artillery Gunner, 1797. (Coloured etching by Dadley after E. Scott.)

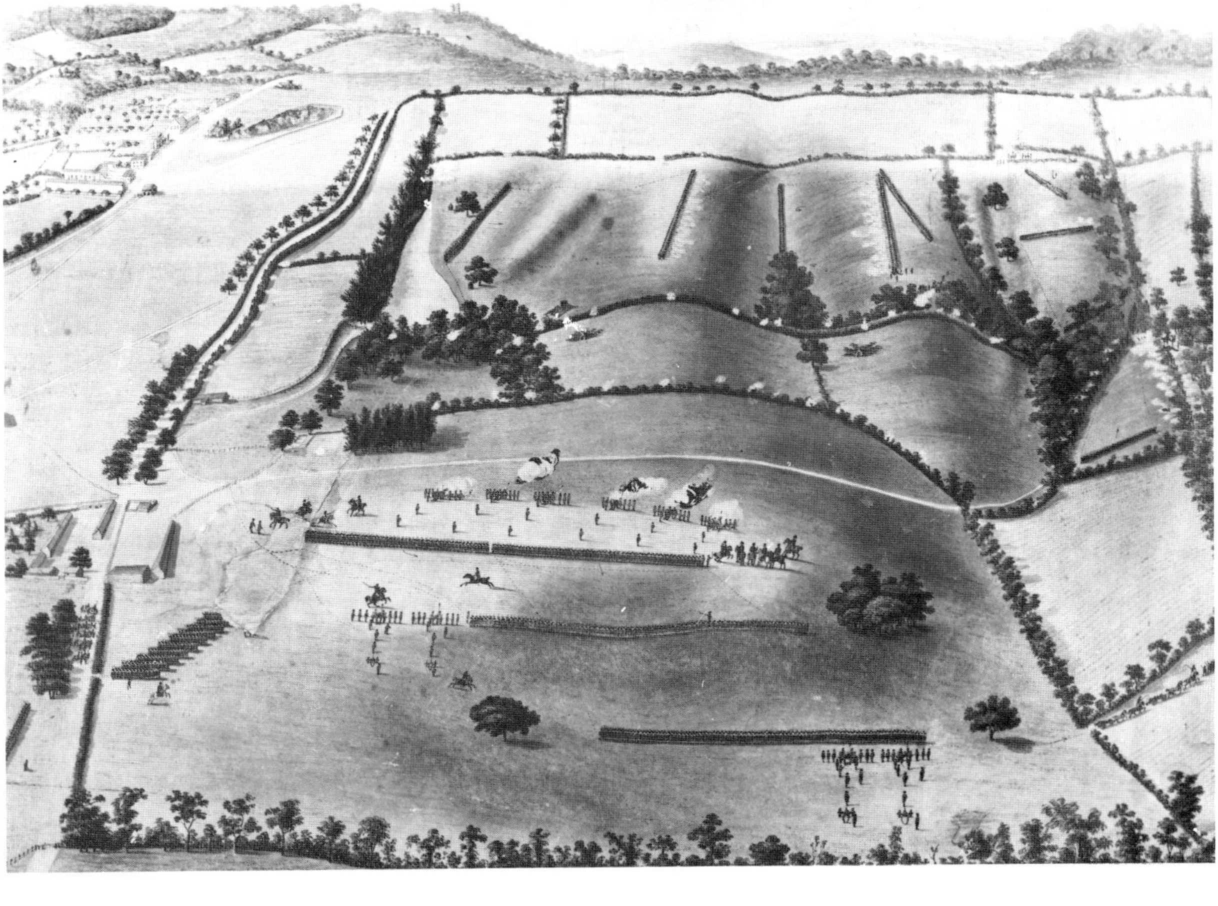

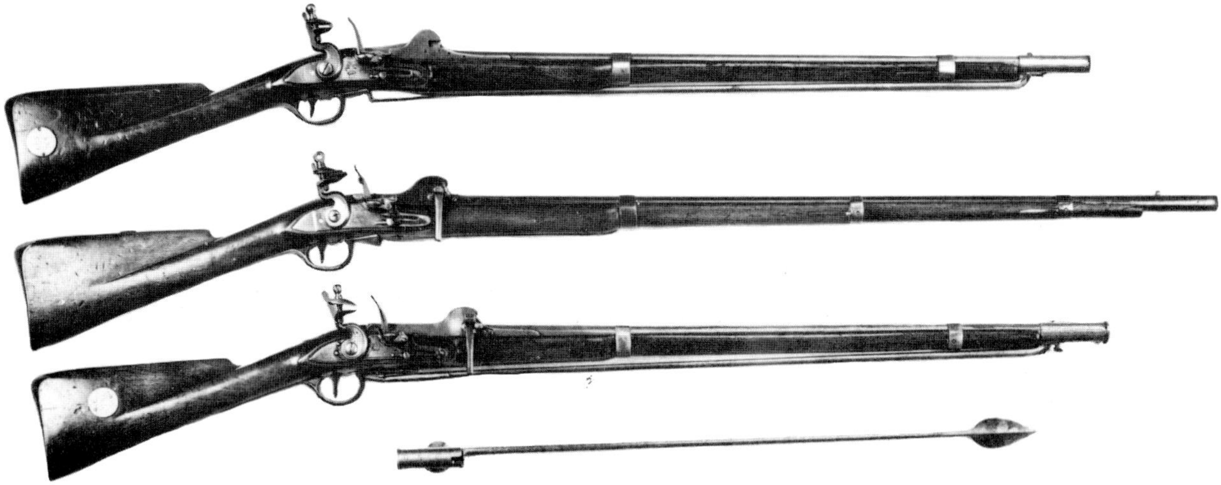

81 One of the third Duke's earliest projects in small arms experimentation: three breech loading cavalry carbines on the Crespi system, made by Durs Egg (with screwless locks by Jonathan Hennem). The breech mechanism consists of a chambered block hinged at the rear to swing upwards, exposing the mouth for loading; the block is held closed by a transverse lever across the front, which itself is hinged to lie along the right side of the arm just ahead of the lock. The spear-bayonets were another experimental feature, although not new to this particular arm. These were issued to the 7th, 10th, 11th, 15th and 16th Light Dragoons in 1786 for extended troop trials, and reports filed in 1788 were generally favourable, especially to the rifled version, for which accurate shooting to 500 yards was claimed. The expense involved, and their susceptibility to damage in service, as well as the traditional conservatism of the military, were responsible for their ultimate rejection.

82 The Duke of Richmond's Musket. The Rammer to the Muzzle pattern resembled the standard design of musket, and formed the bulk of the production. A much simplified design of stock and brass furniture, a heavy steel, rammer, and in particular the Nock modification of Hennem's screwless lock, were the musket's main characteristics. Its 42-inch barrel was browned, probably the earliest use of this finish on a British military arm intended for general issue. The Rammer to the Butt pattern (not shown) was probably derived from a contemporary French idea adopted for one of their carbines. It allowed a lighter fore-end to the stock with less likelihood of damage and fewer rammer pipes, but it was more complicated to manufacture, and clumsier to handle. The Nock lock is fitted with a flash-guard, then current in the Austrian and Prussian armies, and the stud ahead of the trigger guard served to fasten a leather lock-cover for protection against rain. Both types of musket were fitted with a new type of socket bayonet.

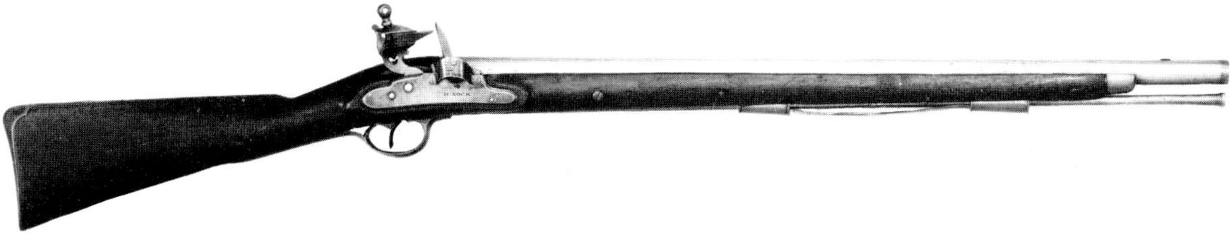

83 The Harcourt Light Dragoon Carbine of 1793. Based largely on the musket design shown above, and using Nock's lock with a flash-guard, the Harcourt (named after the Colonel of the Queen's Light Dragoons) was the first carbine to be issued with a musket (.75 inch) bore rather than the carbine (.65 inch) bore. The heavy steel rammer was held in position by a spring between the two pipes, and the stock was slit (the rammer channel being entirely open) to prevent accumulated dirt jamming the rod. This 28-inch carbine barrel formed the basis for the more widely issued Pattern 1796 carbine, which used the conventional lock and had a 26-inch barrel. The socket bayonet was similar to that of the musket, with a locking ring. This 'musquet-bore carbine' was soon relegated for use by the Heavy Dragoons as being less manageable, although more formidable, than the Elliot Carbine of the Light Dragoons.

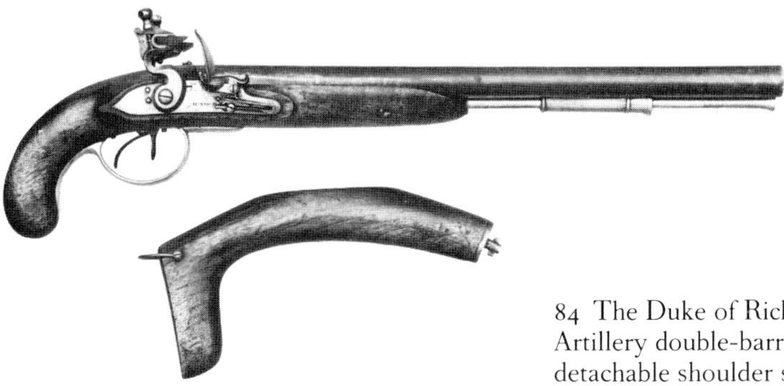

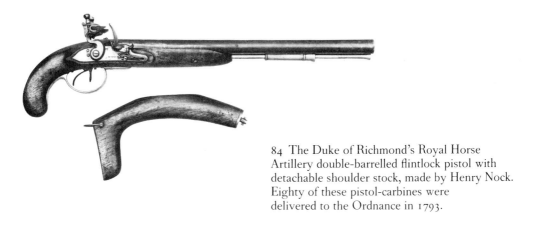

84 The Duke of Richmond's Royal Horse Artillery double-barrelled flintlock pistol with detachable shoulder stock, made by Henry Nock. Eighty of these pistol-carbines were delivered to the Ordnance in 1793.

his slightly patronising tone, but it may also suggest that Richmond helped to promote the Horse Artillery's particular spirit. He did not live to see their magnificent service in the Peninsula, commemorated in his nephew William Napier's *History of the Peninsular War.*

As Richmond left the Ordnance early in 1795 he cannot be said to have greatly influenced the new unit, but his work in general was much in evidence in the Army and the Navy. His enthusiasm for improving the efficiency of military equipment was tempered and abetted by his own military experience and observation, and by travels on the Continent. His innovations were broad in scope, covering both the Land and Sea Services, but his enterprise in the field of artillery was particularly notable.

New metals for casting barrels; the rifling of bores and redesigning of breech and chamber shapes, cannon sights and sight regulating instruments; new ways of manufacturing higher quality and more reliable ammunition for all types of field and naval artillery; new designs of gun carriages and the redesigning of old ones; a sponge and rammer hafted with stiffened rope to make cleaning and reloading cannon easier, quicker and safer for naval gun crews in action; at least two new types of cannon igniting-locks and their more general distribution in the Navy; wide experimentation with strength and granulation of gunpowder following on the Board's purchase of the Waltham Abbey Powder Mills in 1787 – all these and more Richmond either initiated, encouraged, or both, during his Master-Generalship.

The Duke's contributions in the area of small arms was equally diverse, both as regards the weapons and their appendages. They included a new, stronger infantry bayonet scabbard, a new infantry cartridge box magazine with tin containers replacing drilled wooden blocks, and a newly designed pike for infantry sergeants to replace the larger and less useful halbert. Even the issue of the common soldier's gun-cleaning tools was regularised: once every five years each man would receive a worm, turnscrew, pricker and brush, and an annual allowance for emery, brick dust and oil. In 1790 Richmond shifted the source of the Board's gunflint supply from Kent to the town of Brandon in Suffolk, which continues to produce gunflints to this day. The change marked a great improvement in the reliability and useful life of the soldier's gunflint.

The earliest of the small arms innovations overseen by Richmond was the 'screwless lock' designed by Jonathan Hennem, and brought to the Board's attention by the Duke's predecessor, Lord Townshend. The concept, as modified by the Duke's 'favourite' gunmaker Henry Nock, figured in all Richmond's subsequent small arms designs except the Royal Horse Artillery pistol-carbine, and consisted of substituting plain pins or studs rivetted to the lockplate in place of conventional threaded screws. A special tool was required to strip locks built in this manner. Hennem supplied more than 400 of the locks, 308 of which were

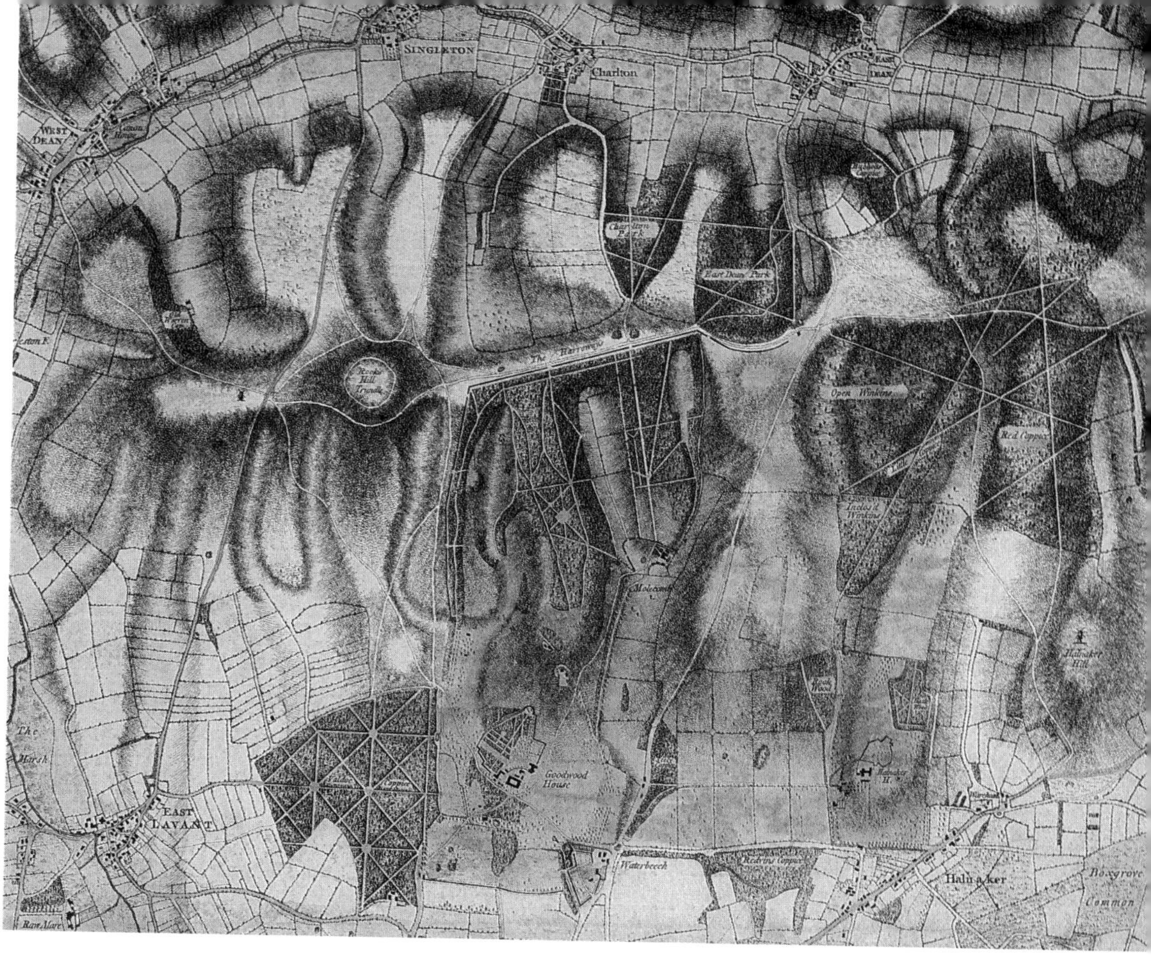

85 (ABOVE) Part of the 1778 map of Sussex by Yeakell and Gardner showing the Goodwood estate, including the villages of Charlton and Singleton. Clearly marked are the Valdoe Coppice; the criss-cross pattern of the woodland drives; the avenues of trees typical of eighteenth-century parkland; and St Roche's Hill (now called The Trundle), site of a pre-Roman hill-fort. On the far right is the Halnaker windmill. The hachuring indicating hills was replaced by contour lines on later maps.

86 (RIGHT) Isometric view of improvements to Fort Monckton at Gosport. The alterations proposed in 1778 were formally approved by the Duke of Richmond on 3 March 1783.

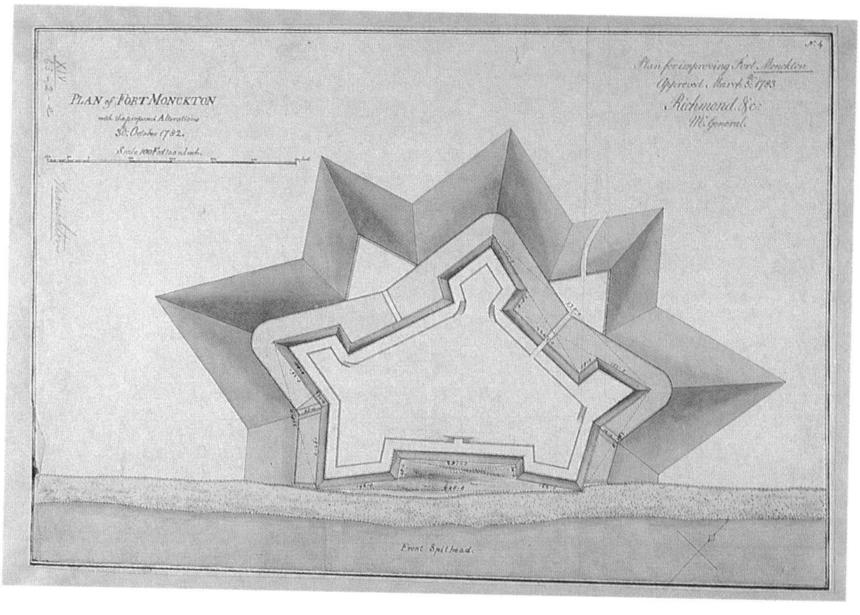

87 Henriette Le Clerc. She came to live at Goodwood at the age of five or six, in 1778. This painting was started by Romney in 1796 and completed after his death in 1801, by Shee.

88 The third Duke as Master-General of Ordnance, by Romney. He is wearing the uniform of Major-General, with the Star of the Garter.

fitted to conventional Short Land muskets and sent with the 20th Foot for trials in 1784. A second use of the Hennem lock was made on thirty breechloading carbines with spear bayonets made by London gunmaker Durs Egg. The breech mechanism was a copy of that designed by Giuseppi Crespi and in issue to the Austrian cavalry between 1770 and 1779. Hennem/Crespi carbines were issued to five regiments of Light Dragoons for trials in 1786.

Richmond was also responsible for the introduction of the steel ramrod on Sea Service muskets, and for the first of a new series of musket-calibre carbines for the heavy dragoons in 1793 – the so-called Harcourt carbine named after the colonel of the first regiment to receive them, which used Nock's modification of the Hennem screwless lock.

It was with the series of infantry muskets which soon came to bear his name that Richmond and the chief manufacturer, Henry Nock, achieved greatest renown in the field of military small arms. Beginning with a small number of experimental muskets (including a breechloading example) in 1786, and proceeding through an initial production order to both Nock and Hennem in June 1790 for several hundred, the project culminated in a contract with Nock for 10,000 'New Pattern' muskets in December 1792. The timing proved catastrophic, and no more than 4000 were completed when the last deliveries were made shortly after the Duke departed office. The arms were basically of two distinct types, one with the ramrod in the conventional position beneath the barrel (which formed the major part of the production) and another with the rod running through the butt to the buttplate, allowing a reduction in the weight of brass furniture used, and a slimmer forepart to the stock. Both variations included a much simplified design of brass furniture and stock outline, and used Nock's screwless lock. Had not the oubreak of war – demanding mass production of arms by the entire workforce of tradition-trained gunmakers – put a sudden end to the fulfilment of the contract, the British army would have been equipped with by far the most modern musket then known. As it was, the Nock locks so favoured by Richmond, proved to be his longest-lasting achievement in the field of small arms, remaining in use on Dragoon carbines into the 1830s, and highly praised by those who used them.

18

'Mr Jones's Little Girl'

BETWEEN 1775 AND 1790 (perhaps a little later) the Duke improved and enlarged his estate. He bought land at East Lavant and outlying property at Itchenor, Barnham, Wittering and Birdham, and he also built kennels for his hounds and put in hand his plans for reconstructing the house itself.

His chief architect was James Wyatt, who in 1772 had converted the Oxford Street Pantheon into an extravagant hall of entertainment, 'a Winter Ranelagh,' with arcades, galleries and refreshment rooms. London Society welcomed its fêtes and masquerades, and although time-worn and much altered in structure and purpose, the building survived until 1937. It is accepted that in 1787 Wyatt built kennels at Goodwood for what Louisa Conolly called her brother's 'cross and pompous dogs'. Costing £6000, this was in its way as strange a building as the Pantheon and in scale as disproportionate to the main house as were Chambers's stables. The rooms 'were very spacious, being about 36 feet by 16 feet, and lofty in proportion, and on one side they were partly lined with large iron plates, which were heated at the back by huge fires when required.'[1] In fact the centrally-heated hounds of the Charlton Hunt were more comfortable than the Duke's guests. The frontage was longer than that of the house as it was then, and there were stores and feeding-rooms. Today the kennels accommodate a golf club.

It is not certain when Wyatt made his other designs for Goodwood, particularly the uncompleted scheme for the house, which may have been as much Richmond's own idea as Wyatt's. This intended the construction of an octagon around a central courtyard, and a wooden model (which has not survived) was prepared at the considerable cost of five hundred guineas.[2] Only three sides of the octagon were built, with domed three-storey towers where the wings meet, and in the central wing a portico with Doric and Ionic columns. At the Duke's insistence only local materials were used in the construction, and the rough flints, mellowing with age, are now partly covered with magnolia and climbing plants.

Because the plan for the house was unfinished when Richmond died in 1806, it has been supposed that Wyatt worked at Goodwood in the years immediately preceding. This has been questioned.[3] The time to improve the house was during the building of the kennels, and there is sufficient evidence of Richmond's financial difficulties to suggest that already the money was running out. Wyatt designed several lodges on the estate, an orangery and a house at Itchenor near by. He also was responsible for interior decoration in the Tapestry Drawing-Room and the Library. It is probable that all this work was done in the years when Richmond was at the Ordnance and before Wyatt entered his 'Gothic' phase. Other improvements on the estate may have originated with Richmond himself. Years previously, Chambers had submitted an account for five guineas for 'attendance on his Grace to teach him architecture,' and in about 1775 Richmond had planned a new prison and gaoler's house at Petworth which, in the words of a local newspaper, 'is calculated to confer lasting benefits on our criminal population.'[4]

This period saw also an addition to the Goodwood household. Returning from a visit to Emily in France in 1778, Louisa escorted a small girl, aged about five or six, who 'spued all the way' on the boat from Dieppe. She told Emily of the child's good fortune, because instead of sending her to boarding-school in Chichester the Richmonds allowed her to stay at Goodwood in the charge of Mr Jones, 'and they have undertaken the care of it 'til its father comes to England. I say "they" because it is impossible for a child or animal to live in the house with my brother without his tutoring it or teaching it.'

Mr Jones presumably was a tutor (reported to be ready to slit any man's throat

89 Nineteenth-century engraving of the kennels at Goodwood, designed by Wyatt in 1787.

90 Watercolour of Henriette Le Clerc, by John Downman.

who assailed his protégée's virtue), and the child was Henriette Ann Le Clerc, generally accepted, although there has never been documentary proof of it, as Richmond's daughter by Madame de Cambis. Henriette has Stuart and Bourbon echoes and Le Clerc is a safe, neutral name in any language into which it may be translated.

Henriette at once became a playmate of Louisa Bunbury, Sarah's child by Lord William Gordon, and Sarah found her 'one of the most enchanting little creatures I ever saw . . . a delightful companion for my Louisa, for she teaches her French and submission and humility – three very good lessons to learn.' Two years later Sarah is telling Emily of the little girl's handling of the Duke. 'Although he does not spoil her (for he makes her obey instantly), yet she gets so about him that, do you know, she has liberty of staying in his room while he is busy, she always will sit next him, be helped by him, and in short she makes a complete nurse of him.'

'The Duchess is as fond of her as he is,' Sarah added. In a letter to her husband in 1793 the Duchess referred to Henriette as 'our child.' This is not to be taken in the physical sense: she could not have borne a child of her own without the sisters writing about it at folio length. It shows her identification with the child that had been brought into her home and her willingness to care for her as though she were her own. In the few surviving letters between 1793 and 1795 the Duchess writes of Henriette in a semi-humorous, semi-caring way that probably expressed her attitude to life in general: in informal company Henriette sang in 'a merry pleasant manner, and it is good for her to sing without accompaniment when with friends who will tell her when she is out of tune.' She wants to stay up too late, but 'I believe she loves and respects me, both in my own account and seeing the affection you have for me [which] certainly raises my consequence in her eyes.'

Henriette does have faults, for which the Duchess is inclined to blame her husband. 'She has *some* ways that do *at times* put me out of humour' because 'you let her run ahead sometimes, till you find the necessity for a check'; and then the sharpness of his temper makes the rebuke too severe. Henriette needs 'a person of sense, temper and steadiness to direct her,' and the Duke is not always steady enough. 'Am not I an impertinent wife?' she guilelessly adds. But a few days later when Richmond is depressed and complaining of 'blue devils', 'there's no better remedy for those than Henriette, who will be happy to attend you.'

From being 'Mr Jones's little girl' Henriette made her first formal appearance in the Goodwood records in the steward's accounts for the Michaelmas quarter of 1785, when £1.2*s*.7*d*. was paid out for 'mercery'.[5] These payments increased as she grew older, rising to £23.6*s*.7*d*. at Christmas the following year for clothes and singing and dancing lessons. They rose to £50 in one quarter when she had shoes, gloves, mercery, muffs, mantuas, as well as expenses for music and coach travel, but the average was lower than this. Richmond's own expenditure on clothing varied from £15 to £87, and averaged about £35.

He clearly was generous to this 'adopted' child, but it may be appropriate to mention here an occasion when, in a different context, he failed in his role of *paterfamilias*. Emily wished her son Robert to go into the Church and Richmond disapproved. Louisa wrote on Emily's behalf:[6] 'I never find that absence abates my affection for those I love,' and she did not know what to wish him 'in the public troubles (for such one must call the employment of a Minister at this time),' but he had offended Emily. 'She cannot be angry with you because she loves you so much, but you both vex'd and distress'd her exceedingly.' With four sons in the armed services 'she was very much set on having no more *red* and *blue* coats in the family. I can tell you a thousand little distresses that I am sure you will be sorry to have given her.'

19

Drama and Devastation

IT WAS A TRADITION OF THE ENGLISH COURT and nobility to stage plays and musical entertainments for their guests. 'Theatricals' had always flourished at Holland House and they were not unknown at Goodwood where at the age of five Richmond had appeared in de Boissy's *Les Dehors Trompeurs*, with Caroline and Emily in the cast.[1] But few of these enterprises were as ambitious and spectacular as the plays which the Duke presented at his London house in 1787–8.

He engaged James Wyatt to convert two rooms at Richmond House into a theatre and a salon. The auditorium seated not more than 150 – fewer when royalty was present – but its decoration, estimated to have cost £500, was 'under the inspection of the Hon. Mrs. Damer.' This unusual lady was the daughter of General Conway, stepsister of Duchess Mary and cousin and god-daughter of Horace Walpole, from whom she inherited Strawberry Hill. After a brief marriage to a wealthy wastrel she made herself known as a sculptress. As already noted, her representation of ancient deities may still be seen on the bridge at Henley-on-Thames, and she gave Richmond the two dogs in white marble which are framed by John Bacon's Classical fireplace in the Tapestry Drawing-Room at Goodwood. (Another of her presents was a bust of Charles Fox, his eloquent admirer, to the Emperor Napoleon: whether as joke or insult or intended compliment is hard to determine.) Eccentricity grew upon her like thickening ivy, and in her old age she sheltered George IV's Queen Caroline during her trial. Meanwhile she was invited to the theatricals because Richmond did not want to use professionals and gathered his casts from relatives and friends. Anne Damer had no experience as an actress but her personality overcame critical objections. Mrs Eleanor Bruce and various Campbell ladies (one of whom delivered harp solos at arbitrary points in the action) were of the Duchess's family, and Emily supplied two sons and a husband. A small professional contribution was given by Elizabeth Farren (who did some coaching and also prompted) and by the celebrated Mrs Siddons, who advised on the ladies' costumes. The newspapers noted that Miss Farren, praised by Hazlitt for her graces, 'at this period began to be noticed, even caressed, by a very long list of Fashionables,' proprietary caresses being already the privilege of the twelfth Earl of Derby, who waited ten

91 Anne Seymour Damer, the well-known sculptress, who supervised the decorations of the auditorium at the Richmond House Theatre.

years for his Countess to die before marrying her. Although portliness detracted from his dignity in youthful or tragic roles, Derby played several leads at Richmond House.

The first play was Arthur Murphy's comedy *The Way to Keep Him* (1760), and on the occasion of its opening night on 19 April 1787 a Commons debate was postponed. The Prince of Wales attended, and for the seventh and last performance on 17 May the King and Queen, with several princesses and foreign ministers, were conveyed in seven carriages. On her harp Miss Campbell performed the national anthem, with variations. The royal guests left soon after midnight, but 'a select company' remained behind for supper and songs that continued until 4 a.m. It may have been on this occasion that the Duke spoke a special prologue, eighty lines of rhyming couplets full of political allusions. Himself he referred to as:

> . . . *a flaming Whig,*
> *Irrev'rend once, unaw'd by regal power,*
> *When spleen had turn'd my milky temper sour.*

Political differences were forgotten in a prevailing air of genteel hilarity. Fox and Pitt entered arm in arm and the patrons included Sheridan, Lord North and Burgoyne, whose comedy *The Heiress* had just been performed professionally.

Opinions varied about the quality of the acting, but décor and costumes were sumptuous. The three sets were by Thomas Greenwood, scene-painter at Drury Lane, and John Downman decorated the walls with six portraits executed for the occasion. Both scenery and costumes were refurbished for the Royal visit. Mrs Damer wore a salmon-coloured chemise with a shining belt and Miss Campbell, formerly in an Indian muslin with gold on a red ground, now appeared in a light-blue striped gauze over a white petticoat looped up with diamonds; on her head a cap of feathers, gauze and a wreath of green leaves with diamond flowers.

Between February and June in the following year the company presented four productions – and now they had a new theatre, designed by Wyatt on the middle floor of an adjoining house which the Duke had bought. Here the audience had the luxury of sitting on seats with backs instead of on benches, but the room was poorly ventilated and accommodated only about a hundred. The first play was Mrs Centlivre's *The Wonder*, or *A Woman Who Kept a Secret* (1714), with *The Guardian* as an after-piece. Lord Henry Fitzgerald, one of Emily's sons, was outstanding as Don Felix, a part played by Garrick. His sister Sophia declared that 'he really was more delightful and more charming than can be express'd. Everybody that had seen Garrick thought Henry equal to him, some parts beyond him ... with one great advantage over Garrick, that of having a remarkably pretty figure and looking more like a gentleman, which I understand was not the case with Garrick.' Even Walpole agreed that he was 'a prodigy' but Mrs Siddons was more taken with the stage-struck and stout Lord Derby. Henry's brother Lord Edward was in the cast and so was William Ogilvie, looking to one observer 'as if Heaven and Earth were coming together.'

Another comedy, *The Jealous Wife* (1761) by the elder George Colman,[2] followed. At one performance the Honourable Mrs Hobart, another overweight performer, was stuck between the wall and the wings and had to be extricated by one of her fellow players. Nathaniel Lee's *Theodosius* (1680) enabled Lord Henry to display his talents in verse tragedy, and a chorus was recruited from local choirs to sing Purcell's music. Greenwood painted three new scenes, the dresses – particularly Mrs Damer's – were magnificent, and a critic commented that tragedy came more easily to the actors than comedy since it was 'much easier to assume the passions than imitate the humours of mankind.'

The final piece was General Conway's translation of *Les Dehors Trompeurs* in which, when it was first presented, the infant Richmond was one of the company. As *False Appearances* it was later played at Drury Lane. Although it was well esteemed, it was the end of the Richmond House 'theatricals'. With four 'first nights' between 7 February and 23 May 1788 the company, in attempting so much, had surely worn out their energy and enthusiasm, and perhaps the appetite of their audiences. Talk of resumption in the autumn came to nothing when the King's health broke down and the politicians were exercised in the Regency crisis. (Miss Campbell died, too.) The theatre was dismantled and Charles Lennox and his wife occupied the house. Next year the Duke assisted in the building of a theatre in Chichester and gave it some of the dazzling scenery from London.

As a dramatic experiment Richmond's theatre won London's attention. The professionals decried it because it might take business from their own theatres, but John Philip Kemble, Mrs Siddons's brother and after Garrick's death the leading actor of the day, attended several performances and admired what he saw. So did Hannah More, a lady whose standards were high. There were the expected criticisms of actors who forgot their lines or were inaudible or took unsuitable roles, but Walpole insisted that no one was better fitted to act genteel comedy than people of high fashion in their natural milieu. 'Actors and actresses can only guess at the tone of high life, and cannot be inspired by it.' The notion of a national theatre in which only kings can act kings, only barons can act barons, and so on down the social scale, is of course ludicrous, but certain outward graces come naturally to those who have been brought up in them and even the most skilful 'imitation' may have recognisable blemishes. These amateur players had a style which many people found attractive.

In the absence of detailed accounts of their hospitality at Goodwood, it is interesting to have this record of the Duke and Duchess as lavish hosts to royalty and the best in London Society. Tickets were eagerly sought and were issued under the Duke's personal supervision. With the lights and costumes, scenery and fees, as well as food and wine, it must have been a very expensive enterprise. The sufferers were the 'Catch Singers' and the 'Sussex Band of Wind-Music', put into scarlet tunics to play for their King. Mostly they were men from Richmond's own militia. In a humble memorial in 1788 they said that when their emolument was discussed, their first demand 'was considered by your Grace as greatly exceeding those Bounds of Economy proposed by the plan for conducting the amusements.' Agreeing to 'leave their reward to the calculation of your Grace's *head* – and the generosity of your Grace's *heart*' – they had settled for a weekly salary, the use of the kitchen when the lower servants dined, and a room over the stables to sleep in. But they had quarrelled with the cook, who said they ate too much, and the Duke then agreed to pay them board wages of 5*s*.3*d*. a week.

Subsequently, on the Duke's instructions, they were supplied 'with victuals from the cheapest cook-shop in Porridge-Island in the Strand,' and they estimated that the daily cost of the meals thus provided was 8¼*d.* per head. They humbly requested that this dietary rigour be relaxed and also that they be allowed some liquid refreshment in the music-room in view of the intense heat in the theatre during performances:

> The very high opinion your Memorialists maintain – in common with the rest of mankind – of the *unbounded* generosity, unaffected candour and accomplished affability of your Grace's character affords them the flattering hope that their present *insupportable* situation will be amply redressed, and your Memorialists, as in duty bound, will PLAY and PRAY.

The reply was brief: 'The Duke of Richmond is very particular in paying punctually all his mechanics, tradesmen and others with whom he has any dealings; but as the Memorial he has received demands more than is expressed by the contract, it is impossible for him to comply with it.'

IN DECEMBER 1791 RICHMOND HOUSE was destroyed by a fire that broke out on the second floor while the Duke was breakfasting in the library. The scene was described with journalistic vigour in *The Public Advertiser*. The Duke of York and some of his regiment assisted the watermen and restrained the encroaching spectators. The Duke of Clarence, the future William IV, gave valuable help throughout the day, 'particularly with the floating engines; he was frequently up to his knees in water.' Other noblemen and gentlemen who gave assistance included Charles Lennox and Sir Charles Bunbury, while the Duke himself 'was very active in assisting personally and giving directions where to throw the water.'

The fire broke out in the apartment of Miss Henriette Le Clerc, described as 'a lady of fashion and received in the first circles.' It was a crippling blow, because the house was not insured and Richmond could not afford to rebuild it. His London base in future would be a neighbouring house which he had made available to Lord George. Reports suggest that a fair amount was salvaged, including official Ordnance papers, books, correspondence, busts and the duke's 'valuable museum.'

20

Dismissal

RICHMOND HAD ONCE BEEN ADVISED BY BURKE that he should keep one object principal in his mind instead of diffusing his energies among a variety of interests. The Ordnance gave him this concentration of purpose, and as long as he was Master-General he was a safe 'government man'. Nothing now was heard about corrupt ministerial habits, and indeed it has often been said that the younger Pitt freed himself of Royal influence: which is true in the sense that, once established by dubious manipulations in 1783–4, he became the firm leader of a government that did not need to be propped up by the Crown. He could even risk defeat on some of his reforms without significantly weakening his position. Thus although Richmond was an official government speaker in the Lords, he seldom had to fight contentious issues, and gradually he withdrew from routine business more than was wise. This would contribute to his fall.

With the Prince of Wales coming of age in 1782 there was once again a Hanoverian 'reversionary interest,' with Carlton House the centre of opposition – most of them Whigs who had complained consistently of the cost of the Royal Family – who promised him a more liberal allowance once they were in office. In the nine years after his coming of age the Prince overspent his income by the equivalent of a year's yield of the land tax or half the annual cost of the Navy. Men who assured him that the State would settle his debts were assured of his support, and their time seemed to have come when in 1788 the King became so seriously ill that even if he recovered he might never again be fit to rule. If the Prince as Regent were granted his father's full executive powers, Pitt would be overthrown in favour of a Whig government and a blank cheque to improve the royal finances. Fox, who was in Italy, hurried home with the trollop he later married, but he arrived too late: the King made a full recovery. Richmond had supported Pitt's Regency Bill which stipulated that the powers of the Regent, with its vital authority over appointments, should be shared between the Prince and Queen Charlotte.

Passions rose high during the crisis and those who were on Pitt's side earned the disfavour of Frederick Duke of York, who had wanted his brother George to have full powers. It was therefore embarrassing for Richmond when in 1789

York was challenged to a duel by Charles Lennox. The cause was trifling and obscure. It appears that York overheard, and repeated, certain remarks made at Daubigny's Club which Lennox, if he were a man of honour, could not stomach without demanding satisfaction. Lennox claimed that he had heard no such remarks and had been unable, on enquiry, to find any member of the club who had either made or heard them. York was Lennox's commanding officer and after further exchange of letters the two met on Wimbledon Common, scene of many such pig-headed ceremonies. Lennox fired and disturbed a curl in York's wig. York did not fire but walked away, remarking that he had been present to give Lennox the satisfaction he had required and he had discharged his obligation. Shortly afterwards Lennox fought another duel, with Theophilus Swift, an Irish barrister who allegedly had insulted him in a pamphlet. It was agreed that Lennox should fire first 'and the ball took place in the body of Mr Swift, whose pistol, on receiving the wound, went off without effects. The parties then quitted the ground.' Clearly it was time for the excitable young man to be posted north to teach the Scotch to play cricket.

After six years in office Pitt was reconstructing his ministry and Richmond, hitherto quite close to his leader, was losing ground. He had a quarrel with Lord Howe, who as First Lord of the Admiralty (1783–8) had opposed the fortifications scheme as costly and over-ambitious, and Richmond had retaliated by criticising Howe's naval administration and helping to bring about his dismissal. Perhaps in awareness of his own vulnerability he attempted the sort of electoral corruption that had so much upset him in the past. In a few boroughs Ordnance employees might sway the vote, and in the general election of 1790 he interfered at Seaford and Shoreham, adding forty-nine non-residents, including Pitt and himself, to the roll at Seaford. This attempted coup was investigated and overturned.[1]

At the end of that year William Grenville* was given a peerage to become the government leader in the Lords. Although he had never been the official leader, Richmond saw this as a personal reverse. A long complaint[2] to Pitt showed him conscious of his declining influence but unable, or unwilling, to see any reason for it:

> To be of any [use] as a speaker a man must feel for himself and not appear to the world in an unbecoming situation. I trust I have not shown myself a difficult man when, after having had for many years a considerable share in the debates in the House of Lords, I first wished to support your government as an individual and afterwards defended your measures as a minister . . . But to continue to act a second part under every change, and particularly under one which is avowedly made for the sole purpose of giving the House

* William Grenville, Baron Grenville (1759–1834), son of George Grenville; Home Secretary 1789–90; Foreign Secretary 1791–1801; leader of 'All the Talents' ministry 1806–7.

of Lords another leader, would be depriving myself of every sort of consideration which I may hope to have in that House and rendering myself totally useless there.

Thereafter he appeared less frequently in the House or Cabinet even when Ordnance business brought him to London. The French declaration of war in 1793 weakened his influence by leaving more decisions to other men – particularly Grenville at the Foreign Office, Dundas,* a confidant of Pitt, as Secretary at War, and Chatham,** Pitt's elder brother, at the Admiralty. At the Ordnance Richmond still had wide responsibility but all the 'fighting' ministers had their own ideas about strategy. He agreed with Pitt in sending fleets to hold on to the sugar islands and he was in favour of helping the French royalists against the Jacobin government, but he was opposed to the dispatch of expeditions to the Continent under the command of the Duke of York, another 'strategist' with strong views on the conduct of war.

Richmond was also worried at this time by his Duchess's poor health. She wrote[3] that she was 'dry and fidgety,' she was always awake at two or three in the morning, and she suffered from 'rumbling', which she found more inconvenient than anything else. She had lost twelve pounds in weight and the doctor discouraged her from taking beer as it would cause irritation and bile, 'but I get nothing and it keeps me regular.' She in turn was worried by the letters he wrote from London. She feared that he was flogging himself to death by attending to every detail. 'You'll do all the drudgery,' and 'that spirit of yours of seeing all with your own eyes makes you sometimes miss what is important.' How well she knew him.

York's appointment to command British armies in the Netherlands made her angry. 'The nation must be ruined that Master Frederick may have a plaything that I doubt he does not know how to manage, and that will give him a rap on the knuckles ... I look upon this continental war as a most dangerous unpopular measure and I do not think these times for princes to play tricks in.' She was distressed to think of Richmond 'fatiguing yourself for the whims of a foolish boy.'

Dundas persuaded Pitt to sanction an attack on Dunkirk, and before departing to his summer camp Richmond arranged for the dispatch of the artillery, including two additional ships to sail from Woolwich. His orders were not observed: the gunners sailed on one ship but their guns were loaded on another ship and left behind. The siege of Dunkirk had to be abandoned, partly because the promised continental allies failed to appear, but York blamed 'the neglect or the malicious delay of the Ordnance:' thus hinting that Richmond had done it to spite him. One of York's officers echoed his master's voice, writing in a

---

* Henry Dundas, first Viscount Melville.

** Sir John Pitt became the second Earl of Chatham in 1778.

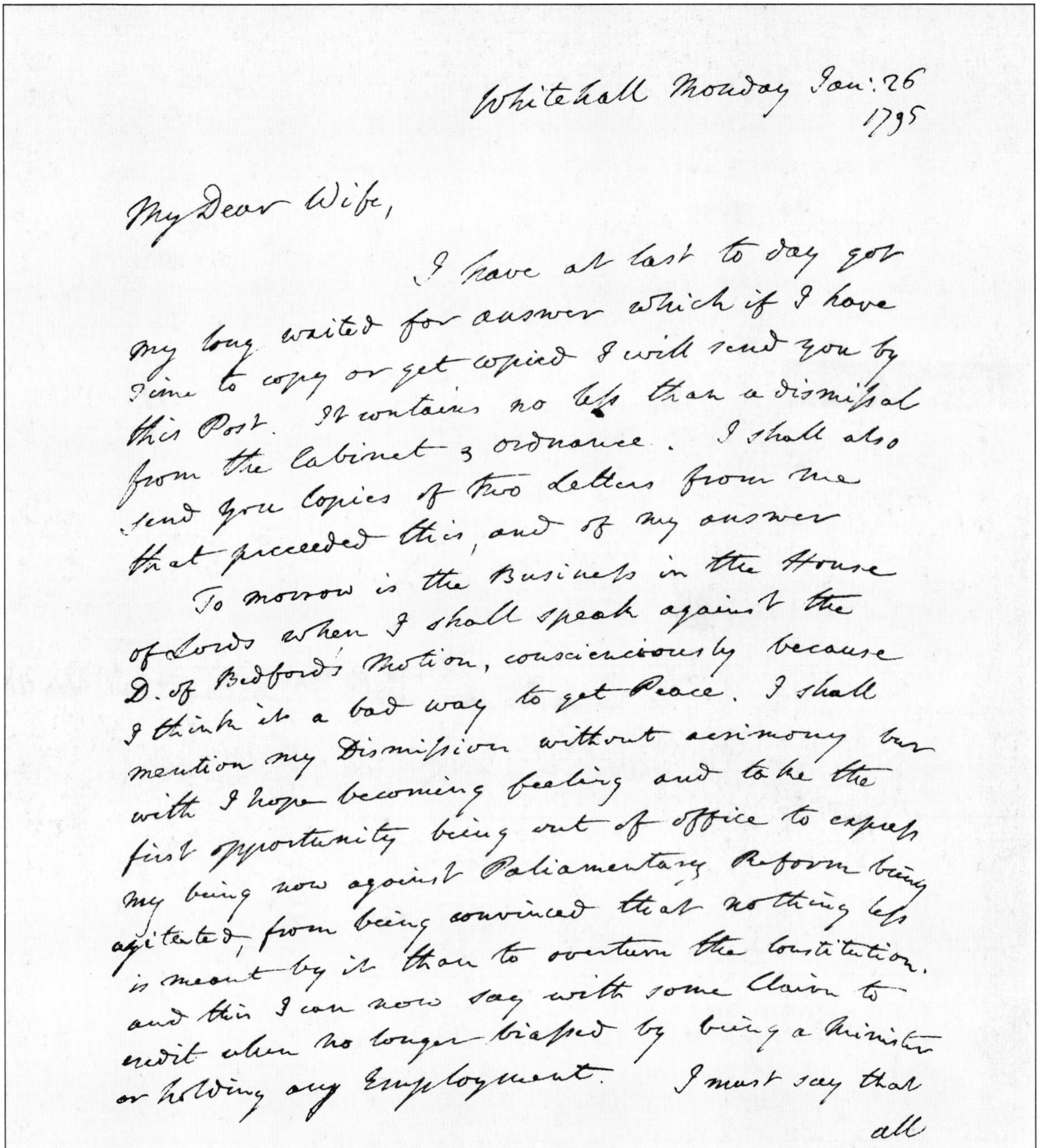

Whitehall Monday Jan: 26
1795

My Dear Wife,

I have at last to day got my long waited for answer which if I have time to copy or get copied I will send you by this Post. It contains no less than a dismissal from the Cabinet & Ordnance. I shall also send you copies of two letters from me that preceeded this, and of my answer

To morrow is the Business in the House of Lords when I shall speak against the D. of Bedford's Motion, conscienciously because I think it a bad way to get Peace. I shall mention my Dismission without acrimony but with I hope becoming feeling and take the first opportunity being out of office to express my being now against Parliamentary Reform being agitated, from being convinced that nothing less is meant by it than to overturn the Constitution. and this I can now say with some Claim to credit when no longer biassed by being a Minister or holding any Employment. I must say that

all

92 (ABOVE) Part of a letter from Richmond to his wife, written on the day that he learned of his dismissal from the Board of Ordnance in 1795.

93 (RIGHT) William Pitt in 1787, by Gainsborough.

newspaper that 'ministers have sacrificed their duty to the holiday mummery of camps or to the amusements of partridge shooting.' Richmond appears to have been blameless for one of those mischances not unfamiliar in history when the British go to war, but he was perhaps impolitic in seeking damage limitation. He answered all criticisms by producing details of his instructions, and he should have left it at that; but he was over-vehement and transferred all the blame to Secretary of War Dundas and First Lord of the Admiralty Chatham.

It was a blow to the professionalism of a department that was proud of its efficiency, and – predictably – it made Richmond ill. For some months afterwards he was at Goodwood with gout and a liver complaint and Louisa was full of maternal concern at finding him so sick. Ordnance work had to be delegated to Lord Howe as Lieutenant-General, and he was no friend to Richmond. The summons to appear, along with Pitt, at the trial of the unlovely Tooke was yet another embarrassment, and during 1794 hints were dropped that some of his Cabinet colleagues were displeased by his absence from their meetings.

A letter in December 1794[4] gave Pitt an opening. The proper course, Richmond wrote, would have been to retire, had it not been for his concern for the nation's political position, his personal regard for Pitt and the desire to support the ministry that he had 'manifested in no equivocal manner on several occasions.' With some ingenuousness he stated that, lest it should be presumed that he was resigning from ill-will towards the ministry, he had hoped that his non-attendance might have passed unnoticed. After more unctuous nonsense in the the style expected in resignations and non-resignations, Richmond came to the point: if after their long association Pitt had solemn reasons for breaking it, 'I have only to beg of you frankly to say so.' He would like to meet Pitt for cordial discussions.

Pitt was neither frank nor cordial. Wise politicians first cover their retreat, and he offered the Ordnance to Cornwallis, leaving Richmond unanswered while he awaited a decision. Duchess Mary implored Richmond to come home, where 'man, woman and beast will exert themselves to amuse you.' Sensing a crisis, Richmond was still in Whitehall as late as 21 December, when in reply to a brief note from Pitt he spoke of returning home. Back in London on 12 January 1795, he hoped that Pitt would soon find 'the leisure hour you promised to bestow' upon answering the letter sent four weeks previously. The Duchess had warned him that 'there's a shuffle somewhere,' but whatever his suspicions, Richmond wrote that he would have 'imputed the neglect I have experienced to an entire change of sentiment' in his old friend and leader had not others assured him that Pitt had spoken of his continuing friendship and regard. (With the Ordnance post not yet filled, no doubt he had.) Richmond went on to probe another possible source of misunderstanding. Although he had opposed too deep a military commitment on the European mainland, and events had 'not been of a nature to

95 (RIGHT) Furniture and porcelain brought from France by the third Duke and now in the Card Room at Goodwood: marquetry commode with fine ormolu mounts; three vases bought when the Duke visited the Sèvres factory with Horace Walpole in 1765; and a chair by Delanois, in what remains of its original cut silk upholstery. The circular Axminster carpet was specially made to match the shape of the room.

94 Satirical print depicting a performance of *The Way to Keep Him*. This play by Arthur Murphy was performed at the Duke's Richmond House Theatre in 1787.

96 (ABOVE) Watercolour of Goodwood House, painted in the 1850s.
97 (BELOW) A painting by Lionel Edwards of Goodwood racecourse, showing the Grandstand of 1904. The present grandstand was opened in 1980.

convince me that my opinions were erroneous,' he undertook not to disturb the Cabinet's unanimity by urging his objections out of season and he hoped to have an early opportunity to declare his loyalty to the government.

A fortnight later he was still hoping. Although the delay was 'mortifying and distressing,' he would not impute it to any of the unpleasant causes it might naturally give him reason to suspect. He proposed nevertheless to call on Pitt at breakfast the following day, or the day after that (a Sunday), because to many disagreeable constructions might be placed on the delay's further continuance.

If only to protect his breakfast from an anxious invading Duke, Pitt at last slunk into the open, six weeks after Richmond's first letter asking for a meeting to explain his long absences from the Cabinet. Pitt may seem to have behaved abominably but his national responsibilities took a higher place than one minister's pique or a vacancy at the head of the Ordnance. Richmond evidently knew all along what was about to happen.

No meeting would be necessary. 'After the fullest consideration, I am under the painful necessity of saying that such an explanation would be fruitless. Your Grace's ceasing to attend the Cabinet, and your breaking off the habits of friendly intercourse between us, proceeded entirely from yourself.' This withdrawal had made it impossible to consult him on recent changes in the ministry:

> . . . and I am bound under the present circumstances to consider how the public service can best be carried on in conjunction with those who now form a material part of government. From the sentiments of some of those persons (wholly unmixed with any personal disrespect to your Grace) I see that your resuming a seat in the Cabinet must prove equally unpleasant and embarrassing to public business.
>
> I communicate it to your Grace with the more pain because I am aware that the consequence does not stop here.

Richmond was to lose the leadership of the Ordnance as well as his place in the Cabinet.

Once the blow had fallen he could reply with some dignity, hoping merely that he would be allowed to keep some employment in the Ordnance. This was granted and he was able to style himself 'G.O.C. Southern District.' He was also (thirty years after it had been promised) made Colonel of the Blues, with an emolument he estimated at £2000 a year, and raised to the rank of Field Marshal. Not all dismissals have been so well compensated. To the Duchess he wrote that in the Lords 'I shall mention my dismission without acrimony but with, I hope, becoming feeling, and take the first opportunity being out of office to express my being now against parliamentary reform being agitated, from being convinced that nothing less is meant by it than to overturn the constitution.'

He reported a very friendly conversation with the King, who thanked him warmly for his services and agreed readily to his remaining on the staff of the

Ordnance. He was sure that the King had not been in any way responsible for his fall, which was entirely due to Pitt. 'After a little cooling,' he told the Duchess, he had tried to find some excuses for Pitt's conduct and he attributed it to 'bad company, distress and over-persuasion . . . He has been distressed and pushed to the greatest degree by his new connections . . . During his long suspense of answering my letter he was struggling hard, but at last gave way, perhaps in a fit of despair and surrounded with other difficulties.' He continued in this vein for some pages, his bitterness at Pitt's ingratitude coming to the surface as he persuaded himself that his dismissal could not have been due to any shortcoming of his own.

Although he was convinced that Dundas and York and possibly Grenville had been the authors of it, these could not in 1795 be described as Pitt's 'new connections.' Richmond could not see that to men unfamiliar with the work he was doing in the Ordnance he had gradually lost credibility as a member of the government. King George informed Pitt that during his conversation with Richmond, 'I thought it but justice to say that Mr. Pitt yielded to the arrangement to prevent a want of concert in the Cabinet which the Duke himself must allow would be highly detrimental to the conduct of affairs at so critical a time.'

This crisis showed the place that Henriette now held in the Goodwood family. 'I confess I do want some of my females just now,' the Duke wrote from London while he was waiting for Pitt's decision. As the Duchess was not well enough to travel, 'please pack off Henriette and her maid.' He took the trouble to make careful plans for the journey, advising that she remain overnight at Godalming as it might take twelve hours in the depth of winter, 'the roads heavy.' To do this in a single day she would have to set out at five, which she would not like. In any case he would send a man to meet her at Kingston.

21

Lord Edward

RICHMOND REMAINED AT GOODWOOD until Duchess Mary's death in 1796, cherishing Horace Walpole's tribute to the unfailing sweetness of her nature, and in the next four years he appeared only twice in the Lords, each time on a private matter. His painful ejection from an office he enjoyed might have given him an Indian Summer of retirement, but his mind was not constituted for tranquillity. His unforgiving hatred of Pitt and the renewed possibility of French invasion were a challenge that drew him back into political intrigue; but first he fought for his family's interests after the disaster of Lord Edward Fitzgerald, fifth son of his sister Emily.

Emily by now was back in Ireland, living at Black Rock, her family's holiday home when the children were young. Carton was occupied by her son William, the Second Duke of Leinster, a man less forceful than his father and less fortunate in his marriage. His first seven children were all girls; on losing two of them his wife had a mental breakdown and in a surge of spiritual excitement installed a Catholic priest with attendant nuns at one end of Carton and a Methodist preacher not similarly attended, at the other. The birth of a son put an end to this ecumenical venture, but the lady had always to be wondered at.

With his father's sense of social responsibility William Leinster provided generous employment on his park of 60,000 acres and he constructed a little township at nearby Maynooth, founding a college there for the training of Catholic clergy, many of whom were bog-ignorant. But he did not take a very active part in the growing struggle for Irish independence. Here he followed Richmond's advice to work only with men who like himself wanted a peaceful solution; and when he accepted Pitt's plan for union (and was handsomely compensated for the loss of his seigneurial rights), it was in the belief that it would be accompanied by reform and toleration.

His brother Edward, born in 1763, was less temperate. As a regular officer he had fought in America and then, a sign of his singularity, been admitted to membership of an Indian tribe. When a love affair foundered on the opposition of the girl's father, Richmond took him on a tour of the Channel Islands, and later Portsmouth and Plymouth, to inspect the defences. 'I grow fonder of him every day,' Edward told Emily, 'and with good reason, for there is no expressing all the goodness and kindness he shows me . . . He not only takes every opportunity of giving me information himself but makes other people inform me also.' Richmond made special efforts to obtain for him an appointment in Cadiz and was not pleased when Edward rejected it because Leinster had procured him a seat in the Irish Parliament.

This intense young man adored his mother: 'You seem to make every distress lighter,' he said in a letter to her, 'and I bear everything better, and enjoy everything more, when with you.' But his life lacked direction and control. When in Dublin on political business he consorted with actresses. In London (where Emily had a house because Ogilvie her second husband, did not like living in Ireland) he had a child by Sheridan's wife and he listened to the chatter of pro-French agitators. In 1792 he went to Paris and was captivated by Tom Paine, in whom he found an incomparable 'simplicity of manner, goodness of heart and strength of mind.' For his revolutionary enthusiasm he was deprived of his commission while at the same time acquiring an aristocratic bride in Pamela Seymour, ward of Philippe Duke of Orléans but believed to be his daughter by the scholarly Madame de Genlis.* Returning to Ireland, Edward was scornful of cautious reformers like his brother William and by 1796 he was seeking French help for a national rising. At the end of the year some 15,000 French troops sailed from Brest. Half of them reached Bantry Bay but did not attempt a landing while the other half, including their commander, Hoche, were separated by a fog and never sighted the coast.

By 1798, when the armies of the European coalition had been defeated, a larger French expedition was confidently expected and the United Irishmen were growing dangerous in numbers and organisation. Lord Edward wanted French arms, munitions and trained officers, but by this time he appears to have had second thoughts about a fully-equipped invasion.[1] If the French came, they might try to take possession of Ireland. Alternatively, he feared they might not come at all – as in fact they did not: Bonaparte sailed instead for Egypt. Edward believed that with the guerrilla tactics used so successfully by the Americans, the United Irishmen would be strong enough to defeat the government forces on their own. Here he overestimated the rebels' unity and strength and underestimated the government's knowledge of their membership and intentions. It was Edward himself who persuaded Thomas Reynolds, a property-owner in Kildare, to join the United Irishmen and take a seat on the provincial committee. Reynolds turned informer and by the end of March most of the leaders had been arrested. Minor outbreaks around Dublin were quickly suppressed, and only in Wexford,

* For his revolutionary enthusiasm Orléans took the cognomen 'Philippe Egalité', but in 1793 he learned on the scaffold how greedily revolutions eat their own children. Paine nearly had a similar fate. He was elected to the National Convention but displeased the mighty Robespierre and was imprisoned. Only Robespierre's sudden fall saved him from the guillotine.

98 Lord Edward Fitzgerald in 1796.

99 Charles James Fox, haunted by the 'ghost' of Lord Edward Fitzgerald. James Gillray's engraving was published in September 1798, some three months after Lord Edward's death.

where 30,000 peasants took up arms, was there any serious resistance. A small French force landed in the summer but soon surrendered at the well-named Ballinamuck in County Longford.

Lord Edward had escaped when the other leaders were arrested and was hiding in Dublin. Out of respect to his family and the honoured name he bore, the government offered him a free passage out of Ireland if he would go away and stay away. He refused, and in May – on the very day when Bonaparte set out from Toulon – troops were sent to take him. He received a bullet in the shoulder when trying to resist, but the authorities would not remove it.* His death from a poisoned wound would spare them the embarrassment and complications of a trial. Louisa visited him in his cell and was on her knees to the Governor, begging that at least he should have medical care. Lord Chancellor Clare 'cried like a woman when he saw him dying,' and he was dead before Emily could come to him from London.

To condone manifest treason was not in Richmond's nature, and Lord Edward's advocacy of armed resistance imperilled his hopes of saving the Irish connection. Even in a letter to the distraught mother he would not hide his feelings: 'His faults were errors of imagination but I am sure no man acted more from principle (mistaken as it was) than he did.' To the innocent, Richmond was all compassion. He welcomed Lady Pamela and her children to Goodwood, with Louisa as their escort, assuring them that they would not be crowding or distressing him. 'It will give me real pleasure to be of any use to you all on so melancholy an occasion.'

In the short period between Edward's arrest and his death, when it was expected that he would be brought to trial, Richmond asked Camden,[2] Lord Lieutenant of Ireland, for it 'to be postponed until a quieter moment than the present' in order that it should not be inflamed by the prevailing passions. He had even appealed to Pitt to this effect, which did not come easily to him. But no trial was necessary, and the Irish Parliament passed an attainder depriving Lady Pamela and her children of Lord Edward's property, which they had expected to inherit. Richmond was outraged by what he regarded as an injustice, and he and the third Lord Holland, Henry Fox's grandson, led a campaign against the attainder. His concern here went beyond personal and family interest. This act of confiscation seemed so iniquitous that it must be reversed for 'the honour of our constitution.' It was the more iniquitous because an official pardon had been granted for all acts of rebellion, or acts in suppression of rebellion, committed before 20 August 1798. Exceptions were made for members of the United Irishmen's national executive and for men imprisoned since 1795 for treason

---

* Ogilvie reported to Lord Holland that the surgeons had said 'the arm was too much inflamed to admit of extracting the balls.'

or murder, and there were two attainders. The impression was given that an example was being made of Lord Edward because of his high social standing as well as his part in the insurrection.[3]

Richmond suggested an appeal to the Attorney-General, by whom measures of the Irish Parliament had to be sanctioned, and to the King on the ground that the attainder was 'contrary to justice and the known laws of the land.'

The unrest in Ireland made it unlikely that assent would be refused to a resolution coming from the Parliament, and Richmond agreed with Holland that 'objecting directly against the principle is the best way to proceed.' He maintained that the law could not pass judgment on a man unable to be heard in his own defence, and in doing this the Irish Legislature:

> . . . is avowing they do what the law must from principles of justice refuse to do. It is said that Bills of Attainder are an exercise of that power which the constitution has reserved to the Legislature expressly for those cases which are necessary for the public safety to make an example of and which the common course of law would not reach. It must be at least confessed that such a power, obnoxious in itself as it is always an *ex post facto* law, ought at least to be exercised with the greatest tenderness possible and never to violate the principles of common justice.

He went on to argue that although 'a man's being killed under arms in actual rebellion might afford undeniable proof of his guilt,' Lord Edward had never been arraigned for any self-evident overt act of treason. This may seem specious as, except that he had never been convicted by a court, Lord Edward's treason was indisputable. But Richmond here was aware that when in March the Irish government had swooped on the leaders and put them in prison, they realised that they had little hard evidence on which to bring these men to trial, and many of them were released in a blanket pardon.

Holland was assiduous in circulating a petition to be laid before the King. Richmond had no great hopes of it at present but it might 'afford sufficient matter for a reversal of the Act in better times.' Lord Edward had lost his life and it was unjust that his children should lose their property when no trial had taken place to prove his guilt. Emily also petitioned the King to restore her grandchildren's property as a mark of favour.

In the turmoil which accompanied and followed the Act of Union, personal injuries of this kind were forgotten among greater ones, and there was enough wealth in the Lennox and Fitzgerald families to protect Lady Pamela and her children in their loss.

22

Money and Mrs Bennett

Among the most interesting documents at Goodwood is a manuscript folio in which the Duke drew up a statement of his financial affairs as they stood in March 1799 and set out his scheme for liquidating his debts. He was then sixty-four and presumably realised that unless he had a policy for reducing his indebtedness, his successor would be heavily burdened.

In the following figures, shillings and pence are omitted and interest payable is given in brackets after the principal. Richmond estimated his current indebtedness at £90,399 (£4366). He then listed his annual outgoings, which totalled £11,457. These included £1310 in additional annuities (£1000 to his nephew Charles Lennox) and payments 'during pleasure' of £200 to Mrs Close, £260 to Madame de Cambis and £20 to Miss Rosewell. (A later entry discontinued the payment to Miss Rosewell.) He estimated his income tax, levied for the first time, as a temporary war measure, at two shillings in £, at £2300, and 'the demand for poor rate at Newcastle' at £3000. The coal duties granted by Charles II to the first Duke orginally yielded about £15,000 a year but by the 1790s this had risen to an average of £21,000. 'The Duke of Richmond takes away as much for himself as would maintain two thousand poor and aged persons' had been Tom Paine's comment on this, and a demand was now being made that he contribute an annual £3000 to the poor rate for the parish of All Saints, Newcastle. He proposed to contest this, as far as the House of Lords if necessary, but he was setting aside £3000 to answer the demand if it were made good. In the event, he made arrangements to commute the duties by selling the grant to the government for £728,333, which would bring him £19,000 a year.

Against the outgoings of £11,457 he estimated his income at £28,550, consisting of the coal duties which he had not yet commuted, £7778 from the landed estate, £2000 from his command of the Blues and £427 as Colonel of the Sussex Militia after deduction of his mess bills. This calculation gave an annual profit of £17,093, but the statement goes on to admit further liabilities, including unsettled debts totalling £10,000 and legacies in his will totalling £27,750; the interest on these two items being £1887. (This refers to the will existing at that time; his final will was not made until 1806.) From the estimated income from the landed estate it was necessary to deduct £1185 which he had left to Miss Le Clerc by his will. The final total of the principal debt would therefore be £143,599, plus £7026 in interest.

How was this to be discharged? The Duke's scheme was based on the assumption that his unsettled landed estate (his personal estate was not to be touched) would yield 7 per cent. If 5 per cent went to pay interest on the debts, the remaining 2 per cent should discharge the principal in twenty-six years. 'This I do not think an unreasonable period to be allowed for such an operation.'

It depended, however, on certain hopeful expectations, such as that holders of annuities would soon die off, that legacies would not be paid until it was convenient to the estate to release them and that some creditors might prefer to leave their money at 5 per cent rather than call it in, or even might advance further loans. Richmond thought that the two main creditors, Lord George at £9540 and his wife at £15,509, would probably not ask for immediate payment. In this way he knocked some £50,000 off the principal debt, reducing it to £93,550, and fresh cash might be raised if some of the estate's tenant farmers were granted leases and persuaded to make loans at 5 per cent.

'The great point then to be considered is how I can so diminish my expenses as materially to reduce my debt, so that my income will pay 7 per cent of it,' and he estimates that 'in order to leave my estate, at my death, in such a situation as to pay off the debt in 26 years, without touching my personal estate, such a saving should be made during my life as will amount to £66,110.' If £5093 were taken from the annual surplus of £17,093, expenditure would have to be curtailed to £12,000. Some of his subsequent calculation is provisional because in March 1799 he did not know what settlement would be made over the coal duties, but by a series of optimistic hypotheses he concluded that the projected saving of £66,110 might be achieved within five years. This would, he concedes, require 'a concurrence of favourable circumstances . . . but these calculations serve to show what with perseverance and good luck may possibly happen.'

Perseverance and good luck did not regularly attend the Duke through life, and at his death he left debts of £180,000, nearly double what he started with in 1799. By then he had spent generously in launching the Goodwood races; and probably several of the earlier debts were incurred in his building schemes and improvement of the estate. His attempt to liquidate his debts and die solvent illustrates his ingenuity and application and his insistence, when his interest was aroused, on investigating the facts and looking for solutions even if, as here, the result fell short of expectations.

Readers not already choked with figures will find more below,[1] but the folio, which covers a period of about eight years, has several interesting items. For example, Richmond and another were trustees for sums invested in 3 per cent Consols for Lord Henry Fitzgerald's natural children; and in 1800 he paid £4000

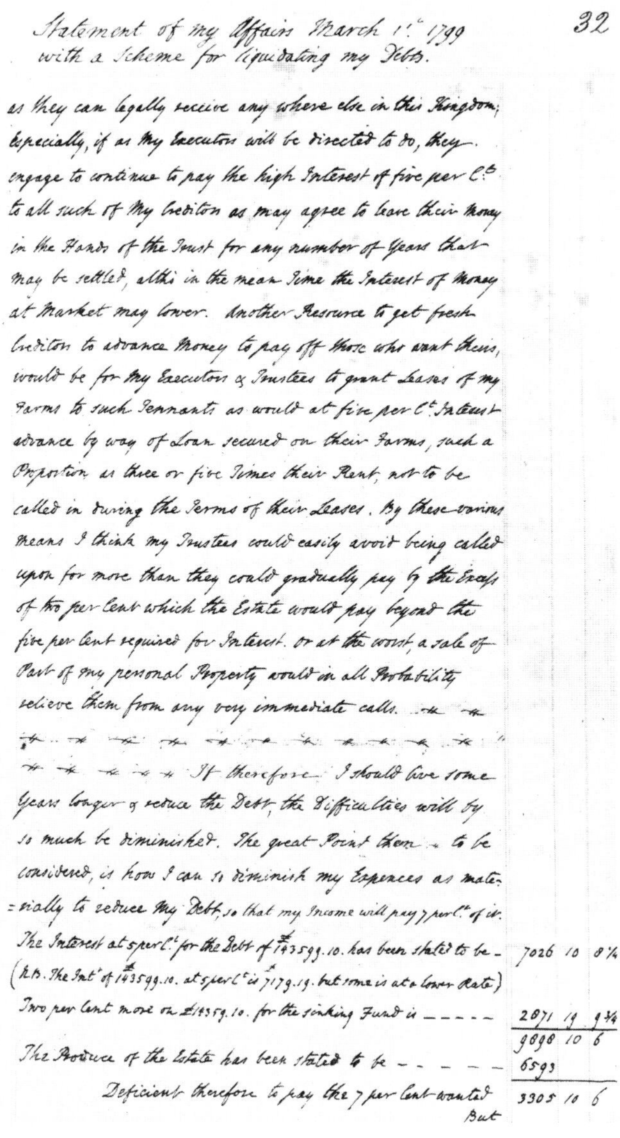

Statement of my Affairs March 1st 1799
with a Scheme for liquidating my Debts. 32

as they can legally receive any where else in this Kingdom; Especially, if as my Executors will be directed to do, they engage to continue to pay the high Interest of five per Ct to all such of my Creditors as may agree to leave their Money in the Hands of the Trust for any number of Years that may be settled, altho in the mean Time the Interest of Money at Market may lower. Another Resource to get fresh Creditors to advance Money to pay off those who want theirs, would be for my Executors & Trustees to grant Leases of my Farms to such Tennants as would at five per Ct Interest advance by way of Loan secured on their Farms, such a Proportion as three or five Times their Rent, not to be called in during the Terms of their Leases. By these various means I think my Trustees could easily avoid being called upon for more than they could gradually pay by the Excess of two per Cent which the Estate would pay beyond the five per Cent required for Interest. or at the worst, a sale of Part of my personal Property would in all Probability relieve them from any very immediate calls.

If therefore I should live some Years longer & reduce the Debt, the Difficulties will by so much be diminished. The great Point then is to be considered, is how I can so diminish my Expences as materially to reduce my Debt, so that my Income will pay 7 per Ct of it.

The Interest at 5 per Ct for the Debt of £143599.10. has been stated to be	7026	10	8¾
(N.B. The Int. of £143599.10. at 5 per Ct is £7179.19. but some is at a lower Rate)			
Two per Cent more on £143599.10. for the sinking Fund is	2871	19	9¾
	9898	10	6
The Produce of the Estate has been stated to be	6593		
Deficient therefore to pay the 7 per Cent wanted	3305	10	6

But

100 A page in the Duke's handwriting from his 1799 account book entitled *Money Matters*.

for Adsdean Farm at Westbourne near Emsworth, which Henriette's son Charles would buy from the fifth Duke as probably his last home. Less easy to explain is that between 1802 and 1805 Madame de Cambis paid in eight instalments a total of £3277, 'which cleared her debt to me which had been advanced to her by my bankers': this when she was in turn receiving an annual £260 'during pleasure.' Possibly Richmond had made loans to a mistress who had borne him a child and might still have favours to offer. Alternatively it is not impossible that she had a natural child by some other man and paid Richmond an agreed sum to take her into his home, educate her and introduce her into society. Whatever the probabilities, Henriette's parentage has never been proved.

That Richmond dearly loved his Duchess and missed her gentle companionship there can be no doubt, but in 1798 Louisa found him enjoying a visit from Lady Elizabeth Foster, a lady notoriously free with her affections; and he had also found consolation in his own household. Among the annuitants listed in 1797 is Mrs Mary Blesard, aged twenty-nine and described as a housekeeper, in the sum of £50. Written later as 'Blizard' and finally as 'Bennett', she rapidly improved her standing and in 1802 she is recorded as contributing £1000 to the £4000 paid for a property at Earls Court, then a country village on the edge of London. The property contained a farm and Mrs Bennett was in charge of it. Documents from later years show payments to her for oats and forage and £142 for servants' wages. Marsden, a gardener at Earls Court, submitted separate accounts for his purchases.

Mrs Bennett appears also in Richmond's final will of 1806 in which minor legacies and annuities were made to servants, including an annuity of £40 to William Young 'for the constant and careful attention he showed to me in my several illnesses.' The largest annuity was £70, apart of one of £450 for Mrs Bennett. The will also instructed the executors to take in trust pieces of land near Goodwood 'for such first-born son as Mrs. Mary Blesard now called Mrs. Bennett, my servant, may be delivered of before my decease or within ten months after.'

If there was a Mr Blesard, or Bennett, he was never mentioned: 'Mrs' was a courtesy title often given to housekeepers and cooks. Although the births were never officially registered, so that the father has not been named, it has been assumed that Richmond was the father of Mrs Bennett's three daughters, the youngest being posthumous. A subsequent arrangement for the Earls Court property left it for the use of the fourth Duke, the trustees and Mrs Bennett and her daughter Elizabeth but to be held in trust for Elizabeth 'until she should attain the age of 21 or be married, which should first happen.'

Elizabeth's future is unknown and probably she died young. Mrs Bennett's two other daughters, Caroline and Mary, like Henriette, were gladly accepted by Lennoxes, Napiers, Conollys and Fitzgeralds, and had happy associations with the family. Caroline married Sarah Napier's son Henry, a naval captain and historian of Florence. They settled in Florence, where by now Mrs Bennett had a house, and mother and daughter were buried in the English cemetery there. Mary married William Light, the distinguished surveyor who mapped the coastline of South Australia and founded the city of Adelaide.[2]

23

Declining Hopes

'I SHOULD BE PLEASED TO SERVE in any part of the world,' Richmond told the Duke of York in 1799[1] in acknowledging an appointment as Colonel Commandant of a battalion of the 35th Regiment. He was not called upon for service more active than training with the militia, but a renewed threat of French invasion drew from him a pamphlet on national defence and angry opposition to the alternative schemes of Pitt. He had no prospect of political office as long as Pitt was alive, but in 1806, when he had only a few months to live, he was hoping to be given some ministerial post by Charles Fox and the Prince of Wales, not his favourite people in by-gone times. The spur, probably, was not ambition, which would have been ridiculous in a man of his age, but simple duty, his knowing that he was not born to be private, his feeling that 'I could be of use.'

When Pitt resigned in 1801 because the King would not emancipate the Irish Catholics, he was replaced by a patchwork ministry under Henry Addington, son of Chatham's doctor and for the past ten years Speaker of the Commons. With Grenville, Dundas and others refusing to join it, Richmond may have hoped for an offer. It is never easy to realise that one has become one of 'yesterday's men' but he did not belong to any of the political groupings, new or old, and only Fox and Portland survived with him from the brave old days of Whiggery under Rockingham's faltering banner. Nor was he suited temperamentally for some honorific post of the kind given to veteran statesman who lend weight to a ministry. He was too individualistic, too often apt to get ideas of his own; and when an idea seized him, he did not mind who was embarrassed by it.

His main confidant now was Henry Vassall Fox, third Lord Holland, who had inherited the barony before he was two years of age and to some extent had been educated by his uncle Charles. He was throughout his life a steadfast and honourable liberal, working for the abolition of slavery, although his wife inherited her father's extensive estates in Jamaica. To him Richmond communicated his reflections on the war, criticizing the attempt to land at the Spanish port of Ferrol and the disastrous Anglo-Russian campaign in the Netherlands in 1799. 'In the retired life I lead I have few opportunities of conversing with officers,' he wrote in February 1801,[2] 'so that my Intelligence is chiefly from newspapers and even those I do not always read.' Nevertheless from friends he had learnt certain 'facts' which had proved 'the shameful ignorance with which that disgraceful expedition was planned, conducted and ended.' He was impressed by the military genius of Napoleon and his defeat of the Austrians at Marengo (1800). 'Those who impute Bonaparte's success to the accidental turn of the day do him an injustice . . . His plan was well conceived, founded on sound judgment of his means and those of the enemy, and he had a right to expect the success he met with.' Here he was perhaps seduced by Napoleonic propaganda, which always sought to overlook Desaix's major contribution on that day.

The defeat of Austria ended Pitt's Second Coalition and left Britain without an ally. Addington had little to bargain with when he agreed to the Peace of Amiens in 1802, acknowledging all France's annexations in Europe with the consequent losses for British trade. Richmond's criticism of the treaty was an undisguised attack on the way Pitt had conducted the war.[3] This had been neither wise nor economical, especially in the price paid for 'running after every petty German prince' who might be hired as an ally. He was not opposed in principle to the payment of subsidies to continental allies, but the nation had hoped to see greater benefit from it. Another old grudge aired itself in an oblique reference to York's ill-favoured outings in the 1790s. In the peace negotiations, Richmond said, the ministry had seemed to expect a French invasion. What else was to be expected when we had 'insulted their coasts and braved them in their ports?'

Forty years previously English politics had been in suspended animation just 'waiting for Pitt',* out of office but bearing such authority that no ministry could survive without him. So it was again. Addington's ministry collapsed as soon as Pitt withdrew the support he had nominally given to it, but in taking office again in 1804 he was a burnt-out man, exhausted by past failures in foreign policy and incapable of devising new initiatives: still quite a young man but in a hurry to die. He patched together a new coalition which at Ulm and Austerlitz, Jena and Friedland, would be blown to pieces by Napoleon.

Against him Richmond fought his last political battle, on the familiar terrain of national defence. The serving conditions of the militia, which differed from one region to another, had raised difficult questions: how the men should be recruited, how long they should serve, whether they should serve outside their county, whether they should be an attachment of the regular army. The Addington government tried to codify the militia laws but were stayed by a memorandum from their own Home Secretary, Lord Pelham, who did not want the militia to be like the Army.[4] Each unit, he proposed, should be situated in its own county, or near to it, so that men who had completed their enlistment could re-join in emergencies. The training would particularly prepare men for the

* Later the first Earl of Chatham.

defence of their own regions, but the militia should be seen as a force only occasionally embodied – for not more than two months even in wartime – in order that men could enter it without being turned into professional soldiers. These in essence had been Richmond's views when in 1779 he had fought Lord North's proposals for raising the militia by ballot. The coincidence is unsurprising, as Thomas Pelham had been then, and was still, a serving officer in the Sussex militia. They had often discussed their ideas and Richmond persuaded him now to retain his rank although as a peer and a minister he could give only 'his name and occasional superintendence.'[5]

The Duke kept his militia at an operational level, including a corps of horse artillery under his direct command.[6] This consisted of about sixty rank and file, armed with two three-pounder curricle guns and two 4½-inch howitzers. (They were to serve only in the district to the west of the Arun.) He protested, however, against laws passed in 1801 and 1803 for the raising of troops and the devastation of the countryside in the event of invasion. A quota was to be set for each county, with a penalty of £20 for each failure to meet it, and crops and livestock were to be destroyed if the enemy landed.

He called a county meeting to reject these proposals, and in 1804 he published anonymous *Thoughts on the National Defence.* The first object of defence was to have always at home a navy and army powerful enough to overcome an enemy. Glorious successes and acquisitions abroad would be useless if our Navy and arsenals were destroyed and the Army 'overcome in the heart of our country.' Since it would be dangerous to rely only on the valour of the troops and the skill of the generals, or on the ability of the Navy to repel a force of 300,000 to 400,000 Frenchmen, he proposed that additional forces should be put in readiness: 'England and Wales alone can have their land force so organised as, without distressing the country, to be able at the shortest warning, to have upwards of 500,000 men to oppose them: not a mere mass of peasantry with pikes and pitchforks, but regularly armed, formed into corps, officered and trained, and under military discipline' (*page 11*).

This force could not be formed from the regular army, which had other duties, and the Army should not be boosted by drafts from the militia, ballots or conscription. Conscription 'would come with but an ill grace to Englishmen, who have been taught to consider it as the greatest stretch of tyranny in France and by no means suited to the people of a free country' (*page 16*). Napoleon was right to regard Britain as a 'nation of shopkeepers, mechanics and money-getting men,' and she could not be converted into a military nation like France without sacrificing our trade, the source of our strength; and the Navy likewise is sustained 'only by that capital which trade produces and by that large body of seamen that a vast extended commerce can alone support.'

Richmond argued that a strong force could be raised without interfering with agriculture (a special problem in a rural county such as Sussex), manufacturing or commerce. His plan (*page 58*) was to raise half a million armed men (ten times the number of the existing militia) by a statute requiring returns to be made of men aged between seventeen and fifty in each parish.* The system proposed would be to keep no man of the militia embodied during the whole year, but by a regular succession of furloughs to allow them leave of absence for a certain time, to work at their different trades at home, during which period they should receive no pay. The scheme was designed to 'preserve the good humour of the soldier and his affection for the service.'

The plan was submitted to Pitt who, if he read it at all, did not discuss it with Richmond or even return it to him. His Additional Forces Bill ignored all its proposals. Opposing the bill in the Lords, Richmond said that he would not carry out its provisions in Sussex, pay the £20 fine for each man short of the quota of recruits, or pay any attention to inspecting officers of inferior rank sent to supervise recruitment and training. On his last appearance in the Lords he supported an unsuccessful motion to set up a committee on national defence.

The immediate crisis passed when in 1805 Napoleon dispersed the invasion force at Boulogne and marched east to deal with the Austrians. The threat of invasion ended at Trafalgar, and was not renewed. Richmond involved himself, however, in an exchange of letters with Charles Lennox,[7] who as Member of Parliament for Sussex had voted for Pitt's bill. He reproached Lennox for disregarding . . .

> . . . the sentiments and inclinations of a person to whom you owe not only your seat but to an uncle who has adopted you as his child, bred you up, and to whom you owe everything . . . I cannot help also recalling to you what Mr. Pitt's conduct towards me has been. He stood much in need of my assistance, and being served by me with all the fidelity of the warmest friendship, he turned me out of office, and in the most shuffling manner, without alleging any cause for it, but evidently to sacrifice me to the Duke of York and Mr. Dundas' jealousy, and you was yourself included in the consequences** . . . Whatever I might feel at such treatment, I showed no resentment, nor enter'd into any opposition against him.

He did not wish to deprive Pitt of the share in government that his abilities deserved but he must 'resist that inordinate ambition of his that will make him expect to be sole and only minister.'

Lennox defended his support of the bill as a trial of Pitt's standing when he had only recently returned to office: 'Should he be turned out, who else are we to look

* This was based on the system used by Frederick II in Prussia and was recommended by Thomas Pelham.

** Lennox resigned his post at the Ordnance when Richmond was dismissed.

101 Charles Lennox, the future fourth Duke at about the age of twelve, by Romney.

to?' He mistrusted the Grenvilles and saw their present alliance with Fox as temporary and short-lived, and he was astonished that Richmond might be thinking, if Pitt should fall, of joining a ministry in which Fox was included. Lennox wrote:

> I believe it would do harm to you in the eyes of the country if they saw you joined in administration with a man whose political conduct you have disapproved of since the death of Lord Rockingham, that is to say for about 22 years . . . I see nothing in Mr. Fox's conduct to make me suppose he is less partial to French Revolutionary principles than he formerly avowed himself to be.

Richmond's reply contained a very curious defence of Fox as a misunderstood man proscribed by the King's prejudices and excluded from office by Pitt's monopolisation of power: 'although often hurried into indiscretions by the eagerness of his temper, yet in reality a sound character.' Richmond wished for 'an administration on the *broadest basis* possible in which all the real talents of the country shall be united, and no one shall take such an ascendancy as shall make all the rest cyphers.' As for Pitt, 'I fear he will be *Caesar aut nullus*, and if we are unfortunately driven to the choice of the two, I must say *nullus*, for usurped as this situation of first minister has sometimes been, and soon abused into being *sole minister*, our constitution knows no such place.'

Fox's attachment to the Prince of Wales explains Richmond's reassessment of his character because, with the King ageing and growing blind, the Prince was coming again to be an important political figure. 'The King's declining health and age will make many, in such a precarious state of things, fly to pay early court to the rising sun'. In such a daybreak Richmond was ready to play the courtier, and the way to the Prince's regard was through Fox. This was a sound judgment because when Pitt died in January 1806 the Prince had some influence in the construction of the new government, and he took Fox's opinions.

It was to be a broad-based ministry, lacking a Caesar, as Richmond had wished, but its calling itself 'All the Talents' did not for a moment conceal its ineffectuality as a plastic coalition incapable either of fighting Napoleon or of gaining from him peace terms favourable to Britain. Grenville was First Lord, Fox Foreign Secretary with a commitment to peace despite a belated weakening in his Bonapartist enthusiasm, but the other ministers indicated the shuffling and compromises required to give the appearance of a broad base. The Prince of Wales put in two of his own followers, Rawdon (now Lord Moira) and Sheridan, neither of them a friend to Richmond, and insisted on the inclusion of some conservative Addingtonians. Pitt's young men like Castlereagh and Canning who would direct the future, stayed away. The group of Foxite Whigs, muting their ambitions until a more opportune season which for them never came, were of a more destructive generation than the remnant of Rockingham Whigs who had followed Portland to Pitt's side in 1794. There could be no place for Richmond, always a positive man, in this soggy compound.

He believed that there *was*, and believed that he had been promised it. Office had become the cordial that 'embalms and spices to the April day again.' 'Had you seen the wonderfully flattering letter I was honoured with from the Prince a few days before the negotiations began ... you would have been still more convinced that I might have expected some further communications,' he wrote to Holland in February, but he had heard no more. 'I make no comments. They would be too painful to my feelings, and I am too proud to complain ... It is hard in the decline of life to find that the longer one lives it is only to experience the oftener how little dependence can be placed on professions of friendship, even in those quarters from whence one imagined one had the right to expect it. If I could obliterate these grating reflections from my memory, I should have no other regret than that if from long experience I have acquired any knowledge of the true interests and resources of this country, I have no opportunity of rendering it useful in a moment so truly alarming as the present.'

Grating reflections were not obliterated and three weeks later they were being directed at Fox. Holland must be distressed at seeing his two uncles (Richmond and Fox) 'so wide asunder; and the blame to lie on him to whom from nearer age, connection and habits you must be naturally more attached.' In a very long and plaintive letter he cannot understand Fox's betrayal of him after their 'reunion in politics as well as private society.' He had been left out of all consultations about the forming of a ministry, and he found a further grievance in the dismissal from two posts in the Ordnance of his former aide Colonel Hopkinson, who had been restored to one of them, 'not on my account but by the solicitation of other friends he got to speak for him.' He was obliged to conclude that Fox and the Prince 'thought my assistance by advice or otherwise could be in no way useful to them since they have so completely done without it.' The Prince's flattering message and letter, in which Fox and his confidential friends concurred, had given him 'some right to expect a very different treatment from that marked neglect which has been shewn me.'

Something must subsequently have happened to change their views, and Richmond attributes it to 'some of those wheels within wheels which I have found by experience to sometimes lead men to think it necessary for political considerations to sacrifice their best friends': the King or the Duke of York perhaps. 'The fault is not in me, and as it is so evident that Mr. Fox cannot in any degree exculpate himself from that which most affects me, his want of candour and friendship, I had rather so far imitate him as to remain silent than distress him for explanations he cannot give.' He did not expect this strange 'coalesced ministry' to serve the public satisfactorily, and there he might have been of some use, having had some experience of politics. The Austrians had now been forced

102 Charles James Fox, by Karl Anton Hickel.

to sign the Treaty of Pressburg,* and he only wished that England likewise 'may not be ruined by ill-concerted alliances and precipitate concessions.'

Fox had proclaimed his intention of seeking peace, but Richmond thought that Napoleon was not to be trusted and would only use the breathing-space to strengthen himself for future attacks. Britain, he suggested to Holland in June, could support a vigorous war if we 'confine the war to our home protection and do not engage in wild continental schemes and connections.' Writing again about the war a few weeks later, he said that it must be conducted with greater economy. The whole system was ruinously expensive and would soon drive the country into bankruptcy. 'If we could once see a ministry resolved to be really economists and punish depredations, the country would feel itself and really be twice as strong as it is.'

He had forgotten perhaps that his own fortifications scheme had been criticised for extravagance, and his observations on the war are unimpressive. In his complaint about being excluded from the ministry it is uncertain what promises or indications, if any, the Prince of Wales had given him. He is unlikely to have been considered. On his own admission he was not in good health, and having been out of politics for ten years, he had not the influence or the all-important 'connections' to give the government significant support.

The ministry's only important achievement was the abolition of the slave trade within the British Empire, heroically carried by Fox just before his death. It is a strange fact that in all the libertarian arguments for supporting the American Colonists in the struggle against the mother country, very little criticism had been heard of the Southern States' dependence on plantation slavery or of the system by which the slaves were provided. Wilberforce's campaign for abolition had made slow progress against powerfully entrenched interests, and abolition seemed imprudent if it would weaken colonial economies in time of war. But Fox held to his beliefs in a course of action that was adopted by other nations after 1815. Richmond, however, was opposed to it, telling Holland that he had 'too much regard for Lady Holland's estate in Jamaica to allow you to do any thing else than give my proxy *against it*.' The consequence would be the loss of our possessions in the West Indies:

I don't say that ought to stop us if we could put a stop to this inhuman practice, and it would be equally moral never to employ spies, never to go to war, and more Christian-like to turn the other cheek. But as it is impossible for us to reform the world one must take it as it is. Others will carry on this slave trade if we do not, and if we confine our endeavours to make their situation as comfortable, or at least as free from injustice, as we can, our carrying it on instead of other nations who may not be so

---

* Depriving her of Venetia, Dalmatia and the Tyrol and setting up the Confederation of the Rhine in place of the Holy Roman Empire.

attentive to these points may serve the purposes of humanity much better than throwing that trade into other hands whereby the poor slaves may be still worse off than they now are.

These were among the standard arguments employed by opponents of abolition. Richmond for once does not hope to reform the world, and in this matter he was not on the side of freedom.

A few weeks later came the news of Fox's death (at the age of fifty-seven), which he had met as courageously as he had lived outrageously, unable now to read but attentive to Lord and Lady Holland as they read to him from Swift, Crabbe and the *Aeneid.* His last words were to his wife: 'It don't signify, my dearest, dearest Liz.'

Richmond's reflections to Holland were conventional. 'To die happy and without pain is all that we can wish for in that dissolution that awaits us all; and, believe me, to avoid old age is to escape from great misery, both of body and mind; for great as Mr. Fox's situation was, it is easy to conceive that had he lived he must have been exposed to many vexations.' He says, quite inaccurately, that Fox's hopes had not hitherto been disappointed and that he was still 'in the full exercise of all his faculties with power to give them effect.' Fox had been ailing for some while, with his upper body wasted and fluid drawn from his abdomen and legs. Nevertheless, 'a death so circumstanced is really more to be envied than lamented as far as the person concerned but must be deeply felt by those who were so attached to him as you was. It is such survivors who are the only sufferers.' This is not the noblest of epitaphs on a man who was capable of gross turpitude but has left a memory that many cherished, and do still.

24

The Last Years at Goodwood

THE DUKE SPENT ALL HIS DECLINING YEARS at Goodwood. London journeys were tiring, and visits to Aubigny were made uncongenial or impossible by the attitude of the French Revolutionary government. For his political comments and aspirations, such as they were, Lord Holland was an apparently willing intermediary, and he would be similarly used when Richmond was concerned for his Aubigny title. Only with the militia and his plan of national defence, costly and somewhat unrealistic, was he personally active. Meanwhile he had financial affairs to set in order, an estate to superintend, a house to be made worthy of his name, a new 'family' to be guided by his compulsion to edify and instruct.

Thoughts of coming decrepitude sometimes occupied him, as was natural at his age. The death of the fifth Duke of Bedford* caused him to reflect that 'the vicissitudes of life are a sad drawback to enjoyment of it, but they prepare us old folks to the approaching necessity of quitting it with less regret.' The family were falling away: Thomas Conolly in 1803, George Napier the following year, then Lord George.

Napier's death brought some unpleasantness with Sarah. Most of their married life had been spent at Celbridge in County Kildare. Napier never earned much money – for a time he was a superintendent at Woolwich Arsenal, a modest position given him by Richmond – and when he died Sarah was left with an annuity of £500 and her younger children still to support. She asked Richmond for a loan so that she would not have to mortgage the Celbridge property. He 'took two sheets of paper to prove he cannot afford it,' although he was spending lavishly on his new racecourse. Relief came to Sarah in a way she may not have expected. The King granted her a pension of £800 for the education of her daughters and for herself as 'the widow of a valued officer.'[1] Old men do not always forget.

---

* Francis Russell (1765–1802), friend of Fox and full of revolutionary affectations. He wore the French 'crop' of powdered hair without a wig, and Earl Fitzwilliam said it made him look like a Bow Street Runner. He demolished Bedford House, his family's home in Bloomsbury built by Inigo Jones, and developed the site as fashionable squares.

Although during fits of depression Richmond was half in love with easeful death, no mood ever stayed with him for long, and he would be busy on the farm or sailing in his sloop at Itchenor or supervising his men as they prepared for the races. His farming methods had been praised by Burke in letters to Charles O'Hara, who was having difficulty in getting good results from his land in Ireland: 'I spoke high things on the Duke of Richmond's farm, and I spoke but the truth. In saying that he did not drill and horse-hoe, I did not mean to insinuate that he did not make clean fallows for his wheat, and hoe his turnips; but this is by the hand, and in the common method.' In general his ideas were 'admirable and very near ordinary practice. He never uses the horse-hoe; but he never raises potatoes or beans.'

Then there was the house. Although he had been forced to relinquish the grand design which he had formed with Wyatt, Goodwood itself was full of treasures: the Gobelins tapestries, the porcelain from Sèvres, Bacon's fireplace, Anne Damer's dogs, curious clock in which he had a special interest, a suite of Louis XV furniture by Delanois, paintings, portraits, engravings by George Vertue, busts by Nollekens, prints, sculptures, ivories and silver. All this was recorded by D. Jacques, the fourth Duke's librarian, whose *A Visit to Goodwood* was written in 1822; since the fourth Duke was not a great collector, and had to retrench financially, the contents of the house would not have changed very much. Jacques in his library had charge of 9000 volumes; the Card-Room, placed in one of Wyatt's circular towers, had a round carpet designed and woven at Axminster, where manufacture had begun in the middle of the century; seascapes, two by the contemporary Samuel Scott, recall Richmond's love of yachting. The portraits* include nearly all the family and their predecessors. The Duke himself was a much painted man, by Reynolds, Romney (twice) and Zoffany as well as by Batoni and Mengs; the Duchess was painted by Reynolds seven times, and she also sat for Gainsborough; three of the sisters (Caroline, Emily and Louisa) are in the collection, and so are the first two Dukes and their spouses. A little farther back in history is the splendid James Stuart, one of the Scottish Lennoxes and third Duke of Richmond of the former creation. An unwavering royalist, he was present at the beheading of Charles I and was permitted by the regicides to take the body to St George's Chapel, Windsor. (The King's shirt and a lock of his hair is now on view at Goodwood.)

While there are several formal Old Master paintings of King Charles II at Goodwood it is a less praiseworthy 'work of art' which brings to life the venality

---

* *Goodwood*, written in 1839 by W. H. Mason, another ducal librarian, lists, with short descriptions, 233 paintings in the house at that date, but some would have been added after the Duke's death. Copies of this book and Jacques's are in the West Sussex Record Office.

103 A bull moose sent as a present from the Governor-General of Canada to the Duke of Richmond, who was interested in domesticating the species. The painting, by George Stubbs, was commissioned by William Hunter and shows the yearling moose near the horns of a fully grown animal. Hunter was making a detailed study of the antlers as part of a comparison of moose with European elk.

of his Court – a lively Edwardian representation of John Evelyn's visit to Whitehall in February 1685:

I can never forget the inexpressible luxury and profaneness, gaming and dissoluteness, and as it were total forgetfulness of God (it being Sunday evening) which this day I was witness of: the King sitting and toying with his concubines, Portsmouth, Cleveland and Mazarine, &c., a French boy singing love-songs in that glorious gallery, whilst about twenty of the great courtiers and other dissolute persons were at basset round a large table, a bank of at least 2000 in gold before them.

Six days later Charles II was dead and 'all was in the dust.'

Imaginative accounts in local newspapers show that rural life had its hazards. The Duke had a narrow escape when a wolf from the menagerie 'flew at him and catched hold of his waistcoat upon the belly', and 'when his Grace was retreating catched hold of the skirt of his coat; but fortunately his Grace, after a long struggle, escaped, leaving part of his coat behind him.' On another occasion the hounds drove a fox 'into a poor woman's hog-pen at Duncton' and she 'went into the pen with a large stick with intent to kill him.' But 'the dogs making a noise are supposed to have terrified the poor woman for as soon as she came out of the pen, she dropped down dead.' In 1803 the *Lewes Journal* reported that a spaniel bitch at Goodwood 'whelped five puppies, three of which had only two legs each, which were situated behind.' Thus two had no forelegs but the third 'had very short stumps, projecting from the shoulder-bones.'*

Many of the works of art at Goodwood had come from Aubigny, and others had been acquired during the Duke's regular visits to France, but this source had now dried up and he was worried about his property. Aubigny had been sequestered by the Republicans in 1795 but restored at the Peace of Amiens (1802), and in August 1806 he asked Lord Holland[2] to be his 'plenipotentiary' in trying to secure his possession in any future treaty. Since 1802 his agents had received the rents but 'owing to the plunder and destruction of the Republicans all the produce has hitherto been employed in necessary repairs, so that I have never touched a shilling, nor do I suppose . . . it will ever produce me above £500 a year . . . But £500 a year is something and such an old possession in France worth retaining.'

Holland had been travelling in Europe between 1802 and 1805 and had met Talleyrand, the Foreign Minister, suave and sinuous, one of the few men who made Napoleon feel uncomfortable. Richmond hoped that Talleyrand would act handsomely in the matter, but the French government still laid claim to the woods, the most valuable part of the property; and French laws of succession

* London, too, had its perils. The Duke was nearly mugged when three footpads stopped his coach in Kensington. He drew his sword 'but on one of the villains putting a pistol to his head, with fearful imprecations, he returned it to the scabbard and delivered his purse, with three or four guineas in it.'

would complicate the inheritance. He doubted whether the possession would ever again be financially rewarding. So it turned out. Napoleon seized Aubigny in 1806, shortly before the third Duke's death. Later, in spite of the fact that the fourth Duke did homage to Louis XVIII, the courts, in accordance with Napoleonic law, subsequently ordered the property to be sold and the proceeds to be distributed among the heirs. Thus the Lennox connection ceased.

The last of Richmond's grand enterprises at Goodwood was the building of the racecourse. Informal racing had probably taken place on the Downs for many years, and it was from such local gatherings of small-time farmers and contests arranged by militias as part of their training that the Goodwood Races were born. In 1800 the Duke invited the officers of the Petworth militia to hold their meeting at Goodwood because for some reason they could not have their usual course. The event must have been such a success that he had the idea of making it a regular occasion, and an official one-day meeting was held in the following April.

A course was laid out under the direction of Henry King, overseer of the woodmen and labourers, who 'had orders to keep strict time, from 7 a.m. to 5 p.m., and not to suffer any irregularities.'[3] It was 'much admired by the acknowledged amateurs of the Turf' when a large company attended and 'five or six roomy tents were pitched, in each of which collations, consisting of every dainty in season, were profusely served up.' A ball was held in the town in the evening but the Duke was not able to be present. Ill with gout, he had not left his tent all day and he retired to bed when the racing was over.

Unmindful of his plans for reducing expenditure, he held a three-day race meeting in 1802 and built a small wooden stand for the spectators. Balls and theatre parties and lavish hospitality attracted distinguished patronage, and the traditions of 'Glorious Goodwood' had been established. (In 1803 the weather was bad – April can be a cruel month 700 feet above sea-level – and before long the date was changed to July.)

A Chichester newspaper wrote handsomely of the meeting of 1802:

> To the efforts of equestrian skill is to be added the princely and almost unprecedented munificence of the noble founder of the Goodwood Races, in providing the new erected stand with a collation which might be entitled a general refrigarium, for the access was as easy as the reception was elegant and hospitable. The thanks of the county in general, and of this city and its vicinity in particular, are largely due to his Grace the Duke of Richmond for having thus munificently and liberally instituted an establishment of most material local benefit in every point of view ... We can only add our wish that the illustrious founder may for years enjoy in health and happiness this promising scion, planted by his own hand, a wish in which we shall be joined by all Sussex patriots.

But August is overtaking July when the Goodwood meeting ends, and local lore has it that the first touch of winter is on the tail of the last horse past the post in the final race. The Duke did not live to see his 'scion' grow from promise into rich fulfilment.

The last months of his life were saddened by disappointment in his heir, Charles Lennox. His letters became longer as he grew older, and a massive remonstrance[4] in June 1804 showed how painful the 'generation gap' could be for a man with a high sense of family responsibility. Richmond had earlier been reproachful over the disagreement about Fox and Pitt. The complaint this time arose from Charles Lennox's decision to continue his army career, but all sorts of little grievances and misunderstandings emerge.

The Duke would have liked to talk over this decision, 'but the extreme reserve you always show to open yourself to me on any occasion is certainly one of those things that hurt me in your conduct towards me . . . You appear to have a regard and a sense of gratitude for former and present attentions but no wish to make an intimate friend of me.' Even on pecuniary matters 'by short answers you endeavour to get rid of it as soon as you could. Such coldness, you must be sensible, will have its effect on the openness and warmth of my disposition.'

Disparity of age may be a bar to complete frankness, but 'a parent under whom one has long been educated makes a difference, and while you are no longer a boy [Charles was thirty-one] I trust I have never been either severe, morose or dry.' The impediment is . . .

. . . in your close disposition, and desire to live in more idle company . . . On my part as I grow old and my time short what have I to look to for the continuation of my family, and the various schemes one forms for its benefit and advantages, but you? In you centres my future pride for the family. I am anxious both for your character and happiness as its probable representative . . . I am not ambitious for you in any way, for I too well know that ambition leads only to vexation . . . I wish you to take care of your numerous family, which is one of the first duties of a father, and for that purpose to be prudent rationally economical and above all things regular, or you will be ruined.

Richmond appears to have feared a disposition to riotous living. Charles may enjoy his domestic life, but:

. . . I do not mean having your house always full of companions inclined to encourage you to drink, which will only promote dissipation and idleness, but a few rational friends, your main resources being always in yourself, your family and your home concerns. Now I confess it is a melancholy prospect to me to see that your turn is very different . . . You suffer foolish passions to interfere with a domestic life. You too often seek in wine to forget care, and sometimes in company that does you no credit.

Because Charles disliked doing accounts he was neglecting his affairs, so that if some accident befell him, his family 'must be left literally without bread.' It was his duty to keep proper accounts and save, at least until he had put them above actual want. The Duke would like with his experience to instruct Charles in the management of the estate. He could provide hunting, shooting and pleasant neighbours, if only Charles would visit more often and not make poor excuses

104 (RIGHT) The fourth Duke of Richmond. Miniature by Charles Robertson. He was Lord-Lieutenant of Ireland and subsequently Governor-General of Upper and Lower Canada, where he died.

105 (BELOW) Hounds of the Charlton Hunt (detail from a painting by Stubbs). After the fourth Duke discontinued the Hunt (by now called the Goodwood Hunt) he gave the hounds to the Prince of Wales.

for staying away. Besides, 'if you were more domestic, Lady Charlotte would be more pleasant.'

Was Charles wise to stay in the Army? 'With the swarms of Princes that we have,' the prospects were not too happy for a man who had not studied military administration or acquired German and other European languages.

He apologises finally for a very long letter, but 'I feel low and uncomfortable and neglected, perhaps soured by perpetual successions of painful disorders which make me the more want the attentions of those I love . . . My notions may be erroneous but I am sure they are dictated by the purest affection for you.' To his nephew, no doubt, this was Richmond's 'intolerable consanguinity' but the old man was lonely, in physical pain, and disappointed in his hopes of being recalled to office. Above all, he was upset because he was not being consulted in his role as head of the family and he felt that his heir lacked a proper sense of filial duty and respect.

In fact his anxieties were ungrounded. Lennox's first obligation as the fourth Duke (which his uncle omitted to mention) was to get the estate out of debt. Partly to this end he discontinued the Charlton Hunt and gave the hounds to the Prince of Wales, after which they developed rabies and had to be destroyed. His wife* bore him seven sons and seven daughters – all but one of whom grew to maturity – and she was hostess at the famous ball on the eve of Waterloo. After a term as Lord Lieutenant of Ireland, the Duke was made Governor General of Canada, where he died from the bite of a rabid fox and was buried under the altar of the Anglican Cathedral in Quebec. For his failure to be a great huntsman he compensated by being one of the outstanding amateur cricketers of his day, playing with great professionals like Beldham, Fennex and Aylward. His son continued the family's patronage of the game and in 1826 was President of the Marylebone Cricket Club.[5]

The third Duke's final will[6] left the bulk of the estate to Lennox and revised earlier arrangments for Henriette. In 1800, when she was about twenty-eight, a property had been bought in her name at West Wittering, and at about the same time the Duke persuaded the ageing Romney, then living near by at Eartham, to paint her portrait. It shows her in the open air stroking a dog, and is similar to an earlier portrait by John Downman. Both pictures are still at Goodwood. By the terms of the will she was to receive a house and park at West Lavant, with other farms and properties amounting to quite a substantial gift of land within a few miles of Goodwood. It was clearly intended that she should continue to be a close neighbour of the family. Personal bequests included furniture from two of Richmond's houses and 'my other repeating timekeeper watch . . . also my curricle & any the harnes, & any six of my horses & six of my dogs she may choose.' She was to be set up as a gentlewoman of some quality.

---

* Lady Charlotte Gordon, daughter of the Duke of Gordon.

Richmond left to her also 'all such Letters, Copies of Letters, Correspondence, Manuscript Books and written papers of every kind belonging to me at my death, whether relating to public or private Affairs and whether found at my House at Goodwood or my House at Whitehall or elsewhere, as bear date or have been written since the decease of my Father and do not concern the Titles to any of my Estates and property'. Henriette is to offer to return to the writers any letters that Richmond has received from them, but the implication is that he wished her to preserve the rest. They, along with a considerable amount of material relating to the Duke's career, have disappeared.

It has been proposed – even assumed – that carelessly, or misguidedly, or maliciously, Henriette destroyed them. She has been such an enigmatic figure that it is possible to believe anything of her, even that she deliberately caused the fire at Richmond House, which broke out in the 'bed furniture' in her room. But Richmond loved her, and the scanty evidence suggests that she loved him; and her subsequent gratitude and attachment to the Goodwood family make deliberate acts of malice very unlikely. Possibly the letters and papers were thrown away, perhaps by her son, many years later because they were thought to be no longer interesting or important.

In 1808 Henriette was married at St James's, Piccadilly, to John Dorrien, the ceremony being performed by the Bishop of Chichester. Dorrien, who was some fifteen years older than his bride, was a professional soldier with long service in the Horse Guards, and he rose to the rank of general. A son born within a year was given the Lennox name of Charles, and the fourth Duke was a godfather.

They lived in Henriette's house at West Lavant and occasional correspondence, particuarly after Dorrien's death in 1815, suggests a continuing link with the Richmonds. Henriette in old age became very maternal about her son Charles, whose deafness disqualified him from a military career. She regretted that he was 'a sad Tory', but he wanted to be painter and she asked the fifth Duke if he might practise by copying some of the pictures at Goodwood. When the fifth Duke inherited the Gordon estates in Scotland he invited Charles to stay at Gordon Castle, and Henriette apologises for his failings as a correspondent. She transferred the lease of the Lavant house to him so that he might always have 'a home in the friendly neighbourhood of yourself and your sons.'

Henriette died in 1846 and was buried in the Dorrien family vault in Hertfordshire. Charles Dorrien, who did not make his name as a painter and perhaps was somewhat ineffectual, seems never to have married. In 1853 he says that he has sent the Duke 'the papers I have been able to find but they are mixed up with other papers of no public importance . . . I felt sure I had more papers somewhere about the defence of the country, also the miscellaneous volume containing the account of Jersey . . . a sheet sent to Mr Pitt.' Maybe Charles was no great judge of what was of 'public importance'.

By 1805 Richmond's health had deteriorated. He was unable to go to Windsor when the King in person was to present the Horse Guards with a pair of silver kettle-drums. These two self-willed men had had a long and confused relationship, and in his last letter to his Sovereign[7] Richmond wrote of his 'extreme mortification' that a severe illness confined him to his bed. 'I can therefore only in this way humbly offer to your Majesty the dutiful sense of obligation I feel for this and every other mark of the immediate protection of your Majesty under which, from their peculiar situation and I hope good conduct, your Majesty has been pleased to take your only Regiment of Horse Guards, in the command of which, under your Majesty, it is the pride of my declining life to have been placed by your Majesty's spontaneous will and pleasure.'

In the following summer he predicted to Holland[8] that William Cobbett, if elected to Parliament, would 'grow too prolix and become tedious and tiresome,' but he could not write very much because in killing his pain he was stupefied with opium. In September he was too unwell to attend Fox's funeral, being 'crippled in my feet,' but it was the gout affecting his right hand that prevented him from completing this letter. Someone else, probably Henriette, explained that he was 'incapable of moving a finger.'

In the last painful months he once again had Sarah with him at Goodwood. Charles Napier, her eldest son, had helped to reconcile them when as an intelligent young subaltern he had enjoyed playing war games with the old man as they studied local maps and planned the defence of Sussex. Sarah afterwards wrote to Lady Susan:

> I shall not dwell much on events of last summer except with respect to my dear brother, who became dear to me as I saw myself more beloved and useful to him. It softened the *past* pains and led me to enjoy the present pleasure of devoting to his age, infirmities and returning love that sacrifice of anger it has cost me so much to make. I have been amply repaid by passing the last four months of his life almost entirely with him.

Richmond died on Sunday the 29th of December 1806. 'He had for some days been insensible, but without pain,' Ogilvie told Lord Holland. 'The Duchess of Leinster bears the account of this melancholy event as well as could be expected. She has for some time looked forward to it as a probable event in view of his health.'

He directed that his body be slaked with lime to absorb the foul air and that the funeral should be carried out in a 'private and inexpensive manner.' He was buried in the family vault in Chichester Cathedral.

25

The Richmond Legacy

VERY FEW OF THE THOUSANDS who every year attend the races and who visit the beautiful house and its treasures know anything about the man who more than any other created Goodwood and its incomparable setting. Of all the eighteenth-century dukes, he was unquestionably the most imaginative, inventive and far-sighted, yet the names of his close associates – Burke and Rockingham – register themselves more readily in the public mind.

This anomaly is probably due more to the diversity of his interests than to anything else, for his achievements were considerable. As a professional soldier he was respected throughout his life. He originated the Ordnance Survey, encouraged innovation in the development of small arms, and sponsored the Royal Horse Artillery. His plans for electoral reform were over a hundred years ahead of his time. He fought for the liberties of Americans, Irish, Catholics, Dissenters, publishers, printers and voters. He opened an academy where young English artists could study the work of the great masters, and later he gave George Stubbs his first important employment. At Goodwood he built the house and stables, which have remained virtually unchanged to this day, and added sixteen thousand acres to the estate; his collection of porcelain, tapestries, furniture and paintings are among England's great art treasures.

Throughout this narrative, enough of his quirks and infirmities have been revealed to explain why contemporaries found him a 'difficult' man. Sometimes he displayed the peacock arrogance of his class, and in all his transactions he could be impulsive, overbearing, and too insistent on the correctness of his own opinions. Sarah was shrewd about this: 'He will try to be so very right that he will be very wrong.' His didacticism would provoke resentment and resistance. Burke had warned him that close adherence to his principles would cause him to be thought intractable. He was too full of rectitude, was 'of little management with the world, and had not troubled to give himself a flattering exterior!'

Burke usually treated him as a rather erratic clock which needed to be kept fully wound, because in some moods he was too sensitive to defeat and after a setback would abandon schemes that had cost him much thought and energy. 'Perseverance, dear my lord, keeps honour bright.'

Richmond was not a rascal but he was unpredictable, and politically, despite his experience, he was always something of an innocent. Never a 'duke of dark corners', he was no match for the Bedfords with generations of intrigue behind them or for Treasury professionals with homely names like Robinson and Jenkinson. Burke told him that he was not born to be private, and he acknowledged his wider responsibilities, but Goodwood always smoothed life's jagged edges and he was calmer there than ever he was in London. As head of the family no man could have done more. He was warm, considerate and indefatigable, championing their interests and working with fine discrimination to make the house and the estate worthy of their name. Nor is there any reason to doubt Kent's assurance that his tenants and labourers were fond of him, even if in his lordly way he bullied them. The willingness of qualified men like Yeakell and Gardner to follow him to the Ordnance, and the respect he won there from a superb professional like Roy, distinguish him as master and employer.

Except in his demand for impracticably small electoral districts, his programme for parliamentary reform was only delayed by war and revolution. In the United States his name is still honoured. From the start of the quarrel with the Colonists he attacked British policy on principle, not just from expediency: they were a free people in a free land with an inherent right to direct their own affairs. Many of his Whig friends moved towards this view only when they realised that the quarrel was having awkward consequences. He failed to save the formal 'connection' he desired, but American goodwill and co-operation were preserved once the 'Sons of Liberty' had been washed out of the system. A connection with Ireland still exists, after a fashion, although poisoned by ancient grudges and alien interference; Richmond would have preserved it more durably by toleration and the correction of abuses, and this lesson took longer to learn than most. Roman Catholics and schismatic Protestants may practise their religion without loss of civil rights, parliamentary debates may be reported and, broadly, the Commons must accept the elected persons the constituencies send to them. All these were issues for which Richmond fought or argued.

Burke was not wrong when he reminded him that: 'Persons in your station of life ought to have long views ... You perpetuate your benefits from generation to generation. The immediate power of a Duke of Richmond or Marquis of Rockingham is not so much of moment: but if their conduct and example hands down their principles to their successors, then their houses become the public repositories and offices of record for the constitution.'

To a great degree Richmond heeded this admonition. He sought to preserve not to deracinate, and, as an enlightened landowner, to strive for improvement. He wanted to save a structure that had weathered storms before and which to him seemed beneficent, deep-rooted and inevitable. Britain's past, if rightly understood, would safeguard the future freedom of her people.

106 One of the few remaining cedars of Lebanon planted by the third Duke.

Today the Goodwood Estate consists of 12,000 acres and employs around 150 people, some of them still engaged in the time-honoured occupations of farming, forestry, and maintaining the racecourse, while others work for such twentieth-century enterprises as the airfield. Families whose names were known to the third Duke – Waymark, Lillywhite, Budd – still live in the neighbourhood. Some of the Duke's one thousand cedars of Lebanon still stand tall. His works of art still furnish the rooms in which he lived. His descendants still make Goodwood their home.

Chronology

Charles Lennox, third Duke of Richmond, Lennox and Aubigny, KG, PC, FRS, FSA

1735	Born London 22 February: Earl of March.
1745	Enters Westminster School as a Town Boy.
1750	Succeeds to the title of Duke of Richmond, Lennox and Aubigny (8 August).
1752	Sets out on the Grand Tour, visiting among other places, Paris, Vienna, Rome, Naples, Hanover, and Geneva. Returns to England in 1756.
1753	Gazetted Captain in the 20th Regiment of Foot, now Royal Regiment of Fusiliers.
	Graduated from University of Leyden.
1755	Elected Fellow of the Royal Society.
1756	Colonel, 33rd Regiment of Foot, now Duke of Wellington's Regiment (West Riding).
1757	Marries (1 April) Mary, youngest daughter of the third Earl of Ailesbury.
1758	Opens an academy at Richmond House for 'any painter, carver, sculptor or other youth to whom the study of statuary might be useful.'
	Colonel, 72nd Regiment of Foot (disbanded five years later, at the end of the Seven Years War.)
1759	Serves with distinction at the Battle of Minden (1 August) in support of Prince Ferdinand of Brunswick.
1760	Lord of the Bedchamber to King George III, but resigned in the same year.
1761	Carries the Sceptre and Dove at the Coronation of George III.
	Major-General.
	Lord Lieutenant of Sussex.
1765–66	Ambassador Extraordinary and Minister Plenipotentiary to the French Court.
	Admitted to the Privy Council.
1766–67	Secretary of State for the Southern Department in the Marquis of Rockingham's first administration.
1770	Lieutenant-General.
1770–75	Tables eighteen resolutions directed at threats to dissolve Colonial assemblies in America if they would not accept certain propositions sent to them in the King's name.
[1774	Death of Louis XV]
1775	Opposes Lord North's Prohibitory Act forbidding New England Trade and Fisheries.
1776	Formally registers his seigneury of Aubigny in the French parliament.
1778	Moves address in Parliament for the recall of British troops from America.
1779	Supports Rockingham's motion for the removal of the causes of Irish discontent 'by a redress of grievances.'
	Proposes (unsuccessfully) reduction in the Civil List.
1780	Formulates proposals for universal adult male suffrage as part of his 'Declaration of the Rights of Englishmen.'
1782	Invested as Knight of the Garter.
1782–95	Master-General of Ordnance (out of office April–December 1783).
1793	Elected Fellow of the Society of Arts.
1795	Colonel, Royal Regiment of Horse Guards, now the Blues and Royals (Royal Horse Guards and 1st Dragoons).
	Field Marshal.
1796	Death of Duchess Mary.
1777	Colonel, 2nd Battalion 35th Regiment, now the Queen's Regiment.
1804	Publishes his *Thoughts on National Defence*.
	Speaks in the House of Lords for the last time (25 June).
1806	Dies at Goodwood (29 December).

Notes and Sources

Abbreviations used for sources repeated throughout the notes.

BM Add.MS	British Museum Additional MS.
Burke *Correspondence*	*The Correspondence of Edmund Burke*, ed. Thomas W. Copeland and others, 1958–70.
Cannon	John Cannon, *Aristocratic Century, The Peerage of eighteenth-century England*, 1984.
Hoffman	Ross F. J. Hoffman, *The Marquis*, 1973.
Ilchester and Stavordale	*The Life and Letters of Lady Sarah Lennox*, ed. Countess of Ilchester and Lord Stavordale, 1901.
Kent	John Kent, *Records and Reminiscences of Goodwood and the Dukes of Richmond*, 1896.
Kynaston	David Kynaston, *The Chancellor of the Exchequer*, 1980.
McCann	Timothy J. McCann, *The Correspondence of the Dukes of Richmond and Newcastle, 1724–1750*, edited for the Sussex Record Society, 1984.
Olson	Alison G. Olson, *The Radical Duke*, 1962.
Parliamentary History	*The Parliamentary History of England.*
Rockingham *Memoirs*	Memoirs of the Marquis of Rockingham and His Contemporaries, ed. George Thomas, Earl of Albemarle. 1852.
Trevelyan	G. O. Trevelyan, *The Early Life of Charles James Fox*, 1880.
Walpole *Correspondence*	*Horace Walpole's Correspondence*, ed. W. S. Lewis, 1937–83.
WSRO	West Sussex Record Office.
Western	J. R. Western, *The English Militia in the Eighteenth Century*, 1965.

NOTES

Chapter 1

1 *The Correspondence of Edmund Burke*, ed. Thomas W. Copeland and others, 1958–70, Vol.II, p.377.

2 Alison G. Olson, *The Radical Duke*, 1962, prints a valuable selection of correspondence relating to Richmond's public career, but this mainly hostile portrait is one-sided and incomplete because it neglects the personal and family affairs that were equally important to him.

3 G. O. Trevelyan, *The Early Life of Charles James Fox*, 1880, p.83, pp.81–90 give a lively account of the consequences of gambling and alcoholic excess. This stylish and entertaining book has an outdated Whiggish bias (the author was Macaulay's nephew and biographer), but as a portrait of a vanished society it is still worth reading.

4 For a closer view of this patrician England, see John Cannon, *Aristocratic Century*, 1984;

Ian R. Christie, *Stress and Stability in Late-Eighteenth Century Britain*, 1984; J. D. C. Clark, *British Society, 1683–1832*, 1985. Books more concerned with the coarse underbelly of the age include T. H. White, *The Age of Scandal*, 1942; Louis Kronenberger, *Kings and Desperate Men*, 1950; John Wardroper, *Kings, Lords and Wicked Libellers*, 1973.

Chapter 2

1 For the Stuarts in France, see Eileen Westmacott, *The Lion and the Lilies*, 1977.

2 John Kent, *Records and Reminiscences of Goodwood and the Dukes of Richmond*, 1896, pages 3–4. Kent was employed at Goodwood for 34 years, mainly in the service of the fifth Duke. Thus his account of earlier years is founded on gossip and traditions that grew up within the household rather than on verified fact. Although in any family such material usually has a substratum of truth, his statements on the early period have to be received with caution.

3 West Sussex Record Office, Goodwood MSS 155–6; Timothy J. McCann, *The Correspondence of the Dukes of Richmond and Newcastle, 1724–1750*, edited for the Sussex Record Society, 1984, pp.xxxi, 276–80; Kent pp.9–13.

4 McCann, pp.279–82, describes Richmond's reluctance to undertake this embassage. He cannot afford suitable standards of equipage and hospitality unless Pelham pays him an advance of £2000, and he feels that the honour of 'being His Majesty's Master of the Horse is as great to me as being appointed his Ambassador.' Newcastle's intervention helped to change the King's mind; 'I am extremely happy in being quit of an employment I never liked.' (The third Duke did not much like it either when he was given a similar employment in 1765, but his reasons were different.)

5 McCann, p.xxix. His edition of the correspondence has a summary of Richmond's career and achievements that has been liberally used in this chapter.

6 Priscilla Napier, *The Sword Dance*, 1971, p.24.

7 McCann, p.xxxiv, writes that 'it is clear from his correspondence that hunting was the ruling passion of his life.'

8 The chase in 1738 is described in WSRO Goodwood MSS 151, and also by Kent, during pp.214–22. For hunting generally, see McCann, pp.xxviii and xxxiv and *passim* throughout the correspondence; and for the third Duke's policies, Kent pp.38–9.

9 WSRO, Goodwood MSS 1883, 1884; John Marshall, *The Duke Who Was Cricket*, 1961.

10 McCann, p.xxxvi.

11 McCann, p.xxx.

Chapter 3

1 Sources for the Lennox sisters and their correspondence, used throughout this book, are: *The Correspondence of Emily, Duchess of Leinster*, ed. Brian Fitzgerald, 1949–53; Fitzgerald, *Emily, Duchess of Leinster*, 1949; Fitzgerald, *Lady Louisa Conolly*, 1950; Countess of Ilchester and Lord Stavordale, *Life and Letters of Lady Sarah Lennox*, 1901; Priscilla Napier, *The Sword Dance*, 1971, and *My Brother Richmond* (unpublished).

2 Holland House Papers, BM Add.MS 51424.

Chapter 4

1 The letters in this chapter, based on papers at Goodwood and Holland House, are taken from *A Duke and his Friends*, by the Earl of March, 1911. The author was later the eighth Duke.

2 Printed in the above (Vol.II, pp.707–11), but not in full, the author finding it necessary 'to make free use of the blue pencil before venturing to place it before the reader.'

3 John R. Baker, *Abraham Trembley of Geneva: Scientist and Philosopher, 1710–1784*, 1952, pp.38–9.

4 *Ibid.*, pp.134–5.

5 *Ibid.*, pp.138–47.

6 Holland House Papers, BM Add.MS 51424.

7 *Horace Walpole's Correspondence*, ed. W. S. Lewis, 1937–83, Vol.21, pp.173–4.

8 Margaret Whitney, *Sculpture in Britain*, Pelican History of Art, 1964, pp.136–41.

9 Quoted in Arthur B. Chamberlain, *George Romney*, 1910, p.43. Richmond was Romney's greatest patron, as his father had been Canaletto's. Romney painted Richmond

several times between 1776 and 1795, and he also painted Henriette Le Clerc. The Duke commissioned Romney portraits of, among others, Burke, Lord George Lennox, Lord John Cavendish and the Hon Mrs Damer.

Chapter 5

1 WSRO, Goodwood MSS 224.
2 WSRO, Goodwood MSS 233.
3 *Ibid.*, MSS 223.
4 *Ibid.*, MSS 206.

Chapter 6

1 *Letters from George III to Lord Bute, 1756–1766*, ed. Romney Sedgwick, 1939, pp.36–9,
2 Holland House Papers, BM Add.MS 51424.

Chapter 7

1 Fox's political memoirs are printed in the Ilchester & Stavordale edition of Lady Sarah's life and letters.
2 WSRO, Goodwood MSS 144.
3 John Harris, *Sir William Chambers*, 1970, pp.41–2, 209.
4 Printed in *The Listener*, 9 April 1964.
5 Kent is discursive. He writes of the third Duke, often repetitiously, on pp.19–42.
6 WSRO, Goodwood MSS 229.
7 *The History of Parliament: The House of Commons 1754–1790*, ed. Sir Lewis Namier and John Brooke, 1964, pp.390–3.
8 Walpole *Correspondence*, Vol.22, pp.148–9.

Chapter 8

1 See Stanley Ayling, *George the Third*, 1972; John Brooke, *King George III, 1972; W. A. Spek, Stress and Stability: England 1714–1760*, 1977; Ian R. Christie, *Wars and Revolutions: Britain 1760–1815*, 1982; J. D. C. Clark, *Revolution and Rebellion*, 1986.
2 John Brooke (above), pp.55–8.
3 For illustrative documents on the powers of the Crown, parties and 'influence' see *The Eighteenth Century Constitution*, ed. E. N. Williams, 1965, pp.67–89, 173–86.
4 See Ian R. Christie, 'George III and the Historians', *History*, Vol.71, p.232, 1986. The article criticises earlier Whig and Marxist interpretations and demonstrates the continuity in George III's methods.
5 Bute's involvement is suggested in Basil Williams, *The Whig Supremacy*, revised edition 1965, pp.354–6.
6 Quoted by P. D. G. Thomas in 'George III and the American Revolution', *History*, Vol.70, p.228, 1985. Professor Thomas argues that throughout the conflict the King was careful not to initiate personal policies. He only regretted having consented to the repeal of the Stamp Act.
7 Parliamentary History, Vol.XXII, p.149.
8 Probably every statement in it would be challenged by one or other of the scholars who have lately studied aspects of the period. A thunderous 'revisionism' has disturbed the once-placid waters, and no one is safe any longer – not even Lewis Namier.
9 Ross S. J. Hoffman, *The Marquis*, 1973, pp.10–28. This is a full biography by an American scholar, of a statesman who until recently has been strangely neglected.
10 Quoted in Hoffman, p.176.
11 *Ibid.*, p.220.
12 *Ibid.*, p.262.
13 Quoted in Trevelyan, p.124.
14 Burke *Correspondence*, Vol.IV, pp.235–6. The editors note that the occasion when Richmond gave this 'public approbation' has not been identified. Hoffman shows (pp.232–6) that Rockingham proposed a publication to give 'right ideas to the public' and was critical of Burke for taking so long to produce it. Some members of the party, Savile especially, feared that the pamphlet would do more harm than good. It is likely, however, that Richmond approved of its general principles.
15 Quoted in E. N. Williams (Note 3, above), pp. 75–6.

Chapter 9

1 WSRO, Goodwood MSS 208.
2 Holland House Papers, BM Add.MS 51424.
3 Olson, p.111.
4 Walpole *Correspondence*, Vol.7, pp.279–80.
5 Joseph Massie, *Observations on the New Cyder Tax*, 1764.
6 Paul Langford, *The First Rockingham Administration*, 1973, pp.238–45.

7 WSRO, Goodwood MSS 192.
8 Walpole *Correspondence*, Vol.30, pp.228–32.
9 Cannon, p.176.

Chapter 10

1 McCann, pp.89, 107, 110.
2 Walpole *Correspondence*, Vol.31, p.301.
3 Burke *Correspondence*, Vol.II, pp.544–5; Vol.III, pp.26–7, 198–200.

Chapter 11

1 *The Marquis of Rockingham and his Contemporaries*, ed. the Earl of Albemarle, 1852, Vol.I, pp.59–63.
2 David Kynaston, *The Chancellor of the Exchequer*, 1980, p.18.
3 WSRO, Goodwood MSS 225.
4 Quoted in Olson, p.130.
5 Burke *Correspondence*, Vol.II, pp.66–7.
6 Quoted in Olson, p.141.
7 Gibbon's *Autobiography*, ed. Birkbeck Hill, 1900, Appendix 43.
8 Burke *Correspondence*, Vol.II, pp.67–8.

Chapter 12

1 Burke *Correspondence*, Vol.I, pp.220–1.
2 *Parliamentary History*, Vol.XVII, pp.214–6.
3 Olson, p.151.
4 Burke *Correspondence*, Vol.II, pp.370–1.
5 *Ibid.*, pp.372–8, from a rough draft amended by the editors.
6 *Ibid.*, Vol.III, pp.39–40.
7 Olson, p.155.
8 Trevelyan, p.47.
9 Kynaston, p.19.
10 See P. G. Mackesey, *The War for America, 1775–1873*, 1964, for the complexities of the war and North's efforts to deal with them.
11 Burke *Correspondence*, Vol.III, p.365.
12 Walpole *Correspondence*, Vol.31, p.188.
13 N. A. M. Rodger, *The Admiralty*, 1978, pp.71–81.
14 Mackesey (above), pp.51–4.
15 Rockingham *Memoirs*, Vol.II, pp.360–1.
16 For the Fighting Instructions and the importance of 'the line', see Michael Lewis, *The History of the British Navy*, 1957, pp.44–5, 131–6, 161; Oliver Warner, *The Navy*, 1963, pp.24–5, 63–4.
17 WSRO, Goodwood MSS 212.
18 Burke *Correspondence*, Vol.IV, p.113.
19 *Parliamentary History*, Vol.XX, pp.979–85. For a general study, see J. R. Western, *The English Militia in the Eighteenth Century*, 1965.
20 Osbert Sitwell and Margaret Barton, *Brighton*, 1935, pp.83–5.
21 Petworth House Archives 69.

Chapter 13

1 *Parliamentary History*, Vol.XVI, pp.1010–14.
2 Burke *Correspondence*, Vol.III, pp.218–9.
3 Hoffman, p.328.
4 *Parliamentary History*, Vol.XVIII, pp.1065–78.
5 Charles Greville, *Journal*, ed. Henry Reeve, 1874, p.129.
6 Rockingham *Memoirs*, Vol.II, pp.308–9.
7 *Ibid.*, pp.310–11.
8 WSRO, Goodwood MSS 210.
9 *Parliamentary History*, Vol.XXIX, pp.1012–21.
10 *Ibid.*, Vol.XXII, pp.966–71.
11 These two extracts from magazines are in a group of miscellaneous, unclassified documents at Goodwood House. In the second, the source is missing and only two pages of a longer article are present. The pages are not consecutive.

Chapter 14

1 See Christie, *Wars and Revolutions*, pp.80–6, for a summary of a complex problem.
2 Hoffman, p.279.
3 Olson, pp.38–9, 154–6, 159–67.
4 Walpole *Correspondence*, Vol.41, pp.300–01.
5 Burke *Correspondence*, Vol.I, p.390.

Chapter 15

1 Olson, p.185.
2 *Parliamentary History*, Vol.XX, pp.649–51.
3 Olson, p.157.
4 Burke *Correspondence*, Vol.IV, pp.165–8.
5 *Parliamentary History*, Vol.XXI, pp.664–72.
6 Goodwood Miscellaneous.
7 Burke *Correspondence*, Vol.II, p.419.
8 *Ibid.*, pp.429–30.
9 G. S. Veitch, *The Genesis of Parliamentary Reform*, 1965 edition, p.70.

Chapter 16

1 Rockingham *Memoirs*, Vol.II, p.467.
2 Hoffman, pp.378–9.

3 Rockingham *Memoirs*, Vol.II, pp.467–8.
4 *Correspondence of King George the Third*, ed. Sir John Fortescue, 1927, p.165.
5 Michael Lewis, *The History of the British Navy*, 1957, p.182.
6 *Parliamentary History*, Vol.XXII, pp.188–9.
7 Walpole *Correspondence*, Vol.25, pp.295–6.
8 *Parliamentary History*, Vol.XXIII, pp.154–6.
9 *Memorials and Correspondence of Charles James Fox*, ed. Russell, 1853, Vol.I, p.455. For a more detailed account of events in this chapter, see John Cannon *The Fox-North Coalition: Crisis of the Constitution 1782–1784*, 1969.

Chapter 17

1 R. A. Skelton, 'The Origins of the Ordnance Survey of Great Britain', in the *Geographical Journal*, 1962, Vol.XXVIII, pp.415–26.
2 Public Record Office, WO/18.
3 *Historical and Posthumous Memoirs of Sir Nathaniel Wraxall*, ed. H. B. Wheatley, 1884, Vol.IV, p.104.
4 The Annual Register, *History of Europe (1786)*, Vol.XXVIII, pp.96–108; *Parliamentary History*, Vol.XXV, pp.1096–1156.
5 *Parliamentary History*, Vol.XXVI, pp.589–95.
6 *Ibid.*, Vol.XXIX, pp.1517–22.
7 Goodwood Miscellaneous, source not stated.
8 As well as containing important information Skelton's article (see above) reproduces some of these maps. See also Sir Charles Close, *Early Years of the Ordnance Survey*, 1969 edition.
9 WSRO, Goodwood MSS 229.
10 Skelton (above), p.422.

Chapter 18

1 Kent, p.37.
2 Anthony Dale, *James Wyatt*, 1956, pp.54–7.
3 Kent, p.26.
4 WSRO Goodwood MSS 228.
5 *Ibid.*, MSS 244.
6 *Ibid.*, MSS 227.

Chapter 19

1 Sybil Rosenfeld, *Temples of Thespis*, 1978, makes a detailed study of private theatres and productions between 1700 and 1820. The Richmond theatricals are described pp.34–52.
2 Rosenfeld, p.47, wrongly attributes this play to Murphy.

Chapter 20

1 Olson, pp.86–8.
2 *Ibid.*, pp.214–18.
3 WSRO, Goodwood MSS 228.
4 The correspondence for 1794–5 is in the Goodwood archives.

Chapter 21

1 R. B. McDowell, *Ireland in the Age of Imperialism and Revolution, 1760–1801*, 1979, p.595.
2 Holland House Papers, BM Add.MSS 51802.
3 McDowell, p.654.

Chapter 22

1 A few miscellaneous items from the accounts illustrate the responsibilities of a noble household. In 1797 rents from the estate farms brought in £5429, coppices £654, quit-rents £73; yearly rents from 50 cottage tenants yielded only £164, much the highest figure being £12 from the tenant of the Waterbeach Inn (now the Goodwood Park Hotel).

In December 1799, nine months after launching the scheme to liquidate his debts, the Duke made an exhaustive 'recapitulation' of his expenditure. (It included a few items for 'London Buildings', the house he used in Whitehall in place of Richmond House.) Wages paid to 29 house servants at Goodwood came to £960, of which £150 with a house was the salary of the manager or principal agent; wages at Itchenor were £142; 30 employees in the stables received £764 with a further £154 for liveries; 5 hunt servants £184 with £153 for liveries; 4 gamekeepers £105; the lady who looked after the Pheasantry £15; 5 servants at 'Mr Lennox's' £304, of which £200 went to one man; £2179 to 75 assorted joiners, carpenters, bricklayers, sawyers and masons; £327 to 14 gardeners; and £286 to 15 'extra labourers'.

The Duke estimated his taxes at £2903, of which £2200 was for the income tax introduced in 1799; lesser dues were imposed on such items as windows (even for the kennels), hair powder, wheeled carriages, servants, horses, dogs, one pack of hounds, kitchen gardens and boathouses. He was also paying annuities and pensions totalling £2123 and a further £40 in subscriptions, including local schools, clergy widows, clubs, coffee-rooms at Chichester and Lewes, the Society of Arts, and prisoners at Horsham Gaol.

As a final outgoing he recorded £1321 in wages to 51 persons constantly employed on the Goodwood farm and £209 to 8 employed at Itchenor.

2 Mrs Bennett and her family were researched by Lawrence Ward in his unpublished 'The Third Duke of Richmond'.

Chapter 23

1 WSRO, Goodwood MSS 224.
2 Holland House Papers BM Add.MSS 5182 for all the correspondence with Holland in this chapter.
3 *Parliamentary History*, Vol.XXXVI, p.731.
4 Western, pp.236–7.
5 Western, p.311.
6 *Victoria County History of Sussex*, Vol.I, p.535.
7 For the correspondence with Charles, see Olson, pp.222–36.

Chapter 24

1 Stanley Ayling, *George the Third*, 1972, p.84.
2 Holland House Papers, BM Add.MSS 51802.
3 Kent, pp.34, 40. The construction of the racecourse may account for an enquiry by Richmond about the new technology. In 1804 he wanted a steam engine that would 'raise 30 hogsheads of water per day to the height of 160 feet', and he applied to James Wyatt's partner, Matthew Boulton, at Soho, Birmingham. In a courteous and helpful reply (WSRO 1892) Boulton said that this would be like using a hammer to crack a nut, or a mill to grind a bushel of corn. A one horse-power engine would be sufficient. His company supplied engines ranging from 2 to 200 horse-power to great houses needing power, but a project on a smaller scale would not be economic.
4 WSRO, Goodwood MSS 224.
5 In *The Cricketer Quarterly*, Summer 1986, Robin Simon discusses 'the Richmond Dynasty' as patrons of cricket, with special reference to Charles.
6 A copy of the will is at Goodwood.
7 *The Later Correspondence of George III, 1802–07*, ed. A. Aspinall, 1968, Vol.IV, p.315.
8 Holland House Papers, BM Add.MSS 5182.

Illustration acknowledgements

The illustrations are reproduced from the collections at Goodwood, with the exception of the following:
1, 46, 52, 68, 85 By courtesy of the County Archivist, West Sussex Record Office.
11, 31 Royal Academy of Arts.
17, 39, 45, 49, 50, 51, 91, 98, 102 National Portrait Gallery, London.
18 Mansell Collection.
24 Guildhall Library, City of London.
36 Private Collection © 1987 The Art Institute of Chicago. All rights reserved.
42 Aerofilms Ltd.
48, 69, 73, 94, 99 By courtesy of the Trustees of the British Museum.
61, 66, 80 National Army Museum.
70 Peter Newark's Western Americana.
71 Tate Gallery, London.
77 By permission of the British Library.
78 © The Trustees of the Science Museum.
79 (LEFT and CENTRE) By permission of The Army Museums Ogilby Trust. (RIGHT) By permission of the Royal Artillery Institution.
81, 82, 83, 84 Board of Trustees of the Royal Armouries.
93 The Iveagh Bequest, Kenwood (English Heritage).
101 Beaverbrook Canadian Foundation, Beaverbrook Art Gallery, Fredericton.
103 Hunterian Art Gallery, University of Glasgow.

Index

Page numbers in *italics* refer to illustrations

Index

Due ~~14~~ 28 Days From Latest Date

APR 8 1988			
APR 22 1988			
MAY 9 1988			
MAY 24 1988			
JUL 27 1988			
Ren Aug 10			
SEP 1 1988			

WITHDRAWN

R4145R

Redwood Library and Athenaeum

Newport, R. I.